WITTGENSTEIN AND PHENOMENOLOGY

SUNY Series in Philosophy
Robert C. Neville, Editor

WITTGENSTEIN
AND PHENOMENOLOGY

A Comparative Study of the Later Wittgenstein,
Husserl, Heidegger, and Merleau-Ponty

NICHOLAS F. GIER

State University of New York Press
ALBANY

Published by
State University of New York Press, Albany

For information, address State University of New York
Press, State University Plaza, Albany, N.Y., 12246

Library of Congress Cataloging in Publication Data

Gier, Nicholas F   1944–
    Wittgenstein and phenomenology.

    Bibliography: p. 249
    Includes index.
    1.   Wittgenstein, Ludwig, 1889–1951.   2.   Phenomen-
ology.   I.   Title.
B3376.W564G53   192   80–26980
ISBN 0–87395–518–8
ISBN 0–87395–519–6 (pbk.)

10   9   8   7   6   5   4   3   2

TO N. J. Y., WHO GOT ME STARTED

Contents

Ja, wenn wir der Sprache die Zügel überlassen und nicht *dem Leben,* dann entstehen die philosophischen Probleme.

—Wittgenstein, The Big Typescript, p. 521

Acknowledgments

In Denmark I would like to thank the following people and institutions:

The philosophy institute at Odense University, who hired me as a visiting lecturer in 1970−71 to teach Heidegger and Gadamer. Their suggestion that I lecture on "The Link between Existentialism and Linguistic Analysis" was the seed for this project.

The philosophy institute at the University of Copenhagen, who graciously accepted me as a visiting professor in 1978−79. I was given full library privileges and I also taught one seminar on the topic of this book. I want to especially thank Peter Kemp and Paul Lübcke for their help and encouragement. I am grateful to Mr. Lübcke for the invitation to speak to the Society for Philosophy and Psychology about my book.

The research librarians at the Lynby-Taarbaek County Library, who did an excellent job in acquiring all of the books and articles that I needed. They also provided me with a fully furnished study cell. This particular county library was as good as any American college library.

Jens Glebe-Møller, formerly professor at Roskilde University, and now professor of dogmatics at the School of Theology at the University of Copenhagen. His book *Wittgenstein og Religionen* is one of the best studies in this area, and it is a shame that Basil Blackwell was not able to accept an English translation for publication. I am heavily indebted to Glebe-Møller for criticisms, comments, and bibliography.

At the University of Idaho, I would like to thank the following people:

Jill Holup, Marilyn Rabe, Theresa Beloin, and Dayle Williams for their patience with my messy rough drafts and their very competent typing.

Professor Francis Seaman, for his help and encouragement. As my department chairman, he arranged many of the tedious details, proof-reading, typing, etc., that go with the writing of any book.

Vicki Leonard, former philosophy student, now law student at the University of Washington. Ms. Leonard did a superb job of proof-reading the typescript.

Professor Marvin C. Henberg, colleague and friend, who has helped me with Wittgenstein since the beginning of the project. For the final rough draft, Henberg offered good suggestions for revising Chapter Four.

Professors James Reece and John Sullivan of the Foreign Language Department for their help in checking my German translations and de-ciphering Wittgenstein's handwriting.

The University of Idaho administration, for granting me a sabbatical leave to research my book in Denmark.

I also wish to thank Carolyn Black of San Jose State University for her comments on Chapter Seven, which at one time was a paper read at the Pacific Division meeting of the American Philosophical Association, March, 1980.

I want to especially thank Barry Smith, formerly of the University of Sheffield, now professor of philosophy at the University of Manchester (replacing Wolfe Mays). Professor Smith was a great store of informa-tion in both areas, phenomenology and Wittgenstein. I am also grate-ful for his invitations to speak at the Seminar for Austro-German Phi-losophy, once at the University of Manchester and then again at the London School of Economics.

I want to acknowledge the help of Professor Dagfinn Føllesdal, pro-fessor of philosophy at Stanford and Oslo. I met him at the University of Oslo where I was invited to speak by the philosophy institute.

Although most of his comments were negative, I wish to thank John Hunter of Toronto for constructive criticism, his prompt attention to the letters which I sent him, and for permission to quote from one of these letters.

I also benefited from the criticism and encouragement of Henry Leroy Finch of Hunter College, as well as from Herbert Spiegelberg of Washington University, the great historian of the phenomenological movement.

I would like to note the excellent comments that Walter Gulick of Eastern Montana made on my Kant chapter. I am also indebted to

George Seidel of St. Martin's College; Jerry H. Gill of Eastern College; Madelein Keys, formerly University of Idaho graduate student, now Ph.D. candidate at the University of Texas.

I owe my gratitude to the National Endowment for the Humanities for awarding me a summer stipend to finish the writing of the book.

I must also acknowledge that the editors of *Philosophy of Social Sciences, Metaphilosophy,* and *Tijdschrift voor Filosofie* have granted permission to use material from my articles published in these journals.

Basil Blackwell has allowed me to use material from the *Philosophical Investigations, Philosophical Remarks, Philosophical Grammar, The Remarks on the Foundation of Mathematics,* and *Wittgenstein's Lectures, Cambridge, 1930–32.* Harper & Row, University of California Press, Macmillan, and Rowman and Littlefield have given permission for the American rights they hold on these titles.

Finally I am grateful to Miss G. E. M. Anscombe and G. H. von Wright for allowing me to read the Wittgenstein papers in the original at the Wren Library in Cambridge. I am also indebted to Michael Nedo, head of the Wittgenstein Archives, who helped me locate *Nachlass* materials and was a good source of information.

PI = *Philosophical Investigations,* trans. Anscombe. New York: Macmillan, 3rd ed., 1958.

PR = *Philosophical Remarks,* trans. R. Hargreaves and R. White. Oxford: Blackwell, 1975.

RF = "Remarks on Frazer's *Golden Bough.*" Original German in *Synthese* 17 (1967), pp. 233–53. New, complete translation in *Wittgenstein: Sources and Perspectives,* ed. C. G. Luckhardt. Ithaca, N.Y.: Cornell University Press, 1979.

RFM = *Remarks on the Foundation of Mathematics,* trans. Anscombe. New York: Macmillan, 1956.

RLF = "Some Remarks on Logical Form," *Proceedings of the Aristotelian Society* (Suppl.) 9 (1929), pp. 162–171.

T = *Tractatus Logico-Philosophicus,* trans. D. F. Pears and B. F. McGuinness. London: Routledge & Kegan Paul, 1961.

VB = *Vermischte Bemerkungen,* ed. von Wright. Frankfurt: Suhrkamp, 1977.

WK = *Wittgenstein und der Wiener Kreis,* ed. B. F. McGuinness. Frankfurt: Suhrkamp, 1967.

Z = *Zettel,* trans. Anscombe. Berkeley: University of California Press, 1970.

Pagination for PR and PG are the same in German as in English.

WITTGENSTEIN'S UNPUBLISHED WORKS

MS = manuscripts; TS = typescripts

MS 105. *Philosophische Bemerkeungen.* Begun February 2, 1929. 135 pp.

MS 106. Undated and untitled. 1929. 298pp.

MS 111. *Bemerkungen zur Philosophie.* July 7 to September, 1931. 200pp.

MS 113. *Philosophische Grammatik.* November 28, 1931 to May 23, 1932. 286pp.

MS 119. Untitled, but some of the second half of the *Investigations* taken from this volume. September 24 to November 19, 1937. 295pp.

TS 208. Typescript based on MSS 105, 106, 107, and first half of 108. 1930. 101pp.

TS 213. The "Big Typescript." Probably 1933. vii + 768pp.

TS 220. Typescript, probably based on MS 142, of approximately the first half of the prewar version of the *Investigations.* 1937 or 1938. 137pp.

TS 226. English translation by R. Rhees of beginning of prewar version of the *Investigations*. 1939. 72pp.

TS 229. A continuation of TS 228 entitled *Bemerkungen I*. 1945 or 1946. 272pp.

Nachlass information has been taken from von Wright's article "The Wittgenstein Papers," *Philosophical Review* 78 (1969), pp. 483–503.

EDMUND HUSSERL

CM= *Cartesian Meditations,* trans. Dorion Cairns. The Hague: Nijhoff, 1969.

EB = "Phenomenology," Husserl's *Encyclopedia Britannica* article, trans. Richard Palmer in the *Journal of the British Society for Phenomenology* 2 (1971), pp. 77–90.

EJ = *Experience and Judgment*, trans. J. S. Churchill and K. Ameriks. Evanston: Northwestern University Press, 1975.

FTL = *Formal and Transcendental Logic*, trans. Dorion Cairns. The Hague: Nijhoff, 1969.

Ideas = *Ideas: General Introduction to Pure Phenomenology*, trans. W. B. Boyce-Gibson. New York: Macmillan, 1962.

K = *The Crisis of European Sciences and Transcendental Phenomenology*, trans. David Carr. Evanston: Northwestern University Press, 1970. Some passages from the original German have not been translated and are therefore cited by the German pagination marked "g."

LI = *Logical Investigations*, trans. J. N. Findlay. New York: Humanities Press, 1970.

PhP = *Phänomenologische Psychologie*. Volume Nine of *Husserliana*. The Hague: Nijhoff, 1962.

PRS = "Philosophy as a Rigorous Science," trans. Quentin Lauer in *Phenomenology and the Crisis of Philosophy*. New York: Harper Torchbooks, 1965.

MAURICE MERLEAU-PONTY

PrP = *The Primacy of Perception*, ed. James Edie. Evanston: Northwestern University Press, 1964.

PP = *Phenomenology of Perception*, trans. Colin Smith. London: Routledge & Kegan Paul, 1962.

WITTGENSTEIN AS A CONTINENTAL THINKER

In *The Decline of the West*, Oswald Spengler declares that "all genuine historical work is philosophy, unless it is mere ant-industry" (DW I, p. 41). The following study deals with the history of 20th Century philosophy and it is my hope that it succeeds in being more than just "ant-industry." With the exception of a few modest attempts at original analysis or criticism, the present work is principally historical and expository. It does not generate an independent philosophical problematic, and therefore it does not completely fulfill Spengler's ideal. Nevertheless, I trust that my work will shed new light on problems in both Wittgenstein and phenomenology.

Spengler is certainly correct in holding that "every thought lives in an historical world" (DW I, p. 46), and it is therefore imperative to place the thoughts of Wittgenstein in the existential space of his own lifeworld. I agree with Allan Janik and Stephen Toulmin's thesis in their *Wittgenstein's Vienna* that we must re-interpret Wittgenstein in terms of his specific Viennese roots and general continental milieu. The result is a Wittgenstein quite different from the philosopher hailed the logical positivists and many analytic philosophers. I am also confident that this "new" Wittgenstein is not the questionable hybrid that the neo-Platonic "Plato" is or the neo-Kantian "Kant"; rather, it is the analytic or positivist Wittgenstein who is the odd creature.

We shall see that there are many aspects of Wittgenstein's thought that separate him from the general analytic philosophical tradition. Hubert Schwyzer believes that it is a mistake to include *any* ordinary language philosophy in the school of British Empiricism:

> [Ordinary language philosophers] seem to be regarded as belonging, in a new and refined way, to the tradition of British Empiricism. I would have thought that this was a mistaken view, even if some of them so regard themselves. Surely no empiricist (discounting Locke) can take how we speak as any sort of *datum*. In this respect, the ordinary language philosopher is much closer to the rationalist . . . than he is to the empiricist.[4]

Although Wittgenstein could not stand to read much of philosophical writing, I believe it is significant that Karl Britton reports that "he could not sit down and read Hume—he knew far too much about the subject of Hume's writings to find this anything but torture."[5]

Wittgenstein's explicit rejection of nominalism (PI, §383) also alienates him from the empiricist tradition, and so does his holism and acceptance of internal relations, topics we shall discuss in Chapter Four.

The idea that Wittgenstein must be seen in terms of his intellectual and cultural background on the Continent has met with stiff resistance among some scholars. They counter that most of the connections are tenuous and speculative, and even if there were such influences, they would have very little philosophical significance. The critics remind us of Wittgenstein's lack of interest in the history of philosophy, and they would be pleased to read that Wittgenstein told his students in 1931 that in philosophy "we can tackle the subject direct, without any need to consider history" (L 1, p. 75). Just because many of the great philosophers do not do historical philosophy does not mean that they rejected it. M. O'C. Drury reports that Wittgenstein once said to him that he regarded "the great metaphysical writings of the past as among the noblest productions of the human mind."[6] Confessing that Wittgenstein had a different "Weltanschauung" than the positivists, Rudolf Carnap relates that once when Moritz Schlick "made a critical remark about a metaphysical statement by a classical philosopher (I think it was Schopenhauer), Wittgenstein surprisingly turned against Schlick and defended the philosopher and his work."[7]

In letters to me John Hunter of Toronto strongly objects to relating Wittgenstein to Spengler, even though Wittgenstein explicitly states that he has been influenced by him and uses his method (220, p. 85). Hunter also cannot accept the fact that Wittgenstein wrote "Phänomenologie ist Grammatik" and contends that the two disciplines cannot possibly have anything to do with one another. Wittgenstein may be wrong in this identification, but Hunter simply cannot ignore the fact that Wittgenstein explicitly made the claim. This is reminiscent of Gilbert Ryle's famous quip at a conference of English and French philosophers in 1962. In response to a suggestion by Merleau-Ponty that both parties were engaged in a common enterprise, Ryle is supposed to have said: "I hope not!"

"I begin," states Merleau-Ponty, "to understand a philosophy by feeling my way into its existential manner, by reproducing the tone and accent of the philosopher" (PP, p. 179). Otherwise, one ends up reducing the philosopher in question to a caricature, one that fits our own preconceptions, but one that does not do justice to the philosopher himself. In his excellent and sympathetic book on Sartre, the analytic philosopher, Arthur Danto, evidently has followed Merleau-Ponty's advice. He says, "I have quarried Sartre's work like a Barbarini over the

years" so that "he is part of my own history and world. . . ."⁸ Similarly,
it has been my goal in this book to work my way into Wittgenstein's
"existential manner" and reproduce the "tone and accent" of his work.

The *Tractatus* and the *Philosophical Investigations* have been taken by
many commentators as unique and original works that have no prece-
dent in the history of thought. For some orthodox Wittgensteinians it is
an insult to even intimate that a genius like Wittgenstein could have
appreciated or could have been influenced in any significant way by
lesser thinkers, especially obscurantist continental ones. In 1929
Wittgenstein seemed to give support for this view of a hermetically-
sealed genius: "It is good that I don't let myself be influenced" (VP, p.
11). But in 1931 he wrote that "it appeared to me at that time
[1913–14] I had created new ways of thinking . . . whereas now I appear to be just applying the old" (VB, p. 45). A concession from the
preface to the *Investigations* is also pertinent: "For more than one reason my work may have something in common with other work done
today" (PI, p. x).

In 1931 he discussed the idea of Jewish "genius" and concluded that
even the greatest Jewish thinkers are not really geniuses but only "tal-
ented." He includes himself among the lesser ranks of Jewish thinkers,
because he is only a "reproductive" thinker, who has not founded an
intellectual movement, but simply has come up with new "compari-
sons." He then states that he has been influenced (apparently in
chronological order) by Ludwig Boltzmann, Heinrich Hertz, Arthur
Schopenhauer, Gottlob Frege, Bertrand Russell, Karl Kraus, Adolf
Loos, Otto Weininger, Oswald Spengler, and Piero Saffra (VB, p. 43).
In 1940 he compared himself to Felix Mendelssohn, whom he calls a
"reproductive" artist, who, like himself in designing his sister's house in
Vienna, simply produces objects that reflect the culture of the period.
What the reproductive artist fails to do is to bring out "the primal life,
the wild life" (VB, pp. 77–8). This last comment clearly reminds one of
the exhortations of the 19th Century Romantics and *Lebensphilosophen.*

Gershon Weiler has offered an intriguing, yet highly tenable, thesis
that an obscure Viennese thinker, Fritz Mauthner, was probably an important influence on Wittgenstein.⁹ Mauthner anticipated the idea that
linguistic rules are analogous to the rules of games, formulated an argument against private language, emphasized ordinary language and
meaning as use, and spoke of philosophy as grammar and as therapy.
Mauthner also believed that both language and logic are subject to a
Völkerpsychologie, an amalgam of psychology and anthropology pro-

posed by Adolf Bastian and Moritz Lazarus. The latter was the teacher of Wilhelm Dilthey, the *Lebensphilosoph par excellence*.

In his foreword to the Schlick-Waismann conversations, McGuinness reports that there were discussions, "about ideas of Husserl, Heidegger, and Weyl" (WK, p. 19). An English translation of a short section on Heidegger was published in the *Philosophical Review*, but edited so that Heidegger's name did not appear. (Was this text "sanitized" for the *Review's* audience of analytic philosophers?) The excised portion was at the beginning of a conversation Waismann had with Wittgenstein on December 30, 1929. Wittgenstein begins by saying that he "can readily think what Heidegger means by Being and Dread" (WK, p. 68). We are not sure if Wittgenstein is referring to something of Heidegger he has read or simply responding to a short summary statement, which Waismann was inclined to do when asking Wittgenstein questions during this period. Michael Murray is convinced that Wittgenstein was speaking with a reading knowledge of Heidegger's *What is Metaphysics?*[10] Whether Wittgenstein actually read Heidegger or not is not of ultimate importance for us. What is significant is that Wittgenstein apparently did not have any difficulty understanding Heidegger's concepts of Being and Dread, something that a positivist like Rudolf Carnap thought was the culmination of philosophy gone mad.

When Wittgenstein's *Philosophical Remarks* appeared in 1964, the various reviews were inexplicably silent about a surprising development in Wittgenstein's philosophy: his explicit and positive use of the term "phenomenology." Herbert Spiegelberg called attention to this significant fact in an excellent article in 1968,[11] but still most Wittgenstein scholars were either unconcerned or unaware of Wittgenstein's acceptance of a phenomenological method. Spiegelberg makes a good case for the thesis that Wittgenstein's phenomenology was not just a momentary lapse, but the underlying method (*viz.*, philosophical grammar) of all the later works. Wittgenstein's consistent identification of phenomenology and grammar during the period 1929–1933 tends to support this thesis, as does the fact that in the recent publication of Wittgenstein's very last work (*On Color*), one finds again the terms "phenomenology" and "phenomenological." The task of this study is to discuss in detail what Wittgenstein means by phenomenology and compare this with the thought of Husserl, Heidegger, and Merleau-Ponty. We shall discover that Wittgenstein's own phenomenology follows the development of 20th Century phenomenology in general: from a more Husserlian stage to a full life-world phenomenology.

THE DIFFICULTIES OF WITTGENSTEIN INTERPRETATION

The writings of Wittgenstein confront the interpreter with severe hermeneutical problems. Heidegger and the other phenomenologists are certainly difficult to read, but at least they write full paragraphs (sometimes too full!) and usually give us sustained, detailed, if not complete, discussions of the issues involved. (I must exclude most of the later Heidegger, which I find to be virtually unreadable in places.) Although much of Wittgenstein's analysis is clear, the interspersed pronouncements and quasi-conclusions are for the most part dense and cryptic. Generally speaking, Wittgenstein's writings are fragmentary, disjunctive, repetitive, and many times inconsistent. In the Preface to the *Investigations* Wittgenstein characterizes the book as an "album" of "sketches" and he admits that he had to "make a sudden change, jumping from one topic to another" (PI, p. ix). Although the *Tractatus* is more structured, it too presents problems. G. J. Warnock states that the *Tractatus* is "a work of impressive subtlety and power which presents difficulties of interpretation not less than and indeed very similar to those sometimes presented by a sacred text."[12]

F. Kerr's description of Wittgenstein as a "hermetic aphorist"[13] is apt, because he, like others of this genre (notably Nietzsche) rarely ever gives a sustained argument, but makes pronouncements accompanied by a few examples and analogies. As he once told his students: "Now you may question whether my constantly giving examples and speaking in similes is profitable" (L 3, p. 50). Rudolf Carnap recognizes that "his point of view and his attitude toward people and problems, even theoretical problems, were much more similar to those of a creative artist than to those of a scientist; one might almost say, similar to those of a religious prophet or a seer."[14] Like the prophets of old, Wittgenstein continually complained of being misunderstood, even by those closest to him. In some respects Wittgenstein resembles Nietzsche's Zarathustra, whose message about the "death of God" fell on deaf ears. This prompted Zarathustra to conclude that he had come too early—the time was not yet right for his message. Wittgenstein's message is not about the death of the deity; on the contrary, he says that he would have dedicated his *Philosophical Remarks* to the "glory of God." He did not do so primarily because of his fear that such a dedication would be misunderstood by a culture whose spirit he did not share (PR, p. 7). This point is confirmed by Norman Malcolm: "He once said that he felt as though he were writing for people who would think in a quite different way, breathe a different air of life, from that of present-day men. For people of a different culture, as it were."[15]

Another problem with Wittgenstein is that it is sometimes hard to take him seriously. Many good discussions are rudely interrupted by a Wittgenstein who has no respect for any thinking, including his own. A beautiful example of this type of tactic appears in a rare English passage in MS 119:

> This book is a collection of wisecracks. But the point is: they are connected, they form a system. If the task were to draw the shape of an object true to nature, then a wisecrack is like drawing just one tangent to the real curve. But a thousand wisecracks closely drawn to each other can draw the curve (119, pp. 108–9).

Does Wittgenstein mean to say that one joke cannot cover the essence of philosophy, but that a thousand interconnected jokes would do the job?

In the face of such problems, I offer the following study as *an interpretation* of Wittgenstein's thousands of remarks, wisecracks or not. My interpretation depends heavily on the "middle works," which are, quite frankly, a hermeneutical quagmire. There are some commentators who make much of the verificationist tendencies in some of this work. There is still much Tractarian doctrine here: e.g., the picture theory, that "grammar is the mirror of reality" and that "thought must have the logical form of reality to be thought at all" (L 1, pp. 9, 10). At the same time there are explicit critiques of the *Tractatus*, centering on a full semantic holism, which we shall discuss in Chapters Four and Ten. Most importantly there are the passages on phenomenology and grammar, which I link with a decided turn towards some form of *Lebensphilosophie*. These data become the principal emphases of my Wittgenstein interpretation.

In my discussions I assume, perhaps rather presumptuously, that readers are generally familiar with both Wittgenstein and phenomenology. Because of the scope of the work, I could not take time to lay out all the doctrines of the *Tractatus*, the middle works, or the *Investigations*. I refer to the Wittgensteinian corpus mainly to support my thesis and not to give any comprehensive view of Wittgenstein's philosophy. The expository nature of my discussions may give the false impression that I always agree either with Wittgenstein or the phenomenologists. Some of the solutions to traditional philosophical problems, which I claim that Wittgenstein and the phenomenologists share, are usually presented as such. There has generally been no attempt to either criticize them or to support them with sustained argument. For example, I state the Kantian-Wittgenstein thesis that there are no judgments without language, but I share Jonathan Bennett's suspicion about whether this is true or not. I present Wittgenstein's concept of internal relations, but I do not assess its merits. I prove that Wittgenstein resurrects the synthetic *a priori*, but my task is not to show whether he was right in doing so. Furthermore, I am especially uneasy about the Wittgensteinian-Heideggerian claim that humans have *unique* forms of life or "existentials." This appears to be an unfortunate return to the Cartesian distinction between humans and brutes.

Some of the readers of early drafts of this work have complained that a pedestrian listing of the places where Wittgenstein uses the term "phenomenology" is a rather superficial way of substantiating my thesis. If I had simply made an inventory of these passages and others that sounded like phenomenology, I would certainly agree with these critics. But I have made a determined effort to back up terminological coincidences with substantial, methodological parallels, in addition to the similar doctrine I have found. This is the reason why I spend so much time and effort on Wittgenstein's Kantian background and his attempts at a transcendental method. Phenomenology without a transcendental method would collapse into phenomenalism, and I show why this should not happen in Wittgenstein's philosophy. We shall see that Wittgenstein's transcendental method does have its weaknesses and inconsistencies.

I must apologize for the inordinate number of passages cited, especially from Wittgenstein. Because of the controversial nature of the topic, I felt that I needed to document as many of the claims as possible. I do not want to be in the position of some commentators who say "Wittgenstein believes this but doesn't explicitly state it." With few exceptions I trust that I have cited specific passages to back up the claims of what I think Wittgenstein believes.

The principal danger in all Wittgenstein interpretation is the temptation to make Wittgenstein's remarks into "doctrines." For example, some are inclined to think that the later Wittgenstein must have some type of coherence theory of truth. But in a 1931 lecture he did not want to commit himself to any one theory of truth: "Thus it is nonsense to try to find *a* theory of truth, because we can see that in everyday life we use the word quite clearly and definitely in these different senses" (L 1, p. 76). The idea that meaning is use essentially prevents one from holding any philosophical theory. But Wittgenstein even hesitates about the universal application of this "doctrine," reminding us that only "for a large number of cases" is meaning use (PI, §43). As I argue in Chapter Eight, the concept of analyticity is dissolved and Wittgenstein's logical propositions collapse into grammatical propositions if meaning is always use. If my attempt to make Wittgenstein into an existential phenomenologist sometimes appears to overlook this proviso, I simply wish to stress now that I am fully aware of this particular danger of Wittgenstein interpretation.

Readers of previous drafts have proposed that some contemporary Anglo-American philosophers, notably Nelson Goodman and W. V. Quine, have *Weltanschauungsphilosophien* much like Wittgenstein's, which are also at odds with prevailing analytic philosophy. I do mention Quine briefly in Chapter Eight, and I do cite Philip J. Bossert's comparison of Goodman and Husserl. But I simply have not had time to do the necessary reading to do justice to the inclusion of these thinkers in a meaningful way. Besides, the inclusion of Goodman and Quine would go beyond the scope of the current study. Two other philosophers who could have been included are William James and Michael Polanyi. Some may object that I have not paid enough attention to Gottob Frege. I do qualify what I believe to be exaggerations of Frege's positive influence on Wittgenstein, and I do include a section in the Bibliography on Husserl, Frege, and Wittgenstein.

USE OF THE *NACHLASS* AND TRANSLATIONS

As far as I know, Herbert Spiegelberg and I are the only scholars who have worked with Wittgenstein's unpublished works (*Nachlass*) on this topic of phenomenology. He has worked with the Cornell microfilm edition of the *Nachlass*, and I have worked both with the microfilm and the originals in the Wren Library in Cambridge. I now wish that I had had more time with the originals, because the microfilms of certain materials are very difficult to read. For example, Spiegelberg found passages on phenomenology in MS 111 on the enlargements at Cornell that I was unable to find on the version sold to many university libraries. In addition, the original MS 119, which I read in Cambridge, appears to have different pagination than the microfilm version, which has no pagination after p. 146. Because of these and other problems, definitive scholarly work with the *Nachlass* will have to await the publication of the critical edition of the *Nachlass*, which is being prepared by Michael Nedo at the Wittgenstein Archives in Tübingen.

Despite this qualification, the combined efforts of Spiegelberg and myself can now offer a better, if not yet complete, account of Wittgenstein's phenomenology on the basis of the *Nachlass*. Some have argued this unpublished material, and even the middle works as a whole, should not be given much weight for two reasons: (1) Wittgenstein did not have any of this material published; and (2) it represents a philosophically unsatisfactory transition period to the mature works of post-1933. At least four points can be made against these objections. First, if Spiegelberg's thesis about the continuation of phenomenology as grammar is correct, then these works are at least of great historical significance. Second, although Wittgenstein was definitely unhappy with some of the first work that he did when he first came back to Cambridge (he ordered some of the material burned and refused to read the paper entitled "Remarks on Logical Form"), he did feel confident enough about the *Philosophical Remarks* to give a typescript copy (probably TS 209) to both Russell and Moore.

Third, von Wright declares that the "Big Typescript may be regarded as being, next to the *Tractatus*, the most outwardly finished statement Wittgenstein ever succeeded in giving to his philosophic position at any time."[16] In a controversial article "From the Big Typescript to the *Philosophical Grammar*," Anthony Kenny reports that at one time Wittgenstein was getting the Big Typescript ready for publication. Taking strong exception to the way in which it was edited as our *Philosophical Grammar*, Kenny declares that "the Big Typescript represents a single, reasonably coherent, stage of Wittgenstein's development—the *Philosophical Grammar* as published does not. . . ."[17] He goes on to assert that the "chapters on philosophy, phenomenology, and idealism present as clear a text to the reader as those on logic and the foundation of mathematics. Strange that they were omitted." The three chapters mentioned were not included in the *Grammar*, but the material on logic and mathematics was.

There are some scholars who suspect that the chapter on phenomenology in particular was excluded because of a bias against that discipline on the part of the three executors of the *Nachlass*. Although I agree with Kenny and many others who believe that the Big Typescript should be published in full, I can also appreciate the exigencies of the situation which forced the editor to cut certain sections. (The typescript is 755 pages long!) The chapter on phenomenology is certainly important, but what Wittgenstein says there is generally the same as what has been published in the *Philosophical Remarks*. Because of this fact, the deletion of the chapter on phenomenology, in order to make the *Grammar* a manageable length, was probably a defensible editorial decision.

The fourth reason why I believe the major works of the *Nachlass* are legitimate data depends upon a thesis I hold about why Wittgenstein refused to publish so little during his lifetime. We have already mentioned that he burned a lot of material that he evidently found worthless. Although much of the material left was either not ready or suitable for publication, I believe that it was largely his fear of being misunderstood that kept him from publishing the rest of this work. Malcolm gives support to this hypothesis: "That [fear of being misunderstood] was *one* reason why he did not himself publish his later works."[18] Wittgenstein not only thought that his works would be misunderstood, but that they would be badly misused. For example, Wittgenstein was so disappointed in Russell's introduction to the *Tractatus* that he was willing to give up the whole idea of an English translation. He was also definitely upset about how the Vienna Circle was using the *Tractatus*. We know from Carnap's own account that Wittgenstein found him so disagreeable in personality and thought that he insisted that both Carnap and Feigl be excluded from the regular visits of Schlick and Waismann.[19] It must have pained Wittgenstein greatly that these men were proclaiming the *Tractatus* as the "Bible" of positivism, and he probably thought that if he published the *Remarks* or the Big Typescript these thinkers and others would misuse them in a similar way.

In addition to those who believe that the *Nachlass* should be given less weight in Wittgenstein interpretation, there are those who propose that the published lectures should be treated likewise. As I rely heavily on lectures from 1930−32 (L 1) and the lectures on mathematics in 1939 (LFM), I must defend the use of this material. The notes from these lectures were essentially *verbatim* and were carefully re-copied. The editors also had the advantage of generally having two or more sets of notes to compare for decisions about the final wording. Malcolm believes that the lectures of 1939 are some of Wittgenstein's best thinking, and the lectures of 1932−35, edited by Alice Ambrose, contain some of the clearest analysis by Wittgenstein that I have read. It is Ambrose's opinion that the "Yellow Book" included in these lectures is a better statement than the "Blue Book" dictation in which she also participated (L 3, p. x).

Those readers who do not know German may be intimidated by the constant use of German terms. Let me therefore give translations of the more frequently used terms, as well as point out those translations that differ from the official versions. The crucial phrase for Kant's transcendental method—*die Bedingungen der Möglichkeit der Erfahrung*—means "the conditions for the possibility of experience." The word *Weltanschauung*, which has already worked its way into our ordinary language, means "view of the world." Heidegger's *"gleichursprünglich"* I render as "equiprimordial." Heidegger's technical term for human Being, *Dasein*, is left untranslated. I have changed slightly the standard translation of Heidegger's *Zuhandensein* from "Being-ready-to-hand" to "Being-ready-at-hand." Things present-*to*-hand are directly in front of us, projected away from our bodies, but things ready-*at*-hand are right *at* our sides, ready to use without thinking and judging.

I have done my own translation of the Wittgensteinian texts that are still in the original German. Otherwise I have followed the official English translations except for the following changes. As Wittgenstein evidently used "synopsis" for *"Übersicht,"* I choose to follow this rendering, rather than "perspicuity" or the much less satisfactory "bird's-eye view" (PR, p. 52). I also prefer "presentation" for *Darstellung*, rather than "representation." Therefore, I use "synoptic presentation" rather than "perspicuous representation." I do, however, follow the official translation of *"übersehen"* as "to survey." I believe that "modes" for *"Modifikationen"* at PI, p. 174 should be replaced by the English cognate "modification." Finally, I translate *Sinn* as the "sense" of a proposition and *"Bedeutung"* as the "meaning" of words, a distinction which Wittgenstein maintains consistently throughout all of his works.

I alternate "forms of life" and *"Lebensformen"* principally for stylistic reasons. This is also partially the reason for the proliferation of the closely related terms *"Weltanschauungsphilosophie," "Lebensphilosophie,"* "life-world phenomenology," and "existential phenomenology." The first two terms, however, are more inclusive than the last two; that is, not all life-philosophers are phenomenologists, primarily because of their penchant for psychologism. Furthermore, it might be said that not all existential phenomenologists are life-world phenomenologists. I am thinking particularly of Jean-Paul Sartre, whose radical subjectivism and existentialism (at least before 1947) would distinguish him from those, like Heidegger and Merleau-Ponty, who definitely believe in the intersubjectivity of the life-world.

WITTGENSTEIN AND CONVENTIONALISM

As the various arguments of this book developed, I became more and more aware of the fact that the most plausible counter-argument would be to interpret Wittgenstein as a "conventionalist." I have therefore decided that a response here in the Introduction would be the best way to pre-empt such criticism. Wittgenstein does claim that when "we strike rock bottom . . . we have come down to conventions" (BB, p. 24), and that "if you talk about *essence*—you are merely noting a convention . . . [and] to the *depth* that we see in the essence there corresponds the *deep* need for the convention" (RFM, p. 23). Michael Dummett claims that "Wittgenstein goes in for a full-blooded conventionalism; for him the logical necessity of any statement is always the *direct* expression of a linguistic convention."[20]

Wittgenstein does accept the Kantian idea that we do not have any direct apprehension of things-in-themselves, but he rejects Kant's assumption that there are innate categories of the mind which insure the universality and objectivity of knowledge. Such assumptions could easily carry one towards "full-blooded conventionalism," but they do not do so in Wittgenstein's case. Let us begin with a crucial passage from a lecture given in 1931: "Grammatical rules are arbitrary, but their application is *not*" (L 1, p. 58, cf. p. 49). For Wittgenstein grammatical rules are arbitrary only because they cannot be given any extra-linguistic justification. They are not arbitrary in the sense that they depend on acts of the human will. The grammar contained in language-games and forms of life is *already* given; generally we are not free to change it. Therefore, Wittgenstein is in direct opposition to the standard conventionalism of J. L. Austin: "We are absolutely free to appoint *any* symbol to describe *any* situation, as far as being merely true goes."[21]

Other commentators support my argument against a Wittgensteinian conventionalism. Derek L. Phillips states that "Wittgenstein is certainly not a realist, in that we can never establish that our own ways of calculating, for example, are true; nor is he a conventionalist, in that our way of calculating is not—*for us*—merely one of an unlimited number of available alternatives."[22] We shall see that both Wittgenstein and phenomenology have overcome the traditional distinction between an interior mental realm and an external nature, and conventionalism is just another way of perpetuating the radical split between the "inner" and the "outer." We shall argue that the principal means of overcoming this dualism is the resurrection of the synthetic *a priori* as a full material *a priori*, in which the "forms of presentation" (*Darstellungsformen*) and the world they reveal are inextricably related.

Contrary to some critics, Wittgenstein knows the limits of his analogy between grammatical rules and rules of a game. The rules of a game are "mere" conventions, but grammatical rules are not, because they have an "application to reality" (L 1, p. 12). This then is the reason for the synthetic *a priori* in the later Wittgenstein. It also means that, although we never have any direct access to nature, "she" nevertheless has something to say: "Indeed she has—but she makes herself audible in another way [other than traditional realism?]. 'You'll surely run up against existence and non-existence somewhere!' But that means against *facts*, not concepts" (Z, §364). A. B. Levison puts it aptly: "Inferring, he says, is bounded *for us* not 'by us' or by an arbitrary definition; there are *natural limits* to what we call 'thinking and inferring.' "[23]

HUSSERL AND WITTGENSTEIN ON "CHANGE OF LIFE"

We shall draw many parallels between Wittgenstein and the phenomenologists, but before we commence the analysis proper let me offer one comparison that is important but did not fit in with any of the chapter topics. Husserl always stresses the point that a successful phenomenological reduction would effect a complete change of attitude towards things, indeed, a complete change of life. Here is one of his most eloquent statements:

> The total phenomenological attitude and the *epoché* belonging to it are destined in essence to effect, at first, a complete personal transformation, comparable in the beginning to a religious conversion, which . . . bears within itself the significance of the greatest existential transformation which is assigned as a task of mankind as such (K, p. 137, cf. 100, 147, 314g).

One of the things that disappointed Wittgenstein most about English philosophers was their attitude towards philosophy and life: they lacked passion, commitment, and moral integrity. For Wittgenstein the questions of philosophy and life involved a Kierkegaardian either/or choice and an attitude that resembled religious fanaticism. An unsuccessful philosophy lecture—Wittgenstein thought that most of his were—was not occasioned by a casual "I'll do better tomorrow" but with an immediate bout of severe depression. Both Husserl and Wittgenstein were perpetual beginners, agonizing over formulations that would not bother most of us, because their standards of truth and excellence were so high.

Wittgenstein's opinions on this point, that a change in philosophy required a change in life, are summed up poignantly in this quote: "The sickness of a time is cured by an alternation in the mode of life of human beings, and it was possible for the sickness of philosophical problems to get cured only through a changed mode of thought and of life . . ." (RFM, p. 57). There is also the mysterious preface to the *Remarks*, which, as we have seen, would have been dedicated to the "glory of God," but that would have been misunderstood by the shallow minds of the time. Wittgenstein claims that the *Remarks* was written in a spirit entirely different from contemporary civilization, with its concerns for progress and scientific advance. Science strives for "larger and more complicated structures," but really works on the periphery. In contrast, the phenomenological method of the *Remarks* works towards the direct apprehension of the structure and essence of experience. The original draft of this preface has been printed in full in *Vermischte Bemerkungen*, and its manner and tone reminds one of Husserl's Vienna lecture. Wittgenstein calls his culture an *"Unkultur"* and he bemoans the fact that this culture, mainly because of positivism and scientism, has lost the means of expressing human values. Wittgenstein's pessimism also reminds us of Oswald Spengler, a figure who will play a central role in our interpretation of Wittgenstein.

1. Forms of Life

One can hardly place too much stress on the importance of this latter notion [Lebensformen] *in Wittgenstein's thought.*

–Norman Malcolm[1]

Human speech and activity, sanity and community, rest upon nothing more, but nothing less than [Lebensformen].

–Stanley Cavell[2]

Here we can only describe *and say: this is what human life is like.*

–Wittgenstein (RF, p. 63)

If I say I believe that someone is sad, it's as though I am seeing his behavior through the medium of sadness, from the viewpoint of sadness.

–Wittgenstein (PR, p. 89)

*What has to be accepted, the given is–so one could say–*forms of life.

–Wittgenstein (PI, p. 226)

Forms of life evidently play the role of a metaphysical ultimate in terms of which the functioning of language is to be understood.

–H. R. Smart[3]

Thus, for both Cassierer and Wittgenstein, philosophy ultimately becomes phenomenological description of the forms of our lives.

–R. S. Rajan[4]

Words are deeds, and deeds are part of the natural history of man.

–Robert L. Arrington[5]

17

FOUR VIEWS OF FORMS OF LIFE

Ludwig Wittgenstein's concept of "forms of life" (*Lebensformen*), though mentioned only seven times in all of his published writings, is, according to leading Wittgenstein scholars, the most significant concept in the later philosophy. Wittgenstein maintains that many traditional philosophical problems can be diagnosed and eventually solved by analyzing how humans use language or how they play language-games. Language-games are intimately related to *Lebensformen*, as can be seen from the following passages where the word is used in the *Philosophical Investigations*, "Lectures on Religious Belief," and *On Certainty*:

It is easy to imagine a language consisting only of orders and reports in battle. . . . And to imagine a language means to imagine a form of life (PI, §19).

Here the term "language-game" is meant to bring into prominence the fact that the *speaking* of language is part of an activity, or of a form of life (PI, §23).

"So you are saying that human agreement decides what is true and what is false?"—It is what human beings *say* that is true and false; and they agree in the *language* they use. That is not agreement in opinions but in form of life (PI, §241).

Can only those hope who can talk? Only those who have mastered the use of language. That is to say the phenomena of hope are modifications of this complicated form of life (PI, p. 174).

". . . mathematics is indeed of the highest certainty—though we only have a crude reflection of it." . . . What has to be accepted, the given is—so one could say—*forms of life* (PI, p. 226).

Why shouldn't one form of life culminate in an utterance of belief in a Last Judgment?" (LC, p. 58).

Now I would like to regard this certainty, not as something akin to hastiness or superficiality, but as a form of life. . . . But that means I want to conceive it as something beyond being justified or unjustified; as it were, as something animal (OC, §§358—9).

In *The Idea of a Social Science* Peter Winch claims that Wittgenstein's concept of *Lebensformen* has created a "genuine revolution in philosophy" that has seminal significance for epistemology and sociology.[6] Several philosophers of religion also find the concept central to their concerns. Each of these thinkers, and all but three of the others involved with this topic, have assumed that forms of life are principally related to social and cultural history. Most of them, however, have not justified this interpretation by any thorough investigation of the Wittgensteinian corpus.[7] Indeed, the only scholar who does any major textual work (John Hunter) concludes that the cultural-historical view is the weakest of four alternatives.

In her book *Wittgenstein and Justice*, Hanna Pitkin offers a good summary definition of forms of life: "Because they are patterns, regularities, configurations, Wittgenstein calls them forms; and because they are patterns in the fabric of human existence and activity on earth, he calls them forms of life."[8] The concept therefore contains a formal dimension as well as a lived one, which can be viewed either in a cultural way or in terms of the natural history of the species. This initial conceptual analysis leads us to at least four possible interpretations of *Lebensformen*. The following is a brief summary of the four possibilities as Hunter describes them:

A. The Language-Game Account. In this interpretation *Lebensformen* are essentially identical with actual language-games. We can conceive of many possible language-games, but we would not necessarily find them being played in ordinary life.

B. The Behavior-Package View. *Lebensformen* are formalized behavior packages (e.g., certain facial expressions, gestures, acts) which are correlated with language-games. As Hunter states: "We are jointly inclined to engage in the behavior (and under appropriate circumstances) to say the words."

C. The Cultural-Historical View. On this account a *Lebensform* "is a way of life, or a mode, manner, fashion, or style of life: . . . it has something important to do with the class structure, the values, the religion, the type of industry and commerce and of recreation that characterize a group of people."

D. The Natural-Historical Theory, or the "Organic" Account. While A, B, and C concentrate on the formal dimension of the German *Form*, this theory emphasizes the biological aspect of the German *Leben*. "It is more like 'something typical of a living being': typical in the sense of being very broadly in the same class the growth or nutrition of living organisms, or as the organic complexity which enables them . . . to react in complicated ways to their environment."[9]

Hunter favors the organic account and does not treat the cultural view as a "serious contender." He is less critical of A and B. His main argument against the cultural view is that it finds no support in the texts. He claims that it does not pass the principal criterion: "To imagine a language means to imagine a form [way] of life." For example, Hunter is at a loss to see how one is able to learn anything at all about the life style or culture of the builders in the "slab" language-game. We shall return to this point and argue in support of the cultural view.

Before we discuss each of these interpretations, it will be helpful to pin down some examples of forms of life. The key passages quoted above appear to indicate that forms of life are particular activities, or states of mind, like giving orders, making reports, and being certain in mathematics or in everyday life. The following quotations give us grounds for believing that pretending and grieving are also forms of life: "Why should it always be pretending that is taking place—this very special pattern which recurs in the weave of our life" (PI, p. 174). In this same passage Wittgenstein also speaks of the "characteristic formation of the pattern of sorrow or of the pattern of joy." With these leads we could begin to make an almost endless list of specific forms of life.

At the same time, Wittgenstein definitely states that *Lebensformen* are more general activities like using language, being religious, and, as we shall see, having a culture (BB, p. 134; LC, p. 8). Hoping, although just like the specific life forms like pretending and grieving, is said to be a *"Modifikation"* of a complicated form of life, presumably the use of language. (Despite Wittgenstein's ambivalence here, I shall continue to refer to hope as a specific *Lebensform*). The references to culture and religion are ambiguous in another way. Forms of life can be religious or cultural in a specific sense: *viz.* a particular religion that believes in the Last Judgment (LC, p. 59), or a culture that has plebian and patrician cases (BB, p. 134).

In the course of this Chapter, I shall develop the concept of *Lebensformen* in terms of four levels: (1) a biological level from which (2) unique human activities like pretending, grieving, etc. are then expressed in (3) various cultural styles that in turn have their formal ground in a (4) general socio-linguistic framework (Wittgenstein's *Weltbild*). Such an interpretation is certainly not as tidy as others which claim one aspect to the exclusion of the others. It does have the virtues of comprehensiveness, flexibility, and as much justice to the texts as possible. I trust that some of the tensions among the levels will resolve themselves in the course of my argument, but I am making no claims about the final coherence of Wittgenstein's various views of *Lebensformen*.

Interpretation B, the behavior-package account, can be discredited fairly easily by posing the example of ironic behavior, in which pretending, a specific life form, is an essential ingredient. In ironic behavior the gestures and expressions would not correlate at all with the concealed intention. In other words, a form of life cannot always be reduced to a form of overt behavior. As Wittgenstein states: "Of course joy is not joyful behavior, nor yet a feeling round the corners of the mouth and the eyes" (Z, §487). Apart from this objection, however, it appears that any valid insights about human behavior and forms of life are already contained in the more comprehensive accounts, C and D. A detailed discussion of Wittgenstein and behaviorism is postponed until Chapter Seven.

Since the specific life forms listed above are sometimes taken as examples of language-games, one could initially make a case for interpretation A. The basic concept would then be language-games (both possible and actual) and various forms of life would simply be various language-games as they are actually played. Afterall, the phrase "language-games" appears 98 times in the *Investigations* as opposed to five occurrences of "forms of life." The basic nature of language-games is evident in this passage: "Our mistake is to look for an explanation when we ought to look at what happens as a 'proto-phenomenon.' That is, where we ought to have said: this *language-game* is played" (PI, §654). It is not surprising to find some commentators proposing the radical thesis that Wittgenstein reduces all reality to linguistic phenomena—the panlinguistic identification of being and language.

To do this, however, would certainly be a mistaken understanding of Wittgenstein. It is clear that hope, as well as most specific life forms, are not possible without language as the general life form. But rather than identifying *Lebensformen* and language-games in the passages above, Wittgenstein is simply being equivocal. The clue to understanding the relationship between the two is found at PI, §23. Here it is not clear whether the speaking of language is a form of life or only part of a more basic activity which is the form of life. The following passages indicate that the correct interpretation must be the latter.

> The concept of the rule for the formation of an infinite decimal is—of course—not a specifically mathematical one. It is a concept connected with a rigidly determined *activity* in human life (RFM, p. 186).

"How am I able to obey a rule?" . . . If I have exhausted the justifications I have reached bedrock, and my spade is turned. Then I am inclined to say: "This is simply what I do" (PI, §217).

We don't start from certain words, but from certain occasions or activities (LC, p. 3).

Disputes do not break out (among mathematicians, say) over the question whether a rule has been obeyed or not. . . . That is part of the framework on which the working of our language is based . . . (PI, §240).

But didn't I already intend the whole construction of the sentence (for example) at its beginning? . . . An intention is embedded in its situation, in human customs and institutions (PI, §337).

Giving grounds, however, justifying the evidence, comes to an end;—but the end is not certain propositions striking us immediately as true, i.e., it is not a kind of *seeing* on our part; it is our acting, which lies at the bottom (*Grunde*) of the language-game (OC, §204; cf. §§110, 403, 411, 414, 559).

I have chosen the passages above in order to link forms of life as activities with the notions of foundation, ground, and bedrock. The word "framework" of PI, §240 is also important in that it indicates the formal nature of forms of life, and also makes it clear that language is based in this framework. The word "embedded" relates to the metaphor of bedrock and shows that Malcolm must be wrong in maintaining that "forms of life [are] embodied in language-games."[10] It is the language-game and its related intentions, emotions, etc. that are embedded in the human situations, customs, and institutions of forms of life. This passage from MS 119 secures our claim: "It is characteristic of our language that it is built on fixed forms of life, regular ways of behaving" (119, p. 148). We must conclude that interpretation A is incorrect, and that we reach bedrock in forms of life that are basic human activities, not just linguistic ones. A panlinguist's motto would be "*Im Anfang war das Wort*"; but Wittgenstein's motto, taken from Goethe's *Faust*, is "*Im Anfang war die Tat*" (OC, §402). Language-games may be autonomous and logically complete only in a narrow sense, because their sense necessarily depends on action in the world.

HUNTER'S "ORGANIC" VIEW

Hunter concedes that many will not be initially inclined to his organic interpretation, primarily because of traditional prejudice that language originates in something mental and therefore unorganic. Learning a language, however, is a type of tacit knowing that involves every little cognition. It is more akin to training and practice, training that is not different in kind from training an animal. Furthermore, the language of pain, for example, is integrally connected with facial expressions and other reactions of the bodily organism. Therefore, humans, because of the natural history of their species, speak a universal language of pain. As Hunter states: "A natural expression of pain . . . is not decided on, but comes as immediately as we cry out or groan."[11]

The following quotations stand out as support for the organic account:

> Commanding, questioning, recounting, chatting, are as much part of our natural history as walking, eating, drinking, playing (PI, §25).

> I want to regard man here as an animal, as a primitive being to which one grants instinct but not ratiocination. As a creature in a primitive state (OC, §475).

> Our language-game is an extension of primitive behavior. (For our *language-game* is behavior.) (Instinct) (Z, §545).

Recall also the connection which Wittgenstein draws between forms of life and "something animal" (OC, §359). There is no question that biology is a necessary condition for human life forms. This fact constitutes yet another decisive counter against interpretation A: nature does have something to say (Z, §364). The fact that color-blind people cannot learn the language-game of normal colors is not due to something cultural (OCo, §112). The same holds for the person who does not have perfect pitch (OCo, §292). James Shekelton quite correctly sees that our reliance on memory is not rule-governed and therefore not dependent upon customs or institutions; nevertheless, it is a necessary condition for human certainty (OC, §632).[12]

But a common biology alone is not a sufficient condition for humans to hope, to be certain, to pray, to obey, or even to have a language. Recall the wolf-boy, biologically a human being, who never learned to speak a human language. Like most animals, human beings can make sounds, but those sounds make sense only in a social context. Or even if a person has normal sight, she is still required to learn the *rules* of a color language-game (OCo, §115). Unlike Shekelton, Hunter fails to see the social conditions which Wittgenstein explicitly lays down for *Lebensformen*. Furthermore, Hunter is definitely wrong in de-emphasizing the formal dimension of life forms, as this disregards the "rule-governed nature of language [that] permeates our life" (OCo, §303); or the fact that Wittgenstein once characterized "certainty" as a "primitive form" (119, pp. 147–8).

Hunter stresses the biological meaning of *Leben* in *Lebensform*; but, as far as I can ascertain, Wittgenstein rarely uses the word in this way. The concept of life in the *Tractatus* is very different from Hunter's "growth or nutrition of living organisms." In a notebook entry on July 24, 1916, Wittgenstein writes that "physiological life is of course not 'Life.' And neither is psychological life" (NB, p. 77; cf. PE, p. 297). In the later works we find a pervasive metaphorical use of the word—e.g., the sense of a sentence is its "life" (BB, p. 5; PG, p. 150); the use of a sign is its "life" (PI, §432); and the "life" of words (PI, p. 209). Wittgenstein does at least once define a "living being" as one which has the capacity to use a sign-language (PG, p. 192), but this is still a linguistic, not a biological definition of life.

According to Wittgenstein, dogs (and presumably all animals) cannot pretend, be sincere, hope, or talk (PI, p. 229, p. 174, §25). If forms of life were, as Hunter claims, "typical of a living being" and "in the same class as the growth or nutrition of living organisms," one would expect that animals could be taught to share some of our forms of life. But as far as I can ascertain, Wittgenstein believes that we do not share any forms of life with animals.[13] Hope, for example, is not at all like hunger, a natural state of an organism. And the reasons why a Christian looks forward to the Last Judgment and an atheist is content with returning to the dust are not to be found in "organic complexities" that are more or less equal. Winch's main thesis is that organic, causal behavior is different from uniquely human behavior because the latter is rule-governed and is based on cultural-historical conventions. Recall this crucial passage: "To obey a rule, to make a report, to give an order, to play a game of chess are *customs* (uses, institutions)" (PI, §199).

In a letter Hunter has responded to the preceding remarks with the following qualification: "I did not mean that any living being would, because it was . . . [a living being], hope, for example. . . . My view was rather that the mastery of the complexities of the use of the word 'hope' is a biological adaptation which, when acquired, just works." Hunter does not clarify what he means by a biological adaptation. He surely does not mean a genetic change, but probably something more like the physiological changes that occur in the nerves and muscles when we learn a new skill. Hunter's case is not at all strengthened by this qualification. When he lays stress on learning, training, and skills, he must realize, like Wittgenstein did, that there is as much *sociology* in such activities as biology. "By being educated in a technique, we are also educated to have a way of looking (*Betrachtungsweise*) which is just as firmly rooted as that technique" (RFM, p. 124).

This idea of "biological adaptation" has the ring of an *Entwicklungshypothese* (a genetic explanation), a type of hypothesis that Wittgenstein categorically rejects. Such a rejection is found in his criticisms of Frazer's explanations of primitive religions, but I am sure this would apply to the whole class of such explanations, including Hunter's theory of "biological adaptation." The method that replaces an *Entwicklungshypothese* is an *übersichtliche Darstellung* (cf. PI, §122) which is designed to grasp the formal connection among things (RF, pp. 69–70). In 1929 Wittgenstein introduces this concept of a synoptic presentation with his phenomenological method (PR, pp. 51–2), and it is significant to note, in view of our subsequent analyses, that Husserl began his *Ideas* with a reminder that "we are not talking here in terms of history . . . either of a psychological causality or of evolutionary history" (*Ideas*, §1fn).

Although we can train a smart dog to do many clever tricks, we can never train him to be sincere, to pretend, or to hope. Why, according to Wittgenstein, are these "adaptations" not possible? It is clear that the reason is not anything organic or anything to do with the capacity for learning. A dog cannot simulate pain because the "surroundings (*Umgebung*) which are necessary for this behavior to be real simulation are missing" (PI, §250). Millions of dogs and humans have lived intimately together for thousands of years in the same physical environment, but dogs have not adopted any human life forms. Like lions who could talk, talking dogs would still be excluded from human *Lebensformen* (cf. PI, p. 223). As we shall see, Wittgenstein's *Umgebung* is much like the *Lebenswelt* of the phenomenologists—a *qualitatively different* "environment" that makes it possible for humans to engage in language-games and forms of life that they cannot share with animals. There is a *formal* difference between an animal world and a human world. Hunter's theory of biological adaptation reduces this difference to an empirical one. I believe that this is definitely un-Wittgensteinian.

Another example of the importance of *Umgebung* is hinted at in this cryptic statement: "And you could almost say that someone could hope in German and fear in English or vice versa" (PR, p. 69). Whatever this means, it does mean that the view that hope is just a biological adaptation is not correct. Further, it strongly suggests that *Lebensformen* have social and cultural bases. Wittgenstein makes a strict distinction between the biological and the ritualistic and states that "an entire mythology is laid down in our language" (RF, pp. 67, 70). In *On Certainty*, Wittgenstein links such a mythology with what he calls a *Weltbild* (OC, §§94–99). What we learn as children—and this is what the wolf-boy missed—is an entire *formal* framework for understanding the world, a *way* of viewing the world, a *Weltanschauung* (cf. OC, §167). This is the sort of non-biological "adaptation" that we should be talking about. New-born infants cannot pretend, because pretending, lying, and all other language-games must be learned in a social context; they do not come naturally (cf. PI, §249).

THE CULTURAL-HISTORICAL ACCOUNT

In the late 1930s, Rush Rhees began an English translation of Part I of the *Investigations*. Wittgenstein wrote extensive corrections on the typescript, which is now a part of the *Nachlass* (TS 226). It is significant that Wittgenstein not only accepted Rhees' translation of *Lebensformen* as "ways of life," but also added "of human beings" at PI, §23. This definitely supports the thesis that *Lebensformen* are uniquely human and again proves that Hunter is wrong in rejecting "ways of life" as a plausible interpretation.

Lebensform is not a word frequently used in ordinary discourse; inded, many dictionaries do not even list the word. The words *Lebenweise* or *Lebensart* (both meaning "way, manner, or style of life") would usually be chosen by native speakers to express the same meaning. *Harrap's Standard German-English Dictionary* has three entries for *Lebensform*, beginning with the cultural "patterns of existence (of tribe, etc.)"; a definition dealing with biological growth; and a psychological meaning: "aspects, traits of personality." *Wahrigs Deutsches Wörterbuch* has two entries for *Lebensform*: (1) *"die Form, Art, sich sein Leben einzurichten"*; and (2) *"ein Leben zu gestalten."* The first meaning is the way one establishes one's life or "settles down," and the second to form or fashion a life.

If Wittgenstein did have ordinary usage or the dictionary meaning in mind when he chose the word, the nuances of "way, manner, or style of life" are very much a part of the cultural interpretation as we defined it earlier. The dictionary meanings above conform most closely with Timothy Binkley's definition of *Lebensform* as "the style of conduct which forms the activities we engage in."[14] Wittgenstein describes being certain as a "manner *(Art und Weise)* of judging and therefore of acting" (OC

§232). In a 1932 lecture he remarked that "causality stands with the physicist for a style of thinking"(L 1, p. 104). One style of thinking is no more rational than another, so it is unfair to criticize a religious "style" of cosmogony with the latest scientific "style."

Decisive proof-texts for the cultural interpretation are found in *Remarks on the Foundation of Mathematics, The Blue and Brown Books,* and "Lecture on Aesthetics":

> And yet we don't call everyone insane who acts similarly within the forms of our culture, who uses words "without purpose." (Think of the coronation of a king) (RFM, p. 45).

> Imagine a use of language (*a culture*) in which there was a common name for green and red on the one hand, and yellow and blue on the other. Suppose, e.g., that there were two castes, one the patrician caste, wearing red and green garments, the other, the plebian, wearing blue and yellow garments. . . . We could also easily imagine a language (*and that means again a culture*) . . . (BB. p. 134, my emphases).

> The words we call expressions of aesthetic judgment play a very complicated role, but a very definite role, in what we call a culture of a period. To describe their use or to describe what you mean by a cultured taste, you have to describe a culture. . . . *What belongs to a language-game is a whole culture* (LC, p. 8, my emphasis).

We will recall that "to imagine a language means to imagine a form of life" (PI, §19), and by simple substitution we have an equivalence of forms of life and cultural forms, styles, and structures.

If we now think if specific forms of life, like praying and being certain, as finding their expression in cultural styles, we find that the initial tension between second and third level *Lebensformen* resolves itself. Praying and being certain are phenomena found among almost all religious peoples. It is therefore general cultural styles that differentiate among various peoples, not the specific life forms (Z, §571). For example, the orthodox Muslim and the American Evangelical Christian have very different *ways* of praying and being certain. The Muslim's prayer is very impersonal and the grounds for his certainty are usually pre-scientific; while the evangelical Christian's prayer is highly personal with the basis for her certainty being a form of pseudo-science, both a reflection of a Western life style.

At PI, §122 Wittgenstein speaks of an *übersichtliche Darstellung* and its fundamental importance for him. Such a "synoptic" presentation "ear-marks the form of account we give, the way we look at things. (Is this a *Weltanschauung?*)" In the original formulation of this passage, Wittgenstein not only answers "yes" to this question, but also states that he means *Weltanschauung* in the sense of the life-philosopher Oswald Spengler (RF, p. 69). In 1942 Wittgenstein again appears to be defining a *Weltanschauung*: "A proposition may describe a picture and this picture [can] be variously anchored in our way of looking (*Betrachtungsweise*) at things, and so in our way of living and acting" (RFM, p. 124).

In the *Philosophical Remarks* Wittgenstein comments: "If I say I believe that someone is sad, it's as though I am seeing his behavior through the medium of sadness, from the viewpoint of sadness" (PR, p. 89). In 1940 he remarks that humor is not just a mood, but a *Weltunschauung*; i.e., humor reveals a certain way of looking at the world (VB, p. 147). Therefore Wittgenstein says that it is not quite right to say that humor was wiped out in Nazi Germany, because "it was not as if people were no longer in good spirits, but something much deeper and more important," i.e., something much more about a cultural style in general.

A FUSION OF NATURAL AND CULTURAL HISTORY

Wittgenstein does seem to equivocate on many points in the *Investigations*, and one of these is on the question of natural history. At PI, §415 he claims that "what we are supplying are really remarks on the natural history of human beings"; but then this passage seems to state the contrary: "We are not doing natural science, nor yet natural history—since we can also invent fictitious natural history for our purposes" (PI, p. 23). He then compares a concept with a style of painting and asks: "For is even our style of painting arbitrary? Can we choose one at pleasure? (The Egyptian, for instance.)" As we have seen above, "an intention is embedded in its situation, in human customs and institutions" (PI, §337). When Wittgenstein tells us to observe how in fact our common lives are structured (cf. PI, §66), he is not only exhorting us to look at ourselves as an animal species, but also to look at our inherited cultural ways of viewing things.

There does not need to be any ultimate conflict between the cultural and organic accounts. If Hunter is correct in interpreting Wittgenstein as saying that language is natural to humans, then surely culture is also part of our natural history. As Pascal once said: "Custom is our nature"; or, as Marjorie Grene puts it, "If . . . our very nature needs culture, then culture is nature, our nature. Even what is natural to us can only become what it is through cultural artifacts. . . ."[15] If commanding, questioning, etc. are as much a part of our natural history as walking, eating, etc., then those cultural styles in which this behavior is expressed are also an aspect of our natural history broadly conceived. If language is not an artificial tool added to the human organism, then culture is not a formal framework externally related to human behavior. Anthony Kenny's organic metaphor is an apt one: "The datum on which language rests, the framework into which it fits, is given not by a structure of unchanging atoms, but by a shifting pattern of forms of life grafted on to a basic common human nature."[16]

Wittgenstein's apparent fusion of natural and cultural history can be seen in his use of the term "convention" in *The Blue and Brown Books*. Some scholars have contended that the word *Lebensform* is a substitute for this earlier use of "convention." If forms of life are the bedrock of the *Investigations*, then this contention is well supported by the following text:

> But what if we went on asking:—"And why do you suppose that toothache corresponds to his holding his cheek just because your toothache corresponds to your holding your cheek?" You will be at a loss to answer this question, *and find that here we strike rock bottom, that is, we have come down to conventions* (BB, p. 24, my emphasis).

Hunter might interject at this point by saying that holding one's cheek while having a toothache is part of a natural language of pain, one which we should share with any animal with an appendage extendable to a locus of pain. But the other reference to conventions in *The Blue and Brown Books* is an example of mapping a country and the convention of dividing certain areas off as counties (BB, p. 57). It is clear that "convention" is not used here in a strict natural-historical sense.

Even with the example of the expression of a toothache, the organic account does not capture the wholeness of the speaking situation. Again we see that a common biology is a necessary but not sufficient condition for meaningful human actions. As P. M. S. Hacker states: "One cannot attain a proper grasp of, e.g., the meaning of 'pain' without appreciating the roles which sentences containing the word play in our life, in entreaties and pleas, requests for mercy, help or alleviation, threats or warnings, expressions of sympathy, prayers and exclamation."[17] Having pain is not a *Lebensform,* for it is a sensation that we share with animals. While Wittgenstein reminds us "that it is a primitive reaction to tend, to treat the part that hurts when someone else is in pain," he like Hacker, emphasizes that the *concept* of pain "is characterized by its particular function in our life" (Z, §§540, 532). ("You learned the *concept* 'pain' when you learned the language" [PI, §384].) If holding one's cheek is simply an animal response, then it is very difficult to explain why Wittgenstein chose the word "convention" to describe it. He must have also meant that it serves as a social cue for eliciting pity or sympathy. Furthermore, it is possible to think of people brought up in such a way "as to give no expression of feeling *of any kind*" (Z, §383; cf. PI, §§142, 257).

It could well be that "all-to-natural" instances of behavior, like our feelings about the "hardness of the logical must," belong, to borrow a metaphor from *On Certainty,* to the mythological hardness of the river banks of our *Weltbild*. The danger of the organic view is that it can easily lead to an illegitimate metaphysics of natural things and events. (This is one of the reasons why Wittgenstein is neither a physicalist nor a behaviorist.) The "natural" boundaries of the world may be just as conventional as the boundaries of the "real" Devonshire (BB, p. 57). The requirements of natural necessity may be grammatical only and not ontological (PI, §373). Note here Wittgenstein's hedge about the "nature" of water: *"Whatever may happen in the future, however water may behave in the future,—we know* that up to now it has behaved *thus* in innumerable instances. This fact is fused into the foundations of our language-games" (OC, §558, first emphasis mine). But doesn't nature have anything to say (cf. Z, §364)? Drawing out some of the implications of Wittgenstein's alleged conventionalism has perhaps vitiated our attempts to reconcile interpretations C and D. We have come dangerously close to what Montaigne once asked: "What if nature were but first custom?"

Let us therefore return to the question of natural history and analyze more closely how Wittgenstein uses the phrase. When he rejects the idea of doing natural history, the phrase always appears in apposition to "natural science," an activity which Wittgenstein consistently eschews (PI, p. 230; OCo, pp. 18, 27, 34). The many other uses of the phrase indicate a broad notion of natural history that clearly includes cultural history. In fact, Sherry and Binkley are probably right in maintaining that "natural history" is a synonym for *Lebensform*. Wittgenstein's statement that hope is a "general phenomenon of natural history" (Z, §469) compares favorably with "phenomena of hope are modifications of this complicated form of life" (PI, p. 174). Also significant in this connection is Wittgenstein's claim that learning a language (i.e., learning a culture) is acquiriing "a knowledge of natural history" (OC, §534; BB, p. 98, 134; PR, p. 59); or when he speaks of the natural history of mathematical objects (RFM, p. 60); or finally, when he speaks of the phenomenon of calculation as "a fact of natural history" (RFM, p. 171). Therefore, natural history is the *entire* record of what we do and what other people have done; and being religious, etc., is just as natural to humans as walking on two legs. (Wittgenstein's "fictitious" natural history is that which we might do, if, for example, certain biological facts were different.) "This simply what we *do*. This is use and custom among us, or a fact of our natural history" (RFM, p. 20).

A PHENOMENOLOGY OF FORMS OF LIFE

In order to clarify the meaning of the cultural interpretation of *Lebensformen,* it will be necessary to delete that part of Hunter's definition which implies that knowing a *Lebensform* will primarily involve gaining *information* about a particular culture. The concept of *Lebensformen* is not to be taken as a *factual* theory, one dealing with certain biological, psychological, or cultural facts. Forms of life are the formal framework that make society and culture possible, but they cannot serve any sociological theory. *Lebensformen* do not answer any "why" questions; they have no explanatory power. They are found as the givens at the end of any chain of explanations.[18] Wittgenstein is concerned with the *meaning* of life and the concepts we use, not their causes, empirical content, or ontological status.

If we did not understand this, we would then be tempted to explicate Wittgenstein's *Lebensformen* in terms of current psychological or sociological theories that attempt to *explain* the relationship between nature and culture. If forms of life could be explained in terms of physiology and psychology, then we *could* understand the lion that talked (PI, p. 223); or, if forms of life could be explained in terms of known cultural facts, then we *could* understand the people of a strange country whose language we have mastered (PI, p. 223); but in each case Wittgenstein claims that we could not understand them. Not even God could tell us about something outside of its proper context, i.e., a human language-game and a particular form of life (OC, §554).

When Wittgenstein convinces us that hope and joy are not reducible to overt behavior, we are then immediately inclined to think of them as inner feelings (Z, §§469, 487). But joy "designates nothing at all," neither outward nor inward; hope is not a "state of mind" (PI, §585) or a feeling (PI, §545), and it surely absurd to think of someone "hoping" for the first time. In other words, hope and joy are not in space or time, and they lack empirical content. As Wittgenstein said in a 1930 lecture; "Hope, fear and doubt are forms of thought" (L 1, p. 24)—or better *forms* of life, not *facts* of life. *Lebensformen* are therefore primarily the formal conditions, the patterns in the weave of our lives, that make a meaningful world possible. They are the existential equivalents of Kant's *Bedingungen der Möglichkeit der Erfahrung*. Understandably, some commentators have proposed that forms of life perform a transcendental function.[19]

As we have seen, Wittgenstein replaces *Entwicklungshypothesen* with *übersichtliche Darstellungen*, which instead of seeking causes and laws, attempt to grasp formal connections. It is significant that the concept of a synoptic presentation is an integral part of Wittgenstein's phenomenological method as he introduces it in the *Philosophical Remarks* (PR, pp. 51–2). The philosophy of the later Wittgenstein can therefore be characterized as a descriptive phenomenology of forms of life, i.e. the formal structures which make a meaningful life possible. In an illuminating article on Wittgenstein and Cassirer, R. S. Rajan proposes, as we cited at the beginning of the chapter, that philosophy for both thinkers "ultimately becomes phenomenological description of the forms of our lives."

2. The Kantian Background

Wittgenstein's philosophy was Kantian from beginning to end.

–D. S. Shwayder[1]

I . . . consider Wittgenstein a Kantian with a vengeance.

–Eva Schaper[2]

Wittgenstein is a true descendant of Kant as any of the rest of Kant's vast philosophical progeny.

–Henry LeRoy Finch[3]

Wittgenstein's philosophy bears deepest affinities to Kant's, despite the fact that he never studied Kant, and despite the substitution of an austere Bauhaus style for the effusions of the Kantian baroque.

–P. M. S. Hacker[4]

Kant's critical method without the peculiar applications Kant made of it . . . is the right sort of approach.

–Wittgenstein (L 1, p. 73)

What in fact does "transcendental" mean? The term implies a Copernican return of subjectivity to itself, but this time with the intention of observing its life and not of discovering in it a logical apparatus.

–Mikel Dufrenne (NA, p. 88)

Like everything metaphysical the harmony between thought and reality is to be found in the grammar of the language.

–Wittgenstein (Z, §55; PG, p. 162)

[Wittgenstein's philosophy] should be properly identified as metaphysical vision . . . [with] . . . Kantian overtones. . . .

–Peter French[5]

33

WITTGENSTEIN AS A KANTIAN PHILOSOPHER

There is now little disagreement among scholars about the fact that phenomenology represents the most significant continuation of the Kantian revolution in 20th Century philosophy.[6] Among Wittgenstein scholars there is a general consensus about the Kantianism of the *Tractatus*, but the claim that the later Wittgenstein is a Kantian is still a controversial thesis.[7] Ross Mandel maintains that both Wittgenstein and Heidegger were involved in a second Copernican Revolution;[8] i.e., an extension of the critical philosophy to a fourth Critique, a "Critique of Language" (the *Tractatus* being a "Critique of Pure Language" and the *Investigations* being a "Critique of Practical Language"). David Pears also sees linguistic philosophy as a "second wave of critical philosophy," doing to language what Kant did to thought.[9]

Alexander Maslow interprets the *Tractatus* as a "kind of Kantian phenomenalism, with the forms of language playing a role similar to Kant's transcendental apparatus."[10] In Chapter One, we have already cited others who claim that Wittgenstein's language-games and forms of life perform a transcendental function. If we realize that the later Wittgenstein expands considerably the concept of a meaningful language, then Erik Stenius aptly summarizes Wittgenstein's Kantianism: "Thus to be possible to theoretical reason corresponds in Wittgenstein's philosophy to possibility in terms of what is describable in meaningful language."[11] Kant taught us that reality conforms to the forms of thought; and Heidegger and Wittgenstein show us that forms of thought are ultimately dependent upon forms of language and life.

How much or how little Kant Wittgenstein actually read is a speculative question that will never be solved. His comments to his students were ambiguous or inconsistent. He told M. O'C. Drury that Kant was a "profound philosopher" and Brian McGuiness heard that the first Critique was a "work of first rank." But G. H. von Wright relates that "from Spinoza, Hume and Kant he said that he could get only occasional glimpses of understanding."[12] S. M. Engel's thesis that Wittgenstein was an avid reader of the Kantian corpus, including Kant's *Introduction to Logic,* is very tenuous. Engel's alignment of parallel texts is interesting, but singularly unconvincing.[13] We do know that Wittgenstein read Schopenhauer with enthusiasm, and his form of Kantianism is a strong influence in the last section of the *Tractatus.*

Stenius is surely correct in arguing that, given Wittgenstein's intellectual background, he did not have to read a word of Kant in order to be a Kantian. The young Wittgenstein was surrounded by neo-Kantian thinkers. We shall discuss the life-philosophers in the next chapter, but probably closest to him were the physicists he studied as an engineering student. For example, Heinrich Hertz speaks explicitly of Kant in the preface of his *Principles of Mechanics*. The only surviving typescript of the *Investigations*, shown to me by Michael Nedo in Cambridge, has a motto from Hertz, and not the motto from Nestroy found in the published editions. It is James Griffin's thesis that most of the fundamental ideas of the *Tractatus*, including the picture theory, were drawn from Hertz.[14] And B. F. McGuinness believes that Wittgenstein was "clearly much influenced" by Hertz, and that "Wittgenstein is said to have thought that Hertz's name ought to have been added to those of Frege and Russell as one of the 'begetters' of the [*Tractatus*]."[15]

Wittgenstein's actual references to Kant are few, with at least two being simply recognition of a Kantian problem or example (NB, p. 15; T, 6.36111). The two other direct references to Kant are much more significant. In 1931, Wittgenstein wrote: "The boundary of language shows itself in the impossibility of describing those facts which correspond to a proposition . . . without just repeating that proposition. We have to do here with the Kantian solution to the problem of philosophy" (VB, p. 27). This appears to be a version of Wittgenstein's doctrine that a proposition cannot "say" its sense, it can only "show" it. Presumably Wittgenstein believes this to be a Kantian solution, i.e., a recognition of the limits of what can be said.

The other crucial reference to Kant is found twice in works in the early 1930s: "Isn't what I am saying what Kant meant, by saying that 5 + 7 = 12 is not analytic but synthetic *a priori*" (PR, p. 129; PG, p. 404; cf. RFM, pp. 125–6). This last claim is nothing short of startling in view of his firm rejection of such propositions in the *Tractatus*, and his inexplicable reiteration of this rejection in a conversation with Schlick in 1929 (WK, pp. 67–8). T. H. Morawetz lists five points that Kant and Wittgenstein share on the topic of certainty and the synthetic *a priori*, and concludes that "if Wittgenstein is concerned to ask the same question as Kant and to answer them in a similar way, he is no more and no less than Kant, doing metaphysics and asking transcendental questions."[16]

There are many Kantian-sounding passages in the later works; i.e., statements that express the Copernican Revolution's thesis that reality must conform to the forms of thought, or to language in the case of Wittgenstein and Heidegger. This assumption is found stated or implied all throughout the later works. Crucial passages are the following: "We predicate of the thing what lies in the method of representing it"

(PI, §104, cf. §§50, 400−1); "the limit of the empirical—is *concept forma-tion*" (RFM, p. 121); and "grammar tells what kind of object anything is" (PI, §373). Stanley Cavell argues that "knowledge of what Wittgenstein means by grammar [is] the knowledge Kant calls 'transcendental.' "[17]

Wittgenstein's insistence that philosophy's task is not an empirical one, but one that searches for the formal structures of possibilities of experience, is also clearly a Kantian concern. "Our investigation, however, is directed not toward phenomena, but ... towards the *'possibilities'* of phenomena. ... Our investigation is therefore a grammatical one" (PI, §90); or "what belongs to grammar are ... the conditions necessary for the understanding of the sense [of propositions]" (PG, p. 88, cf. p. 66). Separating himself off from the scientists and technologists, Wittgenstein contends that "I am not interested in constructing buildings, but in having clearly before me the *Grundlagen* of possible buildings" (VB, p. 22). Kant also uses a building analogy to separate himself from those who remain with the facts of experience. As a transcendentalist, he must assure himself "as to the *Grundlegung* of any building that we propose to erect, not making use of any knowledge that we possess without first determining whence it has come, and not trusting to principles without knowing their origin" (KRV, p. 46).

In a direct attack on an empirical theory of judgment, Wittgenstein states that "experience is not the ground of our game of judging" (OC, §131). In typical Kantian phraseology he states: "*We* may derive it from experience, but experience does not direct us to derive anything from experience" (OC, §130; cf. KRV, p. 41; PR, p. 65). The game of judging, like all language-games, has its source in the *forms* of language and life, not in the facts of experience. When discussing the self-evidence of mathematical axioms, he denies that they derive their certainty from experience. "I mean: experience plays a part; but not the one that one would *immediately expect*" (RFM, p. 113). Mathematical axioms *already* play the role of self-evidence in our language, for as we have seen, certainty is a *form* of life.

In 1931, Wittgenstein admitted that the transcendental method, without Kant's peculiar applications, was the "right sort of approach" (L 1, p. 73). In the same lecture, he charges that Hume and Descartes were wrong in their respective philosophical methods. He observes that "the rationalists were right in seeing that philosophy was not empirical, that is, that as soon as it became empirical it became a question for a science of some sort" (L 1, p. 79). He criticizes the empiricists for not recognizing this distinction, the most crucial one for the transcendental method.

KANT'S ANTICIPATION OF LINGUISTIC PHILOSOPHY

At this point it is instructive to note three specific insights in the works of Kant which anticipate the central issues of this book. First, Kant sets in motion the development of a truly linguistic philosophy; second, he is the principal historical ground for the transcendentalism of phenomenology, a discipline Wittgenstein preferred to call "grammar"; third, he anticipates the contextualism of both Wittgenstein and existential phenomenology.

Kant definitely has an inkling of the "linguistic turn," which comes to fruition not only in Wittgenstein but in existential phenomenology as well. At least twice Kant observes an analogy between the forms of understanding and the forms of grammar. In his *Introduction to Logic* he states:

> The science [logic] which contains these universal and necessary laws is simply a science of the form of thought. And we can form a conception of the possibility of such science, just as of a *universal grammar* which contains nothing beyond the mere form of language, without words, which belong to the matter of the language.[18]

From the *Prolegomena to Any Future Metaphysics*, we find the following passage:

> To search in our common knowledge for the concepts which do not rest upon particular experience and yet occur in all knowledge from experience, of which they as it were constitute the mere form of connection, presupposes neither greater reflection nor deeper insight than to detect in a language the rules of the actual use of words generally and thus to collect elements for a grammar (in fact both researches are very nearly related), even though we are not able to give a reason why each language has just this and no other formal constitution, and still less why any precise number of such formal determinations in general, neither more nor less, can be found in it (P, p. 70).

This passage is instructive in two respects. First, Kant uses the word "grammar" in the uncommon sense that Wittgenstein does, as the "actual use of words." Second, Kant appears to agree with Wittgenstein that one cannot justify grammar, i.e., one cannot prove why these rules rather than others. Wittgenstein believes that the rules of grammar are "arbitrary" and "conventional" (PG, pp. 184, 190; PR, p. 53), and that "I must begin with the distinction between sense and nonsense. Nothing is possible prior to that. I can't give it a foundation" (PG, p. 126; OC, §559). It seems odd that Kant would imply that the rules of grammar are arbitrary in a direct comparison to the rules of understanding, which are definitely not arbitrary.

Although Jonathan Bennett believes that the thesis that "there are no judgments without language is far from being obvious," he attributes this claim to both Kant and Wittgenstein.[19] Janik and Toulmin also emphasize Kant's role in the development of modern linguistic philosophy: "According to [Kant's] account, the logical or linguistic forms of judgment were the forms, also, of any genuine 'experience,' . . . [whose] structure can be characterized only in terms of the forms of judgment, and these forms themselves can be expressed only in terms of the standard forms of logical grammar."[20] Kant's correlation of the Table of Judgments (=logical grammar) and the Table of Categories as the ground for the possibility of experience is therefore the key to the origin of the "linguistic turn." As Engel states: "[Wittgenstein] systematically substituted *forms of expression* for Kant's forms of judgment."[21]

Wittgenstein called his grammar a phenomenology; therefore, it is significant to note that Kant also once used this term in the rough outlines of his critical program. In a letter to Markus Herz on February 21, 1772, Kant announced that he was planning a work on the limits of sensibility and reason, and that the first section of the theoretical part would be called *"Phänomenologie überhaupt."* Bruce Wilshire contends that even though the "natural attitude" of Newtonian mechanics compromises the first Critique as true phenomenology, the "phenomenological spirit" is still there, and that the deduction of the categories is really a *Wesenschau.*[22]

Paul Ricoeur believes that the "Copernican Revolution, disengaged from the epistemological hypothesis, is nothing other than the phenomenological *epoché.*"[23] Because of its heavy reliance on Euclidean geometry, the phenomenology of the Transcendental Aesthetic is weak, but Kant is definitely correct in seeing space as a subjective constitution of our minds. (In Chapter Five, we shall see that Wittgenstein's phenomenology [=grammar] of space will have nothing to do with either Euclidean or non-Euclidean geometry.) In its move from fact to essence, the Transcendental Analytic is sounder phenomenology, but here again Kant's reliance on Aristotelian logic and Newtonian physics takes him away from the true *logos* of phenomena.

Ricoeur praises Kant's "Refutation of Idealism" primarily because of its anticipation of the doctrine of intentionality. Kant states that "our inner experience . . . is possible only on the assumption of outer experience"; and that "the determination of my existence in time is possible only through the existence of actual things which I perceive outside me" (KRV, pp. 244–5). Ricoeur maintains that this "correlation of 'I am' and 'something is' is intentionality itself."[24] As Wittgenstein observes, this means there is an internal relation between what intends and the thing intended (PR, pp. 63–4). Allan Janik believes that Wittgenstein derived this doctrine of internal relations from Schopenhauer, who saw, more directly than Kant, the "inseparable and reciprocal dependence" of subject and object.[25]

Ricoeur offers major reasons why Kant's critical philosophy ultimately cannot be called phenomenology in any sense. Of the two aims of the Critique mentioned at B, 22–3—the limiting of phenomena and the investigation of their internal structure—only the second can be said to be truly phenomenological. Phenomenology cannot be a "critique" in the sense of limiting the field of experience. Ricoeur elaborates:

> Thus, phenomenology has become critical, but in a way opposite to that of Kant. With Kant, intuition refers to the *Denken* that would limit it. With Husserl, "simply thinking" refers back to the evidence that fulfills it. The problem of fullness (*Fülle*) has replaced that of limitation (*Grenze*).[26]

If I understand Ricoeur correctly, then Wittgenstein has expanded the critical philosophy in a similar way. First, Wittgenstein believes that we cannot "talk about the limit of experience, because we should have to experience both sides of the limit" (L 1, p. 86). This is precisely the problem that arises with Kant's concept of "things-in-themselves." Although he insists that we cannot experience them, he nonetheless talks about them and infers certain of their properties.

Second, Wittgenstein merges all three Critiques so that *all* human experience can be subject to the eidetic reduction. This means that some sort of conceptual necessity applies to all experience, not just to "cognitive" or "objective" thought. Keeping in mind the fact that Wittgenstein views conceptual necessity quite differently than Husserl, Hubert Schwyzer phrases the point well:

> Much of the inner world—of pains, itches, moods, smells, tastes, and colors—appear not to be subject to conceptual necessities, and seems to be dismissed by Kant as merely subjective. The realm of human conduct, though by no means dismissed in any way, is also [excluded]. . . . For Wittgenstein there are no exceptions: nothing we can talk about lacks a grammar.[27]

As Wittgenstein once said in class: "So in philosophy all that is not gas is grammar" (L 1, p. 112).

The third point of this section—Kant's anticipation of the contextualism of much of 20th Century thought—revives discussion about Wittgenstein's direct reference to Kant's problem of congruent figures. In the *Prolegomena* Kant offers what he considers to be a decisive argument against the rationalist argument that space and time are qualities in things themselves. Kant challenges the rationalist to explain the difference, *solely in terms of the understanding,* between two otherwise equal triangles on opposite sides of a sphere, or between the images of a right and left hand. Kant is confident that

> there are . . . no internal differences which our understanding could determine by thinking alone. Yet the differences are internal as the senses teach, for, notwithstanding their complete equality and similarity, the left hand cannot be enclosed in the same bounds as the right one (they are not congruent); the glove of one hand cannot be used for the other (P, p. 33).

In the *Tractatus,* Wittgenstein takes up Kant's challenge with his contention that "the right hand the left hand are in fact completely congruent. It is quite irrelevant that they cannot be made to coincide. A right-hand glove could be put on the left hand, if it could be turned round in four-dimensional space" (6.36111). Wittgenstein's answer can be seen as reactionary, in the sense that he initially seems to support the rationalist; but also revolutionary, in the sense that his phenomenology of space is not to be limited in any way by our common experiences of space. As we shall see in Chapter Five, the phenomenology of Wittgenstein's middle period appears at times to be much more ambitious and "pure" than the grammar of the *Investigations*.

In the *Tractatus* and parts of the middle works, Wittgenstein would say that Kant's puzzles of congruity, although *sinnlos* for our world, are nonetheless not *unsinnig*; and that they would be *sinnvoll* in a world of four-dimensional space. As we shall see, the later Wittgenstein collapses the distinction between *Unsinn* and *Sinnlosigkeit* so that he would now agree with Kant. In the *Tractatus* Wittgenstein was apparently unwilling to extend this "semantic holism"—that a word has meaning only within a sentence (see Chapter Ten)—to situations like the puzzles of congruity. But the thorough-going globalism of the later works, I believe, must force this extension. Wittgenstein's favorable remarks in 1939 about the impossibility of superimposing right and left hands readily supports my thesis (LFM, p. 139).

Therefore, Kant's answer to the problem of congruity is a significant anticipation of the most crucial axiom of existential phenomenology: Heidegger's concept of Being-in-the-world and the "hermeneutical circle." (Heidegger even acknowledges Kant's insight on this point [SZ, p. 109].) Kant was correct in his criticism of the rationalists: reason does not operate independently of sensibility. Kant, however, did not follow through radically enough on this insight. That was the achievement of the existential phenomenologists, who claimed that our existential situation always precludes a universal categorial scheme and makes impossible a complete eidetic reduction. Our understanding is thoroughly conditioned by our being in a particular "life-world." One cannot stand outside of this "hermeneutical circle" and make universal claims about all possible worlds.

In the discussion of congruence Kant also mentions another significant point which anticipates a discovery of the later Wittgenstein. The full implication of Wittgenstein's "semantic holism" is the doctrine that "meaning is use." Immediately preceding Kant's discussion of congruence in the *Prolegomena,* he makes the related claim that *a priori* concepts "require, in order to be meaningful and significant, a certain concrete use . . ." (P, p. 29). Concepts are not externally related to one another or to the situations in which they are used. These Kantian insights, even though Wittgenstein and the existential phenomenologists were probably unaware of the specific passages cited in this section, are significant anticipations of a descriptive phenomenology based on a holistic doctrine of internal relations.

SOCIOLOGICAL NEO-KANTIANISM

Following the classification of neo-Kantian thought offered by L. W. Beck, it would be most appropriate to place Wittgenstein among the "sociological neo-Kantians." These include most of the thinkers called *Lebensphilosophen*, such as Wilhelm Dilthey, Georg Simmel, and Oswald Spengler, whose connection to Wittgenstein we shall discuss in Chapter Three. The modern descendants of life-philosophy are the existential phenomenologists, Wittgenstein, and even some neo-Marxists. The Norwegian Wittgenstein scholar Viggo Rossvaer observes that Wittgenstein's interests overlap with Jürgen Habermas and Theodor Adorno, "whose connection to Kant is not through mathematics, but via a study of society."[28]

Beck characterizes the sociological neo-Kantians as having "detranscendentalized" Kant's philosophy by locating the structures of experience in the world itself rather than in the mind. As we shall see, both Wittgenstein and Heidegger have done just this. But a move from the mind to the world does not necessarily mean that the transcendental method is given up. Karsten Harries puts the point this way: "This shift [in Wittgenstein] from an ideal logic to ordinary language parallels the shift from the transcendental subject to the embodied self. In both cases the transcendental approach is not given up: ordinary language and the body can still be called transcendental conditions of experience."[29] Bruce Wilshire concurs: "In becoming existential, phenomenology need not become non-transcendental, and this is particularly true of the most important existentialist of all, Martin Heidegger."[30]

Although Kant does locate the *a priori* in the structures of the mind, this is not a necessary condition in his definition of "transcendental," which is "such knowledge as concerns the *a priori* possibility of knowledge or its *a priori* employment"; or "all knowledge which is occupied not so much with objects as with the mode of our knowledge of objects . . ." (KRV, pp. 96, 59). Wittgenstein's forms of life, language-games, and "framework" facts definitely quality as "transcendental." For Wittgenstein, as Ross Mandel phrases it, "the linguistic community behaves like a transcendental subject for itself. . . . The linguistic practices of a community become conditions through which we see the world."[31] Also appropriate is Dufrenne's definition of the transcendental, which we used as an epigram, and which "fleshes out" beautifully the Kantian version: "The term implies a Copernican return of subjectivity to itself, but this time with the intention of observing its life and not of discovering in it a logical apparatus" (NA, p. 88).

As we shall argue in Chapter Eight, Wittgenstein's grammatical propositions, and the "framework facts" of *On Certainty,* are similar to the Kantian *a priori* synthetic. Grammatical propositions do not derive their sense from experience (otherwise they would not be indubitable). They are not even, strictly speaking, true or false; rather, they *constitute* what is true and what is false. As Wittgenstein states: "Grammar is not accountable to any reality. It is grammatical rules that determine meaning (constitute [*konstituieren*]it) and so they themselves are not answerable to any meaning and to that extent are arbitrary" (PG, p. 184). Kant also believed that the true *a priori* could not be "accountable to any reality" because that would definitely make it contingent and not necessary (cf. e.g. KRV, p. 140). But unlike Kant and Husserl, Wittgenstein's constitution is *in the world* (in *forms* of life) and not in a transcendental subject. The existential phenomenologists believe likewise: e.g., M. C. Dillon affirms that Merleau-Ponty sees "the world horizon [as] a condition for the unity of consciousness."[32]

The key to the transcendental method of phenomenology and Wittgenstein is its emphatic stand against the psychologism of the 19th Century (especially Millian) empiricism. For Husserl, Kant's Copernican Revolution meant the ultimate turning away from any grounding of philosophy in the facts of objective sciences. The transcendental method lays down a strict separation of *Wesen* and *Tatsache*, between philosophical *quaestio iuris* and scientific *quaestio facti*. For Wittgenstein this means a firm rejection of any attempt to reduce the logic (grammar) of a language-game to an association of facts, for "how can we describe the foundations of our language by means of empirical propositions?!" (RFM, p. 120).

The associationism of classical empiricism assumed realistically that the world is prior to humans. But, as Harries points out in the article cited above, the transcendental method assumes that *neither* is prior. This is a clue to why Heidegger always uses the term *gleichursprünglich* when he is talking about "beginnings." *Dasein* is not prior to the world (i.e. idealism) nor is the world prior to *Dasein* (realism)—they are "equiprimordial." I contend that Wittgenstein's method expresses itself in a similar way when he insists that *Lebensformen* cannot be justified— they are the givens that must be accepted (OC, §359; PI, p. 226). As Heidegger would phrase it: we find ourselves *already* in a *Dasein*-world, *already* wrapped up with entities ready-at-hand, which are *already* interpreted for us.

TRACTARIAN AND FUNDAMENTAL ONTOLOGIES

According to Beck's classification, Heidegger's Kantianism was of the "Heidelberg" type, that associated with Wilhelm Windelband and Heinrich Rickert. Heidegger studied under Rickert at Freiburg until Rickert left to finish his career at Heidelberg. (Appropriately, at least for the historical continuity between Kant and phenomenology, Edmund Husserl took Rickert's chair at Freiburg.) Heidegger's first dissertation, *Der Lehre vom Urteil im Psychologismus* (1914), was written under Rickert and contained a strong critique of any attempt to reduce logical procedures and norms to psychological processes. But with the publication of *Being and Time* in 1927 it was clear that Heidegger had been heavily influenced by Wilhelm Dilthey, George Simmel, and *Lebensphilosophie* in general.[33] At the same time, however, Heidegger was critical of Dilthey. Although he did anticipate a phenomenology of

"Gestalten" and *"das Ganze des Lebens,"* Dilthey's work was still a philosophical anthropology based on a type of psychologism (SZ, p. 46).

It is strange then that Husserl rejected *Being and Time* because he thought that the *Dasein*-analysis was a philosophical anthropology. In the same way commentators want to draw a theory of man or society out of the later works of Wittgenstein. These thinkers are overlooking a fundamental Kantian assumption that both Wittgenstein and Heidegger firmly maintain: that their respective philosophies are *not theories* about sociological or psychological facts, but descriptive phenomenologies of *forms* of life. Wittgenstein's *Lebensformen* are the formal framework that make a human society possible, but they cannot serve as the basis for any sociological theory. As we have seen in Chapter One, neither Heidegger's *Existenzialen* nor Wittgenstein's *Lebensformen* can answer any "why" questions—they have no explanatory power.

Originally, Heidegger had planned to introduce *Being and Time* with his work on Kant, but as it turned out, the later appeared as *Kant and the Problem of Metaphysics* two years later. In *Being and Time* Heidegger emphasizes his transcendental method in the strongest possible terms (SZ, p. 38). He also insists that his *Existenzialen* are *a priori* in nature, i.e. they are the *given* forms of human life (SZ, pp. 44, 53). The most important existential, care, is not to be seen as this or that "concernful" behavior, but as the *"Bedingung der Möglichkeit"* for being able to care at all (SZ, p. 317).

In *Kants Theses über das Sein* Heidegger praises Kant's critical philosophy, because it turns us away from a philosophy of Being based on entities (*Seiendes*) to conceiving of Being in terms of the *"Gegenständlichkeit des Gegenstandes der Erfahrung"* (KTS, p. 291). In other words, Being is "that which determines entities as entities," or "that which is 'transcendental' for every entity" (SZ, pp. 6, 208). In similar Kantian fashion Wittgenstein states that "grammar tells what kind of object anything is" (PI, §373). Heidegger's search for the conditions for the possibility of objects has the same Kantian basis as Wittgenstein's philosophical grammar, which is directed toward the *'possibilities'* of phenomena" (PI, §90). Heidegger also maintains a necessary connection between transcendental conditions and language (cf. SZ, pp. 162, 166), which we shall explore in more detail in Chapter Ten.

I believe that Stenius is correct in claiming that the Tractarian "logical form of substance," which is prior to all experience and therefore *a priori*, is equivalent to Kant's *a priori* "form of experience."[34] As we saw above, Heidegger's Being is the equivalent of Kant's "form of experience." Stephen Erickson has also seen this connection between Heidegger's Being, Kantianly interpreted, and Wittgenstein's logical form.[35] It is significant to find Wittgenstein using the word *"Sein"* in a strikingly Heideggerian way in his *Notebooks*:

> My *whole* task consists in explaining the nature of the proposition. That is to say, in giving the nature of all facts, whose picture the proposition *is*. In giving the nature of all *Sein*. (And here *Sein* does not stand for existence—in that case it would be nonsensical) (NB, p. 39).

This is what Heidegger means by the "ontological difference," *viz.* that Being, as the condition for the possibility of objects, cannot be an object itself. For Heidegger only entities exist. Further, here is the Tractarian equivalent of Heidegger's "ontological" knowledge: "If I know an object I also know all its possible occurrences in states of affairs [=Being]. Every one of those possibilities must be part of the nature of the object" (T, 2.0123). Both Wittgenstein and Heidegger agree that an object and its Being are ontologically different, but nonetheless inseparable.

With the preceeding key we can now draw some instructive parallels between the ontology of the *Tractatus* and Heidegger's fundamental ontology. Although there does not seem to be any completely consistent use in *Being and Time* of terms like *Tatsache, Faktum, Gegenstand, Objekt*, one can nevertheless propose that Heidegger's "ontic facts," those which can be represented as present-at-hand (*Vorhandenes*), correspond to Wittgenstein's *Tatsache*, the only things of which we can "make pictures" (T, 2.1). Heidegger's "ontological facts," those which are actually *possible* arrangements of ontic facts, correspond very well with Wittgenstein's *Sachverhalte*. Heidegger would have fully agreed with Wittgenstein when he later told Schlick that "physics . . . does not offer a description of the phenomenological *Sachverhalte*" (WK, p. 63). One of the central assumptions of *Being and Time* is that all entites have Being, and that there is no such thing as a Being-less, i.e., meaningless, entity. This corresponds to the Tractarian doctrine that all substance (*Gegenstände, Sachen, Dinge*) is inseparable from logical form and that only such objects have meaning, or more accurately, *are* meanings themselves (T, 3.203).

But there is an important difference between the Tractarian ontology and the fundamental ontology, which, significantly enough, prefigures the development of Wittgenstein's later philosophy. Heidegger's ontological facts are internally related to one another is a *Dasein*-world, while Wittgenstein's *Sachverhalte* are, following the lead of Russell's logical atomism, externally related. In contrast, the "framework" facts of

On Certainty are internally related. As early as 1929, it is clear that Wittgenstein had given up logical atomism, the independence of elementary propositions, and external relations. In the *Philosophical Remarks* he directly attacks the theories of Russell, Ogden, and Richards and their doctrine of external relations. Intentionality is essential to the functioning of language, and this requires a doctrine of internal relations (PR, p. 63). In Chapter Four, we shall discuss the crucial concepts of *Übersicht* and *Umbegung* which definitely imply this significant turn to internal relations.

A METAPHYSICS OF LIVED EXPERIENCE

Let us now sum up the ways in which Wittgenstein diverges from Kant, but still remains within the transcendental tradition of phenomenology, especially its later forms. He rejects the transcendental ego and the strong emphasis on cognition in favor of the idea of intersubjectivity based in *Praxis* and non-cognitive modes of experience. Husserl's own form of Kantianism led him into the dead-end of a transcendental solipsism (Husserl's own "crisis" as Ricoeur phrases it) to which sociological neo-Kantianism was a ready answer. Both of the major streams of neo-Kantianism, the life-philosophers and the cognitivists of the Marburg School, tended to merge the Transcendental Aesthetic and Analytic, but the former emphasized *aisthesis* and the second and third Critiques, and the latter focused on pure *noesis*.

Although there is a significant parallel between Kant's transcendental logic as the "rules of the understanding in general" (KRV, p. 93) and Wittgenstein's grammar as the rules for meaning and sense, there is also an important difference. (Could neo-Kantian talk about "rules" have partially prompted Wittgenstein to think of "rules" of language-games?) Kant models his transcendental logic on Aristotelian logic; but Wittgenstein, observing that this logic is just one among many possible logical language-games (see Chapter Nine), wishes to free grammar from any one particular system of rules. Wittgenstein contends that one can make sense even if one is contradicting oneself, whereas Kant and most traditional philosophy would not have accepted this. Viggo Rossvaer believes that Wittgenstein's most important insight was that "logic must accommodate itself with the [life-] world and not the world to logic."[36] Therefore Wittgenstein's grammar cannot be like Kant's transcendental logic, which "treats of understanding without any regard to difference in the objects to which the understanding may be directed" (KRV, p. 93).

Contrary to those who have taken the critical philosophy to be a rejection of any metaphysics at all, Kant made it very clear that the Critiques were a propaedeutic for a new, reformed metaphysics which would use reason in a proper way. H. J. Paton's phrase "metaphysics of experience" is used to describe this reformed philosophy, and this phrase has been used for Wittgenstein as well.[37] Mandel describes how such a metaphysics would operate in Wittgenstein and Heidegger:

> Heidegger and Wittgenstein have instigated this great reversal: instead of explanations, theories, and models being used to replace the everyday sense of things, they maintain that we should treat these models and explanations as emerging from the way we ordinarily experience the world and as referring back to that experience.[38]

For Wittgenstein we ordinarily experience the world through language-games and forms of life, and "like everything metaphysical the harmony between thought and reality is to be found in the grammar of the language" (Z, §55; PG, p. 162).

It is true that Wittgenstein often criticizes metaphysics, but this is the pre-critical variety fueled by an overreaching reason "craving for generality" and having a "contemptuous attitude towards the particular case" (BB, p. 17). Traditional metaphysics "obliterates the distinction between factual and conceptual investigations" (Z, §458), but a reformed metaphysics of experience would carefully separate these two questions according to Kant's transcendental method. The following passage is crucial in this regard:

> Perhaps we shouldn't be inclined to say that we had said anything physiological, even psychological, *but something metapsychological, metaphysical. Something about the essence, nature, of pain as opposed to its causal connections with other phenomena* (PE, p. 277, my emphasis).

This is pure transcendentalism and it finds a significant link with the linguistic phenomenology of the *Remarks*: "Philosophy as the custodian of grammar [=phenomenology] can in fact grasp the essence of the world, only not in the propositions of language, but in rules for this language . . . (PR, p. 85).

In "On Man's Need for Metaphysics," Schopenhauer proposes an "immanent" metaphysics—one drawn from experience and not constructed *a priori*—which would give us "the correct and universal understanding of experience itself, the true interpretation of its meaning and content."[39] In the next chapter, we shall see that the influence of Schopenhauer on Wittgenstein was considerable, especially during his early period. Remnants of a purer Schopenhauer-like transcendentalism persist in the middle period in the passages quoted above. Hacker describes the later Wittgenstein's metaphysics of experience more aptly as "generalizing . . . the concept of a 'form of world-description'. . . ."[40] It is significant that Hacker speculates that L. E. J. Brouwer, an intuitionist mathematician whom we shall ally with the *Lebensphilosophen* of the next chapter, was a possible "impetus" for Wittgenstein to move in the direction of a full *Weltschauungsphilosophie*.

Kant requires that any future metaphysics be based on synthetic *a priori* propositions, and Wittgenstein's version of these propositions would be the transcendental grounds for the *Weltbild* phenomenology that is hinted at in *On Certainty*. Wittgenstein's radical pluralism, based as it is on the possibility of different world-views and world-pictures, definitely avoids the denigration of the "particular case" and preserves the fullness and richness of lived experience. In the next chapter, we discuss Wittgenstein's relationship to 19th Century *Lebensphilosophie*. One *Lebensphilosoph*, Georg Simmel, believed that for centuries thinkers had written metaphysics from the standpoint of static being, God, or nature, and had lost sight of the true goal of metaphysics: to do justice to life itself.

3. Life-Philosophy

The absolute is life, *the ultimate reality which we are able to reach, not by dominating it conceptually, but only by* living *it.*

–Georg Simmel[1]

Everything . . . must . . . be the expression of something living.

–Oswald Spengler (DW I, p. 46)

But that which is missing is primal life, wild life, which wishes to vent itself.

–Wittgenstein (VB, p. 78)

Instinctively we use language rightly; but to the intellect this use is a puzzle.

–Wittgenstein (L 1, p. 1)

A true Plato, who first of all fixes in concept things that become and flow and then supplements the fixed concept with a concept of flowing.

–Wilhelm Dilthey[2]

In the veins of the knowing subject, as constructed by Locke, Hume, and Kant, no real blood is flowing, but the diluted juice of "reason" as the mere activity of thinking.

–Wilhelm Dilthey[3]

THE MAIN CHARACTERISTICS OF *LEBENSPHILOSOPHIE*

It is the thesis of this chapter that Wittgenstein's concept of *Lebensformen* can be best understood on the background of *Lebensphilosophie*. Patrick Sherry at Lancaster states that "in so far as anything is basic for the later Wittgenstein, it isn't sense-data or atomic propositions, but forms of life—or simply 'life.' "[5] K. E. Trangy explains Wittgenstein's radical limitation of what we say and his emphasis on what must be shown as a way of insisting "that there is no substitute for life."[6] In his entry on *"Leben"* in the *Handbuch philosophisher Grundbegriffe*. Josef Simon does indeed place Wittgenstein in the camp of Wilhelm Dilthey, Friedrich Nietzsche, Martin Heidegger, and Hans-Georg Gadamer with respect to their views of "life."[7] Of course, Simon did not have the space to defend such a controversial thesis, but this is a task which I shall undertake in that which follows.

Lebensphilosophie is a term which is used to characterize a broad range of philosophical thinking that came into being as an integral part of the Romantic reaction against 19th Century mechanism, materialism, and positivism. It is a blend of Kant's formalism and Hegel's historicity of Spirit. I. M. Bochenski proposes that there are three main schools of *Lebensphilosophie*: Bergsonianism, pragmatism, and a German school dominated by Wilhelm Dilthey, Arthur Schopenhauer, Friedrich Nietzsche, Oswald Spengler, Georg Simmel, and Eduard Spranger. We know for a fact that Wittgenstein read Schopenhauer and Spengler with great enthusiasm and interest.

Except for Spengler, Schopenhauer, most likely Nietzsche, and less likely Spranger, I shall not assume that Wittgenstein actually read any of the major works of *Lebensphilosophie*. This would be a risky assumption given what we know of Wittgenstein's reading habits. But Wittgenstein is still a Kantian, even though he probably read little or none of Kant's works. Similarly, Wittgenstein's *Lebensphilosophie* came to him primarily through a process of intellectual and cultural osmosis. As Bernard Kaplan surmises:

> For someone like Wittgenstein, who did no systematic reading in the classics of philosophy, someone who received his deepest impressions not from academic philosophers, but from writers in the border between philosophy. religion, and poetry, Dilthey would have been an enormously appealing figure, and moreover a figure whose writings were quite likely discussed at some length in his home.[8]

For reasons given below, I have included the Dutch mathematician, L. E. J. Brouwer, as a life-philosopher. Wittgenstein attended two of his lectures in Vienna in 1928 and they made a profound effect on him. After these lectures he decided to return to philosophy and Brouwer's influence after that can definitely be documented. Herman Feigl, who along with Friedrich Waismann persuaded Wittgenstein to attend Brouwer's lectures, describes vividly the effects of the first evening: "It was fascinating to behold the change that had come over Wittgenstein that evening. . . . He became extremely voluble and began sketching ideas that were the beginnings of his later writings. . . . That evening marked the return of Wittgenstein to strong philosophical interests and activities."[9]

Bochenski claims that there are five main characteristics of the *Lebensphilosophen*:[10] (1) "They are absolute actualists. For them, there is only movement, becoming, life." There is at the same time sufficient emphasis on form and structure to avoid the chaos of pure experience. (2) They oppose a mechanism based on Newtonian physics with a holism and organicism drawn from biological analogies. (3) They replace the rational-analytic method with "the test of intuition, practice, and a vital understanding of history." (4) "They are but rarely subjectivists and they assume the existence of an objective reality which transcends the subject." (5) Finally, "they betray a marked inclination toward pluralism and personalism." This shows up as the "perspectivism" of Nietzsche, Wittgenstein, and the existential phenomenologists. (A full discussion of Wittgenstein's holism and intuitive method must wait until Chapter Four.)

The linchpin of the philosophical method of the *Lebensphilosophen* was their attempt to bring philosophy back to concrete actuality—back to life itself. In the *Philosophical Remarks,* written in 1929–30, Wittgenstein states: "This which we take as a matter of course, *life*, is supposed to be something accidental, subordinate, while something that normally never comes into my head, reality" (PR, p. 80). If we consider the context of his discussion, we find that he is criticizing philosophers who, even though life itself and the "world of ideas" (*Vorstellungswelt*) are really closest to them, still persist in assigning reality to only those things of the natural sciences. For Wittgenstein, true philosophy should not go beyond "the stream of life, or the stream of the world" (PR, p. 81); or as he states it in a much later work: "Psychology connects what is experienced (*das Erlebte*) with something physical, but we connect what is experienced with what is experienced (*Erlebtem*)" (OCo, p. 48). This phraseology reminds one of Dilthey's concept of *Erlebnis*, which was taken over by the phenomenologists and the existentialists.

In contrast to the positivists who used physics as their model, the *Lebensphilosophen* favored biology as the principal scientific guide for philosophy. The raw "biologism" frequently found in Nietzsche and Spengler is the most extreme development of this thesis. This biologism can also be found in Wittgenstein, as we saw with the "wild" life quotation above and his claim that all great art comes from primitive instincts and that in such art a "wild animal" has been tamed (VB, p. 77). Wittgenstein states that "being certain" is a form of life and it is based on "something animal" (OC, §§358−9). We have seen other passages of the same sort: "I want to regard man here as an animal, as a primitive being to which one grants instinct but not ratiocination" (OC, §475); or "our language-game is an extension of primitive behavior. . . . (Instinct)" (Z, §545). In Chapter One, we saw that Wittgenstein's biologism is strong enough that John Hunter was able to write an impressive, but incorrect, interpretation of forms of life as non-cultural, "biological adaptations."

But this biologism is really a caricature of *Lebensphilosophie*, for it essentially reduces it to a form of the naturalism and reductionism that it sought to depose. For Dilthey, life is not reducible to biology, for it finds its ultimate expression in the irreducible objective spirit of religion, culture, and the arts. And if one analyzes fully Wittgenstein's use of "life" and "forms of life," one discovers that he too means much more than biology. We have shown in Chapter One that, except for the implications in the passages above, he rarely ever used the term "life" to describe physical life. Therefore, Wittgenstein, like most of the *Lebensphilosophen*, saw forms of life as cultural-historical categories and not as mere biological adaptations.

ARTHUR SCHOPENHAUER

There are already excellent studies relating Wittgenstein and Schopenhauer. All that I can hope to do in this section is to synthesize this scholarship in a way that best supports the general thesis of this book. Wittgenstein read Schopenhauer's *The World as Will and Representation* at the age of sixteen, and he admitted to von Wright that his earliest philosophy was a Schopenhauerian epistemological idealism.[11] It is obvious that during the composition of the *Notebooks* and the *Tractatus* that he had either re-read Schopenhauer or had retained much of the material from his earlier reading. Hacker is convinced that ". . . little sense can be made of his thinking on these thoughts [about death] without presuming that he saw some deep truth in the Schopenhauerian metaphysical vision and the transcendental ideality of time." [2]

A. Phillips Griffiths states that "for while there is only one reference to Schopenhauer by name in the *Notebooks*, some of the remarks there, some of which are repeated in the *Tractatus*, are so exactly Schopenhauerian as to appear almost culled from the text."[13] Hacker has pointed out that the metaphor of the eye to explain the relationship of Wittgenstein's "metaphysical subject" to the world is identical with Schopenhauer's; and Patrick Gardiner suggests that the ladder image of the *Tractatus* is also borrowed directly from Schopenhauer.[14] More generally, Schopenhauer appears to be the source of the early Wittgenstein's insights about the world, the will, the "metaphysical self," aesthetics, and ethics. Like Schopenhauer, Wittgenstein disengages ethics from the world, and joins him in his separation of ethics from reason, a divergence from Kant that other life philosophers follows as well.

Engel is along in arguing that there are recognizable Schopenhauerian influences in the later Wittgenstein. He contend that Wittgenstein's ideas on the nature of philosophy, including the rejection of the "craving for generality," are derived from Schopenhauer's minor works. He also maintains that Wittgenstein follows *The World as Will and Representation* in his thesis that language bewitches us and that this deception can be avoided by attending to particular usage.[15] Again, Engel's alignment of parallel texts is, with some exceptions, not very convincing; furthermore, he assumes that Wittgenstein read many of Schopenhauer's minor works. In addition, Gardiner, although he sees a connection between Wittgenstein and Schopenhauer on language, proposes that it is the *Tractatus*, not the *Investigations*, where this influence might have evinced itself.[16]

Wittgenstein's initially odd remarks about self, life, and world make some sense if interpreted in light of Schopenhauer. Many commentators have despaired in encountering passages such as "The world is my world" (T, 5.641), "The world and life are one" (T, 5.621), and "It is true: Man *is* the microcosm: I am my world" (NB, p. 84). The connecting clue for the tie with Schopenhauer is "As my idea is the world, in the same way my will is the world-will" (NB, p. 85), which is unmistakable Schopenhauerian phraseology. As Hacker observes: "The identification of the individual consciousness with the microcosm, and the microcosm with the macrocosm, is a central Schopenhauerian thesis."[17]

The passages above have at least two significant implications other

than the historical connection to Schopenhauer. They are the source of
the early Wittgenstein's notorious remarks about solipsism, which have
been debated at great length. As we are interested primarily in the later
Wittgenstein, it is sufficient to remark that the later Wittgenstein rejects
solipsism in favor of an intersubjective life-world. The idea of a fully
social world still retains a crucial insight that Schopenhauer claimed he
had discovered: *viz*., the internal relation between will and body, between self and world.

As we have seen in the Kant chapter, it is Allan Janik who has pin-
pointed this important link to Schopenhauer. He shows that
Schopenhauer introduced a new starting point for philosophy—one
that commenced neither with the knowing subject nor the object
known, but with "the *idea* as the first fact of consciousness."[18]
Schopenhauer is definitely lingering in Wittgeinstein's mind in
1929–30 as he emphasizes the primacy of the *"Vorstellungswelt"* and
criticizes those who take actual physical things as the givens (PR, p. 80).
The "stream of the world" (="stream of life," PR, p. 81) is a unified
flow of subject and object in which the Cartesian distinction between
the "inner" and the "outer" has been dissolved. As Wittgenstein said in
a lecture in 1930: "This simile [*sic*] of 'inside' or 'outside' the mind is
pernicious. It is derived from 'in the head' when we think of ourselves
as looking out from our heads and of thinking as something going on
'in our head' " (L 1, p. 25).

The ultimate result of such thinking is the avoidance of the traditional dilemma of realism vs. idealism. It also offers a way of interpreting Wittgenstein's cryptic remarks about e.g. "idealism lead[ing] to
realism if it is strictly thought out" (NB, p. 85; cf. T, 5.64). Wittgenstein
contends that the "idealists were right in that we never transcend experience. Mind and matter is a division *in* experience" (L 1, p. 80). But
he also argues that realists were correct in holding that external objects
do exist. This sounds like the thrust of Kant's "Refutation of Idealism,"
in which he argues that transcendental idealism is the only proper basis
for an empirical realism (KRV, p. 244f).

Hacker calls Wittgenstein's early position, one principally derived
from Schopenhauer, a "transcendental solipsism," which includes "a belief in the transcendental ideality of time (and presumably space) . . .
together with the acceptance of Schopenhauer's reification of the unity
of consciousness [and thus a slip back into traditional metaphysics], and
other related and undigested theories about ethics, the will, aesthetics,
and religion."[19] To this might be added an acceptance of the Kantian
formal *a priori*, but not the synthetic *a priori*. Janik observes that the

early Wittgenstein, like Schopenhauer, believes that logic, mathematics, and natural science are pure, formal sciences whose basic propositions reduce to tautologies. Ironically, it took another life-philosopher strongly influenced by Schopenhauer, L. E. J. Brouwer, to persuade Wittgenstein that this particular position was wrong. Wittgenstein's move to the synthetic *a priori* parallels the move from a purely formal metaphysical subject to the embodied "soul" (cf. PI, p. 178) of the later works. Solipsism, pure formalism, and pure transcendentalism are all left behind as the later Wittgenstein merges with the dominant forces in life-philosophy which rejected these positions.

EDUARD SPRANGER

We have no evidence that Wittgenstein ever read any of the works of Dilthey, the principal and most respected figure in *Lebensphilosophie*. Wittgenstein did, however, spend 1906–08 at the Technische Hochschule in Berlin, which was right after the end of Dilthey's very successful tenure at the University of Berlin. Kaplan contends that "Dilthey's posture and his problems were very close to those of at least the later Wittgenstein. After all, Dilthey was one of the leading neo-Kantians of the day."[20] Dilthey's *Weltanschauungsphilosophie* was the starting point for all the later life-philosophers. Calvin Schrag describes Dilthey's philosophy as "an imaginative interpretation of various world-views arising out of particular life-styles,"[21] which would be directly equivalent to Wittgenstein's forms of life. Karl-Otto Apel observes that in Wittgenstein, Kant's *a priori* forms are replaced by language and forms of life in a way very similar to what Dilthey did with Kant.[22]

A Viennese student of Dilthey's, Eduard Spranger, is a more promising connection to Wittgenstein, although Kaplan suggests that "it was less Spranger than Dilthey who influenced Wittgenstein during the 1920s."[23] Spranger was one of the most popular and widely-read *Lebensphilosophen*, primarily because of his best-selling book, *Lebensformen*, which had sold 28,000 copies by the end of the 1920s. We do not know if Wittgenstein read the book, but he must have at least heard of it. Janik and Toulmin are emphatic in their opinion that "given Wittgenstein's Viennese background . . . he was no more in a position to *invent* the term 'forms of life' than one could today invent the phrase 'territorial imperative'; in the Vienna of the 1920s, this was just one of those cultural commonplaces that did not need explaining."[24]

Spranger's book, translated into English as *Types of Men*, is a socio-psychological study of six principal *Lebensformen*: the theoretical, the economical, the aesthetic, the social, the religious, and the political. There is obviously not a complete match between Spranger's forms of life and Wittgenstein's, which range, as we have seen, from specific forms like hoping and pretending, to cultural styles, religious beliefs, and the use of language in general. The two thinkers do agree on religious and aesthetic life-forms, and Wittgenstein does stipulate that giving commands and obeying orders is a language-game (PI, §19), which would ultimately be based on a form of life involving political authority. The ultimate difference between them is that Wittgenstein would have definitely rejected Spranger's theory that forms of life are structures in consciousness.

Both Spranger and Wittgenstein believe that *Lebensformen* have a biological basis, but they cannot, contrary to Hunter's thesis, be explained solely in terms of biology. As Spranger states: "On a lower level, perhaps, the soul is purely biologically determined. On a higher level, the historical, for instance, the soul participates in objective values which cannot be deduced from the simple value of self-preservation."[25] Spranger criticizes those psychologists who would reduce the psyche and society to the abstract elements of the sciences. Such a method would possibly give us a genealogy but not a morphology, i.e. a "logic of forms" that would allow us to truly understand the uniqueness of humankind and its activities. Positivistic psychology is therefore methodologically unable to do justice to the "superbiological levels in which meaning-contents become significant beyond mere adaptation to conditions which barely preserve life."[26]

Another relevant characteristic of Spranger's methodology is his holism, which he terms "*Ganzheitforschung*." It involves the discovery that "everything is a part of everything else," and that the "totality of mind is present in every act."[27] Spranger contrasts his "structural" psychology based on internal relations with a "psychology of elements," in which the psychic whole is just the sum of externally related parts. Quantitative calculations of sensations, reflexes, and citations from memory are meaningless units that, when synthesized, do not add up to the meaningful whole that we all live. Spranger also synthesizes data, but with a difference: "In the realm of psychology of structure we may consider as building material only what has an independent meaning or a significant attitude."[28] We must keep in mind the fact that Wittgenstein's basic "building blocks" are the unities of meaning experienced in language-games and forms of life.

GEORG SIMMEL

In his essay, "The Conflict in Modern Culture," George Simmel summarizes the main tenets of *Lebensphilosophie*. He lays out the evolution of philosophical concepts from the Greek focus on *being*, the medieval Christian's emphasis on *God*, the Renaissance's resurrection of *nature*, and finally, the discovery in the middle of the 19th Century that *life* is the most fundamental concept in philosophy. Simmel states: "Life has thus reclaimed its sovereignty. . . . The purest expression of life as a central idea is reached when it is viewed as the metaphysical basic fact, as the essence of all being . . . every object becomes a pulse beat of absolute life. . . ."[29] In typically Hegelian style, Simmel claims that life gradually progresses beyond the animal level to spirit, and then the human spirit produces culture and "forms of life."

Cognition is that which is most alienated and independent of the flow of life, and therefore any philosophy based primarily on cognitive data will simply not do justice to human experience. As Simmel declares: "The philosophy that exalts and glorifies life insists firmly on two things. On the one hand, it rejects mechanics as a universal principal. . . . On the other hand, it rejects the claims of ideas to a metaphysical independence and primacy."[30] The life-philosophers and Wittgenstein share with Simmel his mistrust of the unrealistic demands of traditional logic: "Since life is the antithesis of form and since only that which is somehow formed can be conceptually described, the concept of life cannot be freed from logical impression."[31] The Eleatics and Bradley were correct: the intellect cannot understand "becoming"—life itself.

Simmel was a popular Privatdozent at the University of Berlin until 1914, so the young Wittgenstein most likely crossed his path. Guy Oakes, one of his translators, believes that Wittgenstein "shares more common ground with Simmel than has ever been acknowledged."[32] The link between the two, like with Spranger, is found in the use of the term *Lebensform*. R. H. Weingartner states that Simmel's *Lebensphilosophie* "concerns itself with the articulation of, and discrimination among, different forms of life."[33] Simmel refers explicitly to religion as "an autonomous *Lebensform* with its own intrinsic properties," and definitely implies that there are also aesthetic, theoretic, and ethical *Lebensformen* as well.[34] Simmel's life-forms find their expression as a style of art or thought, as specific historical-cultural ways of acting and thinking. Similarly, Wittgenstein, who explicitly states that to imagine a language is at the same time to imagine a form of life and a culture, gives, as we have seen, the hypothetical example of a culture in which the plebes wear blue and yellow and the patrician class wears red and green. He also argues that for us to describe the use of words we use in aesthetic judgment requires us to describe the specific aesthetic tastes of the culture in question.

Simmel, therefore, believes that *Lebensformen* operate at different levels, so that they have a hierarchical relationship and structure. Like Wittgenstein and other *Lebensphilosophen*, Simmel maintains that there is a definite biological basis for all *Lebensformen*: "[There] must be the basis of our acting in a beneficial, life-preserving way, according to the peculiarity of the psychobiological organization of our species."[35] All forms of life arise from an undifferentiated *Erleben* in which concrete, practical needs play the principal role. In this capacity, forms of life function merely as "instruments of life."

Culture is possible, however, only when these forms take on an autonomy of their own, when they "stand forth as autocratic ideas and themselves determine life and its value."[36] Simmel scholar R. H. Weingartner phrases this transition aptly: "Usually . . . men see in order to live. Artists, however, come to live in order to see"; or as Simmel himself states: "At first men know in order to live; but then there are men who live in order to know."[37] Only in the latter cases do we have the appearance of genuine life-forms called the "aesthetic" and the "theoretic."

Lebensformen are unique in the sense that they, in contrast to the formal elements of mathematics and logic, cannot be cognized, but only lived and experienced. This means that forms of life can never be objects of *Erkennen*, but only categories of *Erleben*. This is the reason why Wittgenstein believes that we must take them as givens: they cannot be justified, rationalized, or explained in a theoretical manner. As we have argued previously, they are also unique in the sense that they are confined to categorizing human life only.

Wittgenstein agrees with Simmel, because he, contrary to the Hunter thesis (*viz.* that *Lebensformen* are simply biological adaptations), sees that biology is a necessary but not sufficient condition for human life-forms. Genuine *Lebensformen* allow humans to pursue goals that are sometimes entirely divorced from basic needs. In many instances, specific forms of life like pretending, grieving, etc., actually give negative reinforcement in terms of meeting basic needs. Such life-forms are "non-teleological," as Simmel would say. It is precisely this independence from and transcendence of fulfilling basic needs that gives human culture its brilliance, genius, and freedom.

This is a point on which the life-philosophies of Simmel and Wittgenstein diverge from pragmatism, which has some of its main roots in *Lebensphilosophie*. For the pragmatists, meaning is that which is *useful*, whereas for Simmel and Wittgenstein, meaning is simply *use*, whether or not it serves any pragmatic end. While Simmel admires pragmatism because it "deprives truth of its old claim to be a free-floating domain ruled by independent and ideal laws," it fails to see that human action in the world is not based on purely subjective needs.[38] In *On Certainty*, Wittgenstein argues that we continue to believe in our picture of the world not because it is useful but simply because it is given—it is ours and it is simply what we do. What possible use, for example, is derived from a world-picture which claims that the king can make rain, or that time and the existence of the world began with the coronation of the king? In his remarks on mathematics, there are similar comments against traditional pragmatism: "Do we live because it is practical to live? Do we think because thinking is practical?" (RFM, p. 171). Above the truth that might be found in correspondence with reality and above the truth of what is useful, there is simply the basic fact of what is used (RFM, cf. p. 4).

Wittgenstein and the *Lebensphilosophen* also agree in their definition of "world." It is not a scientific cosmos, but a cultural-historical "world." For Simmel each of the general *Lebensformen* can function as a "world-form" (*Weltform*). And only when all the contents of experience are grasped by such a form do we have a "world":

> A world, in the full sense, is thus a sum of contents in which, from the perspective of the mind, each piece is delivered from its isolated condition and is brought into a unified system, into a form which is capable of encompassing the familiar and the unfamiliar.[39]

Therefore, one can speak of a religious world, an aesthetic world, a theoretical world—each self-sufficient and each with its own inner logic. Furthermore, there is a premonition of the linguistic turn because Simmel suggests that "each [world-form] in its peculiar language already expresses the *entire* world-stuff . . . these worlds are not capable of any mixing, overlapping, crossing."[40] In the *Remarks* Wittgenstein also speaks of a "form of the world" which is so pervasive that we never call it into question (PR, p. 80). (As we shall see shortly, he also uses the term "*Weltbild*" in a similar fashion.) His first talk of language-games is phrased in terms of formal systems or "worlds" (PR, p. 178). Each language-game and form of life has its own inner logic, its own rules of adequacy: one is not superior to another—one is not more truthful than another.

Some of Wittgenstein's most vigorous criticism of another thinker comes in his "Remarks on Frazer's *Golden Bough*." Here Wittgenstein chides Frazer for taking the religious rituals of primitive tribes as a form of naive science. The theoretical world and the religious world do not overlap; the rules of one do not apply to the other. That which is needed is not some phony "historical" or "evolutionary" hypothesis to explain primitive religious behavior, but a formal analysis (an *übersichtliche Darstellung*) of the structures of the rituals themselves (RF, p. 69).

The *Lebensphilosophen* borrowed freely from the Kantian tradition and talked of the *a priori* and the formal conditions for the possibility of experience.[41] Although they emphasized the concrete actuality of lived experience, they, as sociological neo-Kantians, also saw an equally important role for form, structure, and essence. But the fixed Kantian categories became fluid forms of history. Indeed, Simmel believes that new forms may arise from raw *Erleben*. But these forms are not arbitrary in the sense that any single individual could create or change them at will; rather, they are products of an objective spirit which lays down the formal framework for individual action and behavior.

Wittgenstein believes that, although it is possible to conceive of a society whose members gave "no expression of feeling *of any kind*" (Z, §383, cf. PI, §257), this is not *our* natural history and not part of *our* forms of life. Here we can see Bochenski's fourth criterion, that *Lebensphilosophen* are not mere subjectivists, being clearly exemplified. But Wittgenstein would definitely not accept any theory of objective spirit to explain this point. He would simply point to the empirical fact of the intersubjective nature of society, much like Mauthner does in the following: "Where is this language a reality? Where in all the world? Not in the individual. . . . Where is the abstraction 'language' reality? *In the air* . . . in the nation, *between people*."[42]

OSWALD SPENGLER

Oswald Spengler is the least regarded of all *Lebensphilosophen*, but it is he whom Wittgenstein read and quotes favorably, at least eight times in the published works. G. H. von Wright states that "the strength of

Spengler's impact on Wittgenstein should not be underrated."[43] Both
PI, §122 and §131 were originally written in direct reference to Spengler's thought (RF, p. 69; VB, p. 57). In an unpublished manuscript he
writes, "I am thinking of Spengler's method" (220, p. 85), which was a
comparative morphology of cultures. This method, according to W. H.
Dray, is "an inquiry into the typical form of their life, their rhythms,
and possibly their laws."[44]

In 1931 Wittgenstein wrote: "So we could have understood Spengler
better, if he had said: 'I *compare* various cultural periods with the life of
families' " (VB, p. 34). Both Garth Hallett and von Wright suggest that
Wittgenstein derived his rejection of causality in history and the central
concept of "family resemblances" from Spengler.[45] Like Simmel,
Spengler rejects the idea that life had an innate teleology, that it was
progressing towards some particular goal. Spengler thinks that teleology was a disguised form of causality which betrayed the nature of life,
which is, as Goethe held, basically causeless and aimless (DW I, p.
111fn).

As a second generation *Lebensphilosoph*, Spengler was influenced by
Nietzsche and Schopenhauer, but most profoundly by the *Ur-
lebensphilosoph* Goethe. *The Decline of the West* is filled with favorable references to Goethe, who, as Spengler claims, taught him method while
Nietzsche taught him to question. For Goethe, "the become" (*das
Gewordne*) is always founded on "becoming" (*Das Werden*), and "the
natural and cognizable are rooted in the historic . . . [which] leads directly to the fact that everything . . . must . . . be *the expression of something living* (DW I, p. 46). From Goethe Spengler learned to distinguish
between experience as lived (*Erleben*) and experience as learned and
cognized (*Erkennen*), a distinction central to all life-philosophy. With
their emphasis on *Erkennen*, traditional philosophers "could not touch
life" because of "their armory of abstractions" (DW I, p. 119).

Spengler sees cultures as unities of meaning, just as Wittgenstein sees
his language-games and forms of life. (Recall that, for Wittgenstein, to
imagine a language is to imagine a culture.) In fact, Spengler uses
Goethe's word "*Urphänomen*" (primal phenomenon) to describe cultural
styles, the same word that Wittgenstein uses for his language-games
(PI, §654). Goethe stated that "there are prime phenomena which in
their godlike simplicity we must not disturb or infringe (DW I, p. 97).[46]
Finch is convinced that Wittgenstein borrowed this term directly from
Goethe, but it is puzzling to find that Finch quotes Goethe *from Spengler*
and *not* from Goethe himself.[47] For Spengler, the *Urphänomene* of cul-

tural styles express themselves specifically as religious, intellectual, political, and socio-economic, making them "forms of life" as Simmel and Spranger call them.

Spengler also believes that cultures are isolated from one another with respect to mutual understanding. Indians and Chinese may share the Buddhist religion, but each lives the religion very differently. Wittgenstein claims that the symphonies of Bruckner and Mahler are entirely different art forms, and he adds that this is really a Spenglerian observation (VB, p. 45). This Spenglerian background also helps us understand Wittgenstein's claim that we could not understand the people of a strange country even if we had mastered their language (PI, p. 223). In different cultures "life would run on differently" and it is possible that alien cultures would have "*essentially* different concepts" (Z, §§387–88). Wittgenstein expressed the doctrine of cultural isolation most radically in 1950, when he wrote: "One (cultural) period misunderstands the others, and a minor epoch misunderstands all the others in its own ugly way" (VB, p. 172).

This idea of non-overlapping cultures, which we have also seen in Simmel, can be best illustrated by a biological analogy. Spengler compares cultural styles to the *habitus* of a plant, the specific and unique ways in which it develops (DW I, p. 108). Spengler's "high" cultures function like separate biological species which cannot interbreed. And if one culture appears to influence another (like Persian influences on late Judaism), this is imitation only (Spengler called it "pseudomorphosis") and does not constitute a genuine Jewish understanding of Zoroastrianism. Today critics of the "talking" chimpanzees have charged that these apes are just clever imitators and have not, and will never, ever enter a human "world."

Like all life-philosophers, Spengler uses the term "world" to describe a cultural, historical world. We have already seen above that Wittgenstein says he uses the term "*Weltanschauung*" in a Spenglerian sense. Each "high" culture has its own *Weltanschauung*, its own unique way of viewing things or its own *Weltbild*. Spengler states that "a picture of the world (cosmos, universe)" is one "in which the whole of consciousness, becoming and the become, life and what is experienced," is grasped.[48] Although Wittgenstein could have had other sources, it is certainly a good possibility that the *Weltbild* of *On Certainty* is of Spenglerian origin. Here it appears to perform the functions of a form of life at the most general level. Recall this key passage from the *Investigations*:

> "So you are saying that human agreement decides what is true and what is false?" It is what human beings *say* that is true and false and

they agree in the *language* they use. That is not agreement in opinions but in form of life (PI, §241).

In *On Certainty* Wittgenstein states: "I have a world-picture. Is it true or false? Above all, it is the substratum of all my inquiring and asserting"; and "[the world-picture] is the inherited background against which I distinguish between true and false" (OC, §§162, 94).

The context of the above quotations is Moore's famous proofs for the existence of the external world. We are generally inclined to make certain knowledge claims because "nothing in [our] picture of the world speaks in favor of the opposite" (OC, §93). A crucial passage is the following: "The propositions describing this world-picture might be part of a kind of mythology. And their role is like that of rules of a game, and the game can be learned purely practically without learning any explicit rules" (OC, §95). Furthermore, the mythology of our *Weltbild* may change like a river-bed: it is conceivable that "hard" propositions would become "fluid" and "fluid" ones become "hard" (OC, §96). But a change in *Weltbild* is not initiated by subjective whim, but only gradually through intersubjective action. For example, Wittgenstein is obviously correct when he claims that one could not choose the Egyptian style of painting at will (PI, p. 230). Hallett is convinced that again the influence of Spengler can be seen here, because he saw style as "an unwilled and unavoidable tendency" that is part and parcel of the objective spirit of a culture.[49]

Spengler fulfills most all of Bochenski's criteria for *Lebensphilosophie*: (1) he rejects categorically modern physics and philosophy for being sterile, empty, and removed from life; (2) he enthusiastically embraces Goethe's organicism and his concept of "living nature"; (3) he chooses intuition over rational analysis; and (4) he rejects the linearism and progressivism of modern history. A similar rejection is poignantly expressed in Wittgenstein's mysterious preface to the *Philosophical Remarks*. Here he separates himself from the mainstream of European and American civilization, which he condemns as an *Unkultur* that is incapable of expressing human values. This bad "spirit expresses itself in an onwards movement, in building ever larger and more complicated structures" (PR, p. 7; cf. VB, pp. 20–3). It is significant that in yet another reference to Spengler, Wittgenstein excludes him and Otto Weininger from the ranks of *Western* philosophers (111, p. 196).

Therefore, Wittgenstein's general goal is similar to Spengler's morphology of cultures: to get clear, i.e. to have a synoptic view, of the basic structures of experience itself. He also shared Spengler's negative view of 20th Century culture in general. Twentieth Century philosophy cannot be great, because there are no longer any great people. Philosophy requires total dedication, complete ethical integrity, and a complete transformation of the human personality. Wittgenstein not only found these virtues lacking in himself, but also among his colleagues at Cambridge.

L. E. J. BROUWER

L. E.J. Brouwer, the founder of intuitionism in the philosophy of mathematics, has not been called a *Lebensphilosoph*, but there is no question that he ought to be interpeted in terms of this tradition. True to the spirit of Romanticism, a driving force behind all life-philosophy, Brouwer, in an early work, *Life, Art, and Mysticism* (1905), criticizes both logic and science. Science is at the "last flower and ossification of culture," and its "mathematical-logical substratum" is "completely alien to life . . ." (CW I, pp. 5, 7). Brouwer's rhetoric is harsh: he maintains that "man's fall [was] caused by the intellect," a "gift of the devil," and predicts that those who relinquish it will attain an "immediately clear" vision of the true nature of things (CW I, pp. 3, 7).

These remarks appear curiously ironic as one pages through Brouwer's *Collected Works* and observes a life-long devotion to highly sophisticated mathematics, which, although its philosophical foundations are laid in the anti-cognitivism of *Lebensphilosophie*, is still a thoroughly intellectual achievement. (Indeed, most of the life-philosophers made their living by perfecting their brilliant intellects.) The editors of Bouwer's *Collected Works* express this contrast well: "The unimpeachable precision of his argument is reflected in his style; his elaborate and precise formulation frightened and put off whole generations of mathematicians" (CW II, p. xv).

In a lecture in 1928, the one which Wittgenstein so enthusiastically received, Brouwer states that mathematical reflection is rooted in an act of will, which, when directed at the temporal succession of events, produces the *"Urphänomen"* of "the falling apart of a moment of life into two qualitatively different things" (CW I, p. 417). This is the foundation of the distinction of self and world, and, in addition, this "twoness" (*Zweiheit*) is the very source of the entire natural number system. Brouwer explains that this *"Urintuition"* of *"Zweiheit"* is derived from Kant's idea of the apriority of time (CW I, p. 127). He gives up the Kantian apriority of space, primarily because of the "serious blow" dealt it by the discovery of non-Euclidean geometry.

P. M. S. Hacker and other commentators have traced Bouwer's Kantian link through Schopenhauer, whose anti-rationalist voluntarism also stresses temporality.[50] For Brouwer the "forms of representation" are founded neither in the constitution of the mind nor in an *a priori* structure of the world, but in the temporal flow of life itself. In a significant break with Kant, Brouwer believes that phenomena are causally ordered, not because of some innate category in the mind, but because "your colored view wants this regularity" (CW I, p. 2). Although Brouwer never escapes the psychologism that infects virtually all life-philosophy, this idea that "constitution" lies in human needs and action is compatible with the later Wittgenstein.

Drawing on Spenglerian themes and language, Brouwer claims that human destiny is not subject to causality and that we should reject the progressivism of the modern world, which always seeks new organization and new growth. In 1949 (Brouwer's basic views remained consistent for almost half a century), he stated: ". . . if the delusion of causality could be thrown off, nature, gradually resuming her rights, would be (except for her bondage to destiny) generous and forgiving to a mankind decausalized and subsiding to more modest and more harmonious proportions" (CW I, p. 487). Wittgenstein agrees with Brouwer that causality is not an *a priori* category in the mind; rather, it is a "style of thinking" or a "hypothesis," "a way of describing things," which is a part of language (L 1, pp. 79, 104). Therefore, phenomena could be "decausalized" by a change in grammar.

Brouwer embraces Spengler's predictions about the modern world's corruption and decline and his general pessimism. He appears to be even more radical than Spengler on the possibility of genuine communication. As we have seen, Spengler believed that separate cultures could not understand one another. Brouwer contends that individuals within the same culture cannot really communicate. In 1905 he said: "For never has anyone been able to communicate his soul by means of language" (CW I, p. 6). In 1949 he still believes in this notion of subjective isolation, but he hints at a means of real communication that definitely reminds one of the *Einfühlung* of the life-philosophers: "By so-called exchange of thought with another being the subject only touches the outer wall of an automaton. This can hardly be called mutual understanding. Only through the sensation of the other's soul sometimes a deeper approach is experienced" (CW I, p. 485).

We know for a fact that Wittgenstein heard Brouwer's 1928 lectures and we can assume from the numerous references to Brouwer that he was acquainted with his general mathematical philosophy (PR, pp. 176, 210, 212; PG, pp. 238, 458; WK, p. 73; L 2, p. 302; 106, p. 245; L 3, pp. 140, 196; 113, pp. 198–99). As we shall see, he probably derived many insights from Brouwer, or at least confirmed in Brouwer ideas that were incubating in his own mind. In a letter to Moore (May 5, 1930), Russell reports about his first impressions of a typescript (probably TS 209, one of the versions of our current *Philosophical Remarks*), which Wittgenstein had sent him. Russell says that Wittgenstein talks about "the *a priori* in the Kantian sense" and "has a lot of stuff about infinity, which is always in danger of becoming what Brouwer has said. . . ."[51]

Despite some strong influences, it is clear that Wittgenstein rejected the basic philosophical claims of Brouwer's "intuitionism." In 1939 he expressed his opinions frankly: "Intuitionism is all bosh—entirely. Unless it means an inspiration" (LFM, p. 237). This appears to conflict with what he told Waismann in 1932—that mathematics is based on intuition (WK, p. 219)—but we shall return to this point later in this section. (A detailed analysis of Wittgenstein's use of the words *"Einsicht"* and *"Anschauung"* is contained in Chapter Five.)

Wittgenstein's main problem with intuitionism is its introspectionism and its dogmatic metaphysical claim that mathematical objects do not have any independent ontological status. Wittgenstein's attack on intuitionism comes disguised in his critical remarks about finitism, which has absurd consequences just as behaviorism has (LFM, p. 111). One is just as wrong to deny the ontological independence of mathematical objects as to affirm it (LFM, p. 141). Wittgenstein rejects finitism and intuitionism for the same reason he rejects behaviorism: each view is reductionistic—each of them say "all we have here is. . . . Both deny the existence of something" (RFM, p. 63)—mental states in the case of behaviorism and real mathematical objects in the case of intuitionism. Both Wittgenstein and the phenomenologists agree that the traditional battle between realists and idealists is a phony one: there is no pure "inner" sphere and no pure "outer" world—both are fused in a *Lebenswelt*.

In spite of this basic disagreement, Wittgenstein was definitely influenced by Brouwer. We can say with some confidence that the Brouwer lecture convinced Wittgenstein that mathematical propositions are synthetic *a priori* (see Chapter Eight for a full discussion), and that Brouwer was correct in rejecting the law of the excluded middle. As we have seen, Brouwer believes that mathematics contains mental constructions which have been derived from an intuition of time. This means that mathematical propositions are inextricably tied to history.

The proposition "There are three consecutive sevens in the development of π" would have to be either true or false according to the law of the excluded middle. Computer calculations of π have perhaps found three consecutive sevens, but for Wittgenstein in his day this proposition had not been verified. Both Wittgenstein and Brouwer reject the claim that all propositions must be either true or false and propose that some propositions must be either true or false and propose that some propositions are "undecided." Wittgenstein admits that the proposition about could "become true" in ten years' time (L 2, p. 302; cf. L I, p. 107).

Wittgenstein agrees with Brouwer that mathematics is invention not discovery; it is the free creation of the human will at a certain time and place. Wittgenstein claims, just before a discussion with Brouwer, that "we can assert anything which can be checked in practice. It's a question of the possibility of checking" (PR, p. 212). The context of the discussion is Brouwer's idea of "undecidability"—e.g. that one cannot say whether "There are three consecutive sevens in the development of π" is true or false. As a result, both Brouwer and Wittgenstein believe that mathematics can be given no foundation in logic or any other formal system. Its only foundation is mathematical practice itself, or as the intuitionist, Michael Dummett, phrases it: "[mathematics] would wear its own justification on its face."[52] Wittgenstein generalizes this point by insisting that no foundations can be "said," but they can be "shown" in our language-games and forms of life.

In Hacker's insightful discussion of Wittgenstein's connection with Brouwer, there is one misleading inference about Brouwer's belief that language is thoroughly social. Although Brouwer does state in his 1928 lecture that "language is thoroughly a function of the activity of the social person," the overwhelming balance of his comments, despite ones that allude to some objective spirit or the idea of *Einfühlung,* are contrary to this. We have already noted this strong belief in subjective isolation and how this precludes any meaningful communication. Furthermore, he believes that intuitionist mathematics is done "without having recourse to language or logic" (CW I, p. 489). In addition, in the construction of mathematics sets "neither the ordinary language nor any symbolic language can have any other role than that of service as a non-mathematical auxiliary . . ." (CW I, p. 128). V. H. Klenk articulates this divergence from Wittgenstein most aptly:

[Wittgenstein] denies the intuitionist claim that what is essential in mathematics is the internal mental state, and that the external

manifestations of that state, the linguistic accompaniments, are irrelevant. In fact, he will claim that it is precisely the external, overt
use of language which is critical in mathematical operation. . . .[53]

Brouwer's introspectionism tends heavily towards solipsism (cf. the
editors' comments in CW II, p. xv) and this solipsism was probably derived from Schopenhauer, who, on this point, was a minority among
the *Lebensphilosophen,* whose holism and belief in an intersubjective
Lebenswelt were paramount.

When Wittgenstein does state that intuition (*Anschauung*) is necessary
for the solution of mathematical problems, he makes it clear that language and the "process of calculating" (both public activities) "provide
the necessary intuition" (T, 6.233). Frege uses the term "*Anschauung*" in
his philosophy of mathematics, but he finds the foundation in logic
rather than language and other human activities. Wittgenstein continued his Tractarian view in his conversations with Waismann in 1932
in which he admitted that mathematics to some degree is founded in
intuition, but this is the intuition of symbols (WK, p. 219). Wittgenstein
is obviously turning the focus of intuition outwards, *in the world*, not in-
wards on mental states. As we shall see in the next chapter, Wittgenstein believes that we can gain an intuitive grasp of the formal structure
of all grammars by means of an *übersichtliche Darstellung* (a *Weltanschauung,* PI, §122; RF, p. 69), e.g. the grammar of color through
use of the color octahedron.

Although Hacker is certainly correct in proposing that Brouwer's
constructivist *Weltanschauungsphilosophie* has an "obvious deep affinity"
with Wittgenstein's later philosophy, we have been compelled to note
these important differences regarding the nature of intuition and the
effects of social institutions like language. Furthermore, we must point
out another significant difference. In addition to Wittgenstein's strong
criticism of Brouwer's introspectionism, he also chides him for believing that one can reject the law of the excluded middle without rejecting
classical logic entirely. Observe these crucial quotations:

> I need hardly say that where the law of the excluded middle
> doesn't apply, no other law of logic applies either, because in that
> case we aren't dealing with propositions of mathematics. (Against
> Weyl and Brouwer) (PR, p. 176).

> Just as in general the whole approach that if a proposition is valid
> for one region of mathematics it need not necessarily be valid for a
> second region as well, is quite out of place in mathematics, com-

pletely contrary to its essence. Although these authors [Brouwer and other intuitionists] hold just this approach to be particularly subtle, and to combat prejudice (PR, p. 210; cf. PG, p. 458).

This means that Brouwer rejects one fundamental axiom of *Lebensphilosophie* which Wittgenstein maintains fervently: holism and globalism. Dummett clarifies the point well: "Intuitionism rejects . . . a holistic view of mathematics: for it . . . each mathematical statement has a completely specific meaning of its own, a meaning which renders it capable of those applications which are made of it, but which is independent of any supplementary empirical hypotheses upon which such applications may hang."[54] Dummett believes that holism is indistinguishable from formalism, presumably because of formalism's assumption of a doctrine of internal relations. As we shall see in Chapter Four, Wittgenstein accepts both holism and internal relations.

In concluding this section on Brouwer, I wish to note two of his beliefs which have instructive parallels with Heidegger and Merleau-Ponty. First, Brouwer appears to agree with Heidegger that truth is not correspondence, not even coherence, but "revelation" of a particular *Dasein*-world. Brouwer states: The manifestations of the Self within the bounds and in the forms peculiar to this life are irruptions of Truth. Always and everywhere truth is in the air; to the initiated truth is the same wherever it breaks through" (CW I, p. 7). Second, Brouwer also anticipates the idea of a "body-ego," a central theme of Merleau-Ponty's phenomenology of perception: "A further aberration has been the concentration of all bodily awareness in the human head thereby excluding . . . the rest of the body. At the same time man became convinced of his own existence as an individual and that of a separate and independent world of perception" (CW I, p. 4). Here again Brouwer is speaking as the life-philosopher that he generally is, and again we see the significant link between life-philosophy and existential phenomenology.

WITTGENSTEIN VS. *LEBENSPHILOSOPHIE*

It will undoubtedly come as a surprise to many to see this common ground between Wittgenstein and *Lebensphilosophie*, a philosophy that has been ostracized by many, including faithful followers of Wittgenstein. But the evidence of the texts is persuasive. It shows that in Wittgenstein's later philosophy life itself plays the role of what H. R. Smart called the "metaphysical ultimate,"[55] just like it does in *Lebensphilosophie*. For Wittgenstein, *Lebensphilosophie* even takes precedence over *Sprachphilosophie*. In Chapter One, I presented textual evidence that shows that forms of life are more basic than language-games. Not only is life more basic, there is a risk that language can bewitch us, while life itself cannot. Note this crucial passage from the Big Typescript: "If we surrender the reins to language and not *to life*, then the problems of philosophy arise" (213, p. 521). Nietzsche, too, believed that we must trust life rather than language, because the masses had so diluted ordinary language that it ceased to be a vehicle for the transvaluation of values.

We cannot presume that *Lebensphilosophie* will be the key to all the puzzles that lie in Wittgenstein's work. Indeed, Wittgenstein would definitely not have agreed with many of the theories of the *Lebensphilosophen*. He would have rejected their frequent use of speculative concepts (like "objective spirit") and would have not been pleased with their psychologism and idealism. Although they explicitly rejected Kant's "faculty" psychology, they replaced it with something just as speculative and just as untenable. Their genetic theory of *Lebensformen*, that they arise out of the pure process of *Erleben*, and their talk of psychic energies being directed here and there would have alienated Wittgenstein completely.

Another major disagreement between Wittgenstein and most life-philosophers is his rejection of Dilthey's division between the *Naturwissenschaften* and the *Geisteswissenschaften*. Following Dilthey, Spengler believed that there were two major world-pictures, i.e. world-as-history and world-as-nature. The organic, intuitive method must be used to investigate history and society, but the mechanical analytic method is appropriate for nature. Heidegger appears to continue this tradition by implying in *Being and Time* that the "existentials" must be used to explain human behavior and things ready-at-hand, but that the Kantian categories are sufficient for understanding things present-to-hand. But Wittgenstein strongly rejects this bifurcation of method, the prime example being his revolutionary and controversial theories about the foundations of mathematics and logic.

In conclusion, the full context of Marjorie Grene's epigram to this chapter is appropriate. Observing that Wittgenstein's concept of life is very much like the phenomenologists', she states:

Language-games of every style, from mathematics to religion, must be freed from the self-consciousness that philosophical reflection chronically produces and be let to live again, each in its own way.

Philosophy is a kind of stage fright. That is death, or at least the image of death. . . . Philosophy, compared to ordinary goings-on, is death-like; it tries to stop the game in the midst of play. . . . Let life go on.

4. Holism and Internal Relations

We [mistakenly] want to say that there can't be any vagueness in logic.
—Wittgenstein (PI, §101)

I strive not after exactness, but after a synoptic view.
—Wittgenstein (Z, §464)

Formerly, I myself spoke of a "complete analysis" and I used to believe that philosophy had to give a definitive dissection of propositions so as to set out clearly all their connections and remove all possibilities of misunderstanding.
—Wittgenstein (PG, p. 211)

The concept of a synoptic representation is of fundamental significance for us. It earmarks the form of account we give, the way we look at things.
—Wittgenstein (PI, §122)

We cannot think of any object apart from the possibility of its connection with other things.
—Wittgenstein (T, 2.0121)

Wittgenstein arrives at the terms of continuity, such as Praxis and Lebensform, from his insistence upon a vision of the whole . . . [they] evoke the wholeness of the speaking situation [so that we are able to] simultaneously glimpse the internal relations among things.
—J. T. Price[1]

A color "shines" in its surroundings. (Just as eyes only smile in a face.) . . . Something is "grey" or "white" only in a particular surrounding (Umgebung).
—Wittgenstein (OCo, pp. 9, 46)

73

THE LOGIC OF VAGUENESS

A typical response to any comparison between Wittgenstein and any of the phenomenologists is that Wittgenstein always seeks to clarify philosophical problems, whereas it seems the phenomenologists just make them more obscure. This response is based on a view of Wittgenstein's first held by the positivists and later by many analytic philosophers. The goal among these philosophers was a *clarité Cartesienne*, a search for clear and distinct ideas with a basis in the exactness and precision of logic, mathematics, and the sciences. Although there is no question that much of Wittgenstein's conceptual analysis in the *Investigations* is well crafted and clear, it is a mistake to take this for his general method.

To say that "Wittgenstein's central ideas . . . are essentially simple," as David Pole does,[2] is at least only a half-truth, but is completely false if Pole defines "simple" as being "clear and distinct" in the general analytic tradition. I agree with Stanley Cavell, who characterizes the *Investigations* as much like Augustine's *Confessions* and observes that "there is virtually nothing in the *Investigations* which we should ordinarily call reasoning; Wittgenstein asserts nothing that could be proved, for what he asserts is obvious . . . or else concerned with conviction."[3] Further, the work of the later Wittgenstein is unsystematic and repetitious; it contains many obscure and cryptic passages; and the meaning of many of these passages is anything but clear and simple. Wittgenstein warns us to be suspicious of "clear and simple language-games" which ignore "friction and air resistance" (PI, §130).

In criticizing one of C. D. Broad's lectures in 1931, Wittgenstein objects to Broad's distinction between the common use of a term and the philosophically precise use: "This is the very last thing philosophy should do. Broad says that philosophy is endeavoring to get clear; but it is shocking to use words with a meaning they never have in normal life and [this] is the source of much confusion" (L 1, p. 73). In the *Philosophical Remarks*, Wittgenstein exclaims about how strange it is that philosophy must speak in a language that is not ours. "Logical analysis is the analysis of something we have, not of something we don't have" (PR, p. 52); or it is the "unfolding of meaning already known" (L 1, p. 108). Although the results of philosophy are simple, the procedures will be just as complicated as the knots we have tied in our thinking.

If we have correctly understood some of Wittgenstein's basic ideas, then many philosophical solutions envisioned by analytic philosophers are rendered impossible. Both Russell and Moore, two fathers of modern analytic philosophy, finally realized this. Russell read the *Philosophical Remarks* in typescript form and was not very impressed, and his negative comments about the *Investigations* are well-known.[4] G. E. Moore came to Wittgenstein's lectures in the early 1930's, and, according to Karl Britton, he "often seemed very disapproving," his replies usually being "very discouraging indeed."[5] As we shall see, Moore was particularly baffled by the way in which Wittgenstein was using the word "grammar." C. D. Broad, another Cambridge philosopher at the time, was openly contemptuous of what he believed was Wittgenstein's philosophical dilettantism.

Although J. N. Findlay is not an analytic philosopher, his comments on Wittgenstein's "magic" are appropriate: "His personality, like his writing, made an immense aesthetic impact, so great indeed that one was tempted to confuse beauty with clarity and strangely luminous expression with perspicuous truth."[6] Many contemporary analytic philosophers have understandably lost interest in Wittgenstein scholarship. For example, Hilary Putnam is critical of forms of life: "The fondness [of commentators] for the expression 'forms of life' appears to be directly proportional to its degree of preposterousness in a given context."[7] Some of the most hostile criticisms have come in reviews of *Remarks on the Foundation of Mathematics,* which Paul Bernays says betrays a "mental asceticism" devoted to the goal of "irrationality."[8] Even the intuitionist Michael Dummett believes that this work contains comments which are "plainly silly" or "thin and unconvincing."[9]

In the later works Wittgenstein distinguishes carefully between philosophical clarity and exactness. He completely rejects the Socratic method of exact definition. Socrates chastises the pupil who, in answer to the question "what is knowledge?", gives an example of knowledge. But Wittgenstein unabashedly sides with Socrates' interlocutors: "But our answer consists in giving such an enumeration and a few analogies" (PG, pp. 120–1). The following is typical of Wittgenstein's arguments against traditional philosophical methods:

The moment we try to apply exact concepts of measurement to immediate experience, we come up against a peculiar vagueness in this experience. But that only means a vagueness relative to these concepts of measurement. And, now, it seems to me that this vagueness isn't something provisional, to be eliminated later on by more precise knowledge, but that this is a characteristic logical peculiarity (PR, p. 263; cf. PI, §88; OCo, p. 21).

In criticizing the use of geometric method in philosophy, Husserl is in surprising agreement with Wittgenstein when he insists that some concepts "are *essentially and not accidentally inexact*, and are *therefore* also unmathematical" (*Ideas*, §74).

Although I have been unable to read Gordon Baker's Oxford dissertation on Wittgenstein, "The Logic of Vagueness," I suspect that it deals with passages such as the above. The emphasis on imprecision, vagueness, and ambiguity is a part of the inheritance of the tradition of *Lebensphilosphie*, and Matthew Fairbanks has proposed that Wittgenstein was specifically influenced on this point by William James. Fairbanks summarizes his analysis: "Both [Wittgenstein and James] are aware of the fact and importance of 'vagueness' in human communication, and both offer a way out of 'vagueness' by insisting that we look to the practical circumstances of contextual use."[10] Fairbanks misleads his readers, however, in overemphasizing the differences between James and Wittgenstein (there are many, of course) by declaring that Wittgenstein is an "analyst" primarily concerned with logical methods. In 1930, Wittgenstein told his class that philosophy is not analysis if that means taking something apart and discovering something new (L 1, p. 35). He also strongly rejects logico-deductive methods, which start with certain self-evident propositions from which other propositions are deduced, in favor of a dialectical method, which is "very sound and a way in which we do work," and whose goal is "to find out where ambiguities in our language are" (L 1, p. 74).

In an article entitled "The Triumph of Ambiguity," James E. Marsh states that "whereas earlier thinkers, Russell, Wittgenstein himself in his *Tractatus*, and Husserl, tried to overcome ambiguity . . . the later Wittgenstein and Merleau-Ponty accept ambiguity . . . [and] make equivalent moves away from meaning conceived as abstract, univocal, clear, exact, and absolutely certain to meaning conceived as concrete, pluralistic, contextualistic, implicit, and tentative."[11] As Merleau-Ponty himself affirms: "Between my sensation and myself there is always the thickness of a *primordial acquisition* which keeps my experience from being clear for itself" (PP, p. 216). Merleau-Ponty argues that the demand for absolute self-evidence simply does not do justice to experience as lived, and that ironically such demands lead to a declaration that the world is absurd (PP, p. 296). Descartes' quest for "super" certainty leads us inevitably into the "super" doubt of skepticism. On the other hand, the logic of vagueness of Merleau-Ponty and Wittgenstein, though falling short of traditional philosophical expectations, is not at all destructive; and at least it conforms to the ambiguities of lived experience. These ambiguities are grasped by a tacit knowing which only becomes problematic when one attempts to make it explicit. As Samuel B. Mallin phrases it: "The experience of evidence will not, therefore, be of a propositional truth but of a situational truth, and it will be ambivalent and ambiguous to thetic powers of reflection."[12] Merleau-Ponty believes that even the most formal thought comes out of a "qualitatively defined mental situation," and that there can be no such thing as "simple analysis," because "thought is never more than relatively formal" (PrP, p. 8).

ÜBERSICHT AND *UMGEBUNG*

In 1914, Wittgenstein wrote: "Don't get involved in partial problems, but always take flight to where there is a free view over the whole *single* great problem, even if this view is still not a clear one" (NB, p. 23). Much later he declared: "I strive *not* after exactness, but after a synoptic view" (*Übersichtlichkeit*, Z, §464, shortened to *Übersicht* at Z, §273 and RFM, p. 146). Even though the speculative metaphysician A. N. Whitehead uses the idea of a free flight of theoretical imagination and holds that philosophy must sacrifice clarity for the most comprehensive view, one must not identify Whitehead's method with Wittgenstein's. Wittgenstein is not for comprehensiveness because he is "keen on completeness" (Z, §465). Wittgenstein believes that a craving for a general understanding of the universe is an "unnatural desire" that should not be indulged. But this does not mean that we cannot search for an "*übersichtliche Darstellung*," which will enable us to "survey" (*übersehen*) the use of our words and make "possible just that understanding which consists in 'seeing connections' " (PI, §122).

As we have seen, the original wording for this passage appears in Wittgenstein's first set of notes on Frazer's *Golden Bough* written in 1931. These notes give us more clues to the methodological implications of such a synoptic method. Wittgenstein contrasts his synoptic view with Frazer's "*Entwicklungshypothese*" (evolutionary or historical account). Whereas the latter is causal and seeks laws and explanations, the former is descriptive and consists of "arranging the factual material itself into an *übersichtliche Darstellung*" (RF, p. 69). The main purpose of this method is not to explain, but to show *formal* similarities and connections. In his remarks on mathematics in 1942, he states that to consider a proof "surveyable" is to mean that "causality plays no role" and that we have grasped the use of the propositions as a whole (RFM, pp. 125, 115).

According to Wittgenstein, philosophy is therefore the art of "seeing connections," seing synoptically, rather than seeking causal connections, proposing historical explanations, or making speculative claims about the nature of reality. We simply have to "put together what we *know* in the right way, without adding anything" (RF, p. 62), i.e. without adding any causal hypothesis, etc. It is clear from the later works that this seeing of connections, this knowledge of the "right" way, is not cognitive knowledge that can be articulated in traditional philosophical fashion. As Wittgenstein's students heard him in 1931: "Correct use does not imply ability to make the rules explicit" (L 1, p. 53). These rules are tacitly known as we engage in our language-games and forms of life, the pre-reflective bases for an understanding of ourselves and our world.

In his book *Wittgenstein*, Robert J. Fogelin has an illuminating section on *Übersichtlichkeit*. He is persuaded that Wittgenstein derived many of his ideas in the philosophy of mathematics, including this concept of a synoptic view, from Schopenhauer. The notion has its roots in Kant, who believed that intuition is an immediate representation (*Vorstellung*) of objects; and because a number like 1,000 cannot be immediately "surveyed" (*übersehen*), a transcendental schema is required to make it intelligible (KRV, pp. 71, 182). As we have seen, Wittgenstein's *Übersicht* also performs the transcendental function of allowing us to see formal connections. Fogelin elaborates: ". . . it is very difficult to define *perspicuity*. It comes to much the same thing as *clarity*. . . . We can say that when a representation is perspicuous it puts everything right before our eyes; it leaves nothing hidden." Fogelin connects Wittgenstein with continental, even Hegelian, thinking when he claims that "our perspicuous representation shows an *identity in difference*; the identity exhibiting a truth and the difference lending significance to this truth."[13] If I understand Fogelin correctly, I believe that Wittgenstein illustrates this point well when he claims that the color octahedron gives us a synoptic view of the grammar of color, a grammar that will contain contradictions and will not operate in terms of truth functions (PR, pp. 51f, 106).

P. F. Strawson believes that Wittgenstein's idea of *Umgebung* (surroundings) is next to importance behind the all-important concept of *Lebensformen*.[14] Wittgenstein does indeed lay much emphasis on this notion (PI, §§250, 412, 539, 583–4; OC, §237; OCo, pp. 9, 46). The term *Umgebung* is also intimately connected with *Übersicht*, as can be seen in Wittgenstein's insistence above on grasping the whole use of propositions by taking a "wider look around," in this case with regard to mathematical *Umgebung* (RFM, p. 54). Another instructive example of Wittgenstein's use of *Umgebung* is the following passage:

> Now suppose I sit in my room and hope that N. N. will come and bring me some money, and suppose one minute of this state could be isolated, cut out of its context, would what happened in it then not be hope?—Think, for example, of the words which you perhaps utter in this space of time. They are no longer part of this language. And in different *Umgebung* the institution of money doesn't exist either (PI, §584).

In other words, the word "hope" will have a different meaning for every possible situation, i.e. "hoping for money" will be "grammatically" different from "hoping for the Danish sun." Hope, pretense, grief, etc., are not intentional states of mind that can be generalized in any conceptual analysis or any behavioristic reduction. This strong emphasis on contextual relevance is very similar to the holistic philosophy of Gestalt psychology, which probably had some influence on Wittgenstein.[15]

The organic unity of language-games as pre-understood wholes appears to be inviolate: "I shall also call the whole, consisting of language and the actions into which it is woven, the 'language-game'" (PI, §7). Some propositions of language are "hard" (=*a priori*) not because of what they are in themselves, but because they belong to a "nest of propositions" and get their sense from the "rest of our proceedings" (OC, §225, 229). These assumptions do not appear to be too far from Gerd Brand's statement that "phenomenology is a philosophy of a pre-understood whole";[16] or Heidegger's contention that Being-in-the-world "stands for a *unitary* phenomenon. This primary datum must be seen as a whole" (SZ, p. 53).

The analogy of weaving is a frequent one in the *Investigations* (§7, pp. 174, 299), but this passage from *Zettel* is the most striking example:

> Disquiet in philosophy might be said to arise from looking at philosophy wrongly, seeing it wrong, namely as if it were divided into (infinite) longitudinal strips instead of into (finite) cross strips. . . .
> So we try as it were to grasp the unlimited strips and complain that it cannot be done piecemeal. To be sure it cannot, if by a piece one means an infinite longitudinal strip. But it may well be done, if one means a cross strip (Z, §447).

These thoughts are obscure, but let us attempt a brief interpretation. The image that first comes to mind is that of a philosopher with blinders pursuing a particular problem (a longitudinal strip) in a linear way, oblivious to the significance of the surroundings (the cross strips). The parallel strips appear to symbolize a doctrine of external relations, but this is compromised somewhat by the fact that it is the "longitudinal" thinker who wishes to grasp the infinite strip whole, relating each thing with everything else. Hacker is confident that Wittgenstein had Frege and his own early philosophy in mind. Hacker observes that Frege believed that an eternal logical form must be grasped in its entirety and "thought *must* move along fixed lines, otherwise we would have a 'hitherto unknown type of madness.' "[17] This last phrase is taken from Frege's *The Basic Laws of Arithmetic*, which Wittgenstein had read (cf. OC, §494).

This passage from *Zettel* elicits another, even more vague image: that the cross strips are like intersecting "world-lines" of groups of people in particular times and places. If this is at all close to what Wittgenstein means, then philosophy *can* attempt without pretense to describe *our* language-games and *our* forms of life (=our *Weltanschauung*). Bringing Wittgenstein and Brouwer together in a *Weltanschauungsphilosophie*, Hacker agrees: "Each strip can be completely described, although its permanence is not ensured. . . . The unknown types of madness against which Frege expostulated are, in Wittgenstein's view, simply different forms of thought founded upon different forms of life."[18] Those passages in Wittgenstein which appear to reveal him as a "longitudinal thinker"—e.g., "If one item necessary for the synopsis is lacking, we still feel that something is wrong" (L 1, p. 34)—can be re-interpreted so that one's *übersichtliche Darstellung* (synopsis) is limited to one's *Weltanschauung*.

ÜBERSICHT AND HEIDEGGER'S *UMSICHT*

Wittgenstein's *Übersicht* suggests a comparison with Heidegger's *Umsicht*, a pre-predicative, non-objectifying "seeing" that allows things to appear as they really are. "Letting something be encountered is primarily *umsichtiges*, it is not just sensing something, or staring at it" (SZ, p. 137). It is the goal of phenomenological interpretation to make it possible for humans to disclose things "primordially" (SZ, p. 140). Heidegger agrees with Wittgenstein that the principal reason for such an approach is to grasp the formal connections among these phenomena and not take them as facts, fitting them into some prescribed theory.

There are, however, important differences between *Übersicht* and *Umsicht* that must not be overlooked. The most crucial one is based on

Wittgenstein's use of the term *"Darstellung."* If we render this term "representation," as it frequently is, then a large gap looms between Wittgenstein's *Übersicht* and Heidegger's *Umsicht*. The latter is definitely not any form of representation, because *Umsicht* is the ground of all representation. *Dasein's* primordial grasp of things is not though representations, but directly with the things themselves (SZ, pp. 62, 154, 218). One of the major tasks of the later Heidegger is to overcome the effects of *"das vorstellende Denken"* and to cultivate a receptive attunement and openness to Being itself.

Paul Ricoeur claims that Wittgenstein's use of *Darstellung* shows him at his closest to the aims of phenomenology.[19] If Ricoeur is correct, then Wittgenstein's *Darstellung* cannot be seen as a traditional representation, i.e. an image that stands for, or mirrors, things-in-themselves. Ricoeur's thesis is strengthened considerably by the fact that both Wittgenstein and the phenomenologists reject a representationalist theory of perception. In his translation of the *Logical Investigations*, J. N. Findlay renders *Darstellung* as "presentation" and comments: *"if* our conscious intentionality is valid . . . then there is no distinction, save one of aspect, between the object as I conceive it and the object as it is. I am not concerned with a subjective image which merely happens to resemble a reality" (LI, p. 27). Although the word *"Vorstellung"* is sometimes used, phenomenological *Darstellung* is the principal term which stands opposed to the *"Abbildung"* of traditional representationalism. As Husserl warns: "In face of errors such as these [made by representationalism], we must abide by what is given in pure experience, and place it within its frame of clearness just as it comes into our hands" (*Ideas*, §90).

At the beginning of the *Philosophical Remarks*, Wittgenstein appears to be following Husserl's phenomenological program closely. He declares that it is the aim of his phenomenology to give an *"immediate Darstellung"* of "immediate experience" (PR, p. 51). A *Darstellung* is a phenomenological "presentation," and that which is presented is not a sense-datum but a *Phänomen*, a form of experience, not a fact of experience. "A form cannot be described: it can only be presented (*dargestellt*)" (PR, p. 208). In the same way that Husserl believes that the *Wesenschau* is of what is immediately presented, Wittgenstein states that the goal of his phenomenology is "grasping the essence of what is *dargestellt*" (PR, p. 51). Gerd Brand describes Wittgenstein's view of recognition in this way: "What is recognized is *shown* as the same thing that it was. . . . [Even in a picture] we grasp the trees and men precisely as

trees and men" (EW, p. 46). This is a fundamental thesis of phenomenology: we are always in contact with the phenomena themselves.

Wittgenstein calls representationism a "pernicious mistake" (L 1, p.
45), and criticizes representative realism for its belief that "images are
'just subjective copies of things.' It must be pointed out that this rests
on a false comparison between the image of a thing and the picture of a
thing" (110, p. 241). "I don't merely have the visual impression of a
tree: I *know* that it is a tree" (OC, §267). As far as I can ascertain,
Wittgenstein is consistent throughout all of his works in distinguishing
between images (*Vorstellungen*) that represent facts, and pictures or
models which present (*darstellen*) form and structure. For example, the
verb "*vorstellen*" appears only twice in the *Tractatus*. It is the picture
which presents (*darstellen*) its sense directly (2.221), and this insight is at
the bottom of Wittgenstein's life-long insistence on "showing." Janik
and Toulmin heavily emphasize the distinction between *Vorstellung* and
Darstellung, and point out that it is Heinrich Hertz's use of *Bilder* as
models which led to the Tractarian "logical scaffolding . . . that is, an *a
priori* system capable of modeling the whole world and, so, of furnish-
ing the logical structure of all description. It would do for language in
general what the first part of Hertz's *Principles* had done for the language of mechanics."[20]

Wittgenstein's doctrine of "showing" directly is intimately linked with
his emphasis on providing an *übersichtliche Darstellung* which takes in the
whole use and makes our grammar surveyable. It is no accident then
that language-games, which do help us make our grammar surveyable,
are characterized in terms of models and pictures. In philosophy, it is
important to get a "full-blown pictorial *Darstellung* of our grammar. Not
facts; but as it were illustrated *Redewendungen*" (PI, §295). The
language-game of pain can be seen as a picture or a model, and can
never be taken as a *Vorstellung* of private pain. "The *Vorstellung* of pain
is not a picture and *this Vorstellung* is not replaceable in the language-
game by anything that we should call a picture" (PI, §300). Viggo
Rossvaer is correct in observing that the Tractarian *Form der Darstellung*
is the forerunner of language-games and forms of life in the later
period; and he also reminds us that the *Form der Abbildung*, the idea of
picturing directly simple objects, is given up.[21] Pictures and models remain but the realistic Tractarian picture theory is gone.

In his battle against mathematical "experiments," Wittgenstein insists
that a true grammar (=phenomenology) of number would involve
Darstellungen such as Eratothenes' sieve which presents the essence of

indivisibility directly and perspicuously (PR, pp. 240, 247). It is significant that the translators find their usual "representation" for *Darstellung* so awkward that they switch to our "presentation": "It is very odd that for a presentation of mathematics we should be obliged to use false equations as well. . . . If negation or disjunction is necessary in arithmetic, then false equations are an essential element in its presentation" (PR, p. 247). This is another way of saying that the grammar of arithmetic, just like the grammar of any discipline, has nothing to do with the truth or falsity, but only with "the conditions necessary for the possibility of sense" (PG, p. 88).

Returning now to our comparison between Wittgenstein's *Übersicht* and Heidegger's *Umsicht*, we find that there are still unresolved difficulties. Although the object of both concepts is to grasp essential connections, it is clear that an *übersichtliche Darstellung* is a *conscious* arrangement ("a piecing together") (*Gruppierung*, RF, p. 69, *zusammenstellen*, RF, p. 62) of facts so as to attain an *intuitive* vision of the whole. In contrast, Heidegger's *Umsicht* is pre-reflective in nature, not just a means to an intuitive "seeing of connections." Therefore, Wittgenstein sometimes sees an *übersichtliche Darstellung* as a contrivance, i.e. a technique (PR, p. 263), for giving in an immediate and comprehensive fashion the formal connection of things. This is clear when he speaks of making plastic *Darstellungen* of his memories (PR, p. 97) or when he claims that one can just as well see the essence of the basic colors by replacing the color octahedron with another model, a double-cone (PR, p. 278). Janik and Toulmin correctly describe *Darstellungen* as "logical constructs," consciously constructed schema and models, which are "totally different from reproductions of sensory experience, or *Vorstellungen.*"[22] It is difficult to reconcile Wittgenstein's *Übersicht* and Heidegger's *Umsicht*, even if we follow Husserl's suggestion that logical constructions, although artificial, still belong to the concrete *Lebenswelt* and therefore are no less genuine phenomena than other presentations (K, §34a).

INTERNAL RELATIONS

J. T. Price, who sees a synonym for *Lebensform* in the term *"Praxis"* (PI, §§51, 197, 202, 208), contends that "Wittgenstein arrives at the terms of continuity, such as *Praxis* and *Lebensformen*, from his insistence upon a vision of the whole, and they thus stand as important evidence of his philosophical concern." As we quoted him at the beginning of this chapter, Price believes that Wittgenstein used these terms in order "to evoke a wholeness of the speaking situation." Situated as we commonly are in the *Praxis der Sprache*, we are able to "simultaneously glimpse the internal relations among things." Price definitely has Wittgenstein's support in these speculations: "If there were only an external connection, no connection could be described at all, since we only describe the external connection by means of the internal one" (PR, p. 66).

Price is therefore correct in seeing an intimate connection between Wittgenstein's holism and a doctrine of internal relations. But the early Wittgenstein evidently did not see this link. Wittgenstein does believe in "semantic holism" from the very beginning, does make general holistic statements like that quoted as an epigram, and does hold that simple objects have "internal properties" (2.01231). But the logical atomism of the *Tractatus*, in which elementary propositions and their corresponding states of affairs are strictly independent of one another, is definitely based on a doctrine of external relations.

As early as 1929, Wittgenstein explicitly rejects this position, represented by Russell, Richards, and Ogden, in favor of internal relations. In contrast to most analytic philosophy, but in agreement with phenomenology, Wittgenstein argues that intentionality is essential to the functioning of language and this requires a doctrine of internal relations (PR, p. 63). Other passages in the *Remarks*, and classroom lectures after that, reveal clearly his move from the Tractarian view to a belief in internal relations. When I make the statement "I have no pain," I am presupposing "the capacity for feeling pain, and this can't be a 'physiological capacity'—for otherwise how would we know what it was a capacity for—it's a logical possibility" (PR, p. 110). If this is true, then one cannot say that our painless states have nothing to do with our painful ones; indeed, one must conclude that painless and painful states are internally related. This means that the "language-game" of pain is an organic "system of propositions" whose elements are necessarily related.

In notes appended to the *Remarks*, taken down by Waismann during the writing of the book, Wittgenstein discusses the same theme. Here he is explicit in his divergence from the *Tractatus*. Instead of each proposition corresponding to each state of affairs in complete isolation from all others, he now prefers to say: "*a system of propositions* is laid like a yardstick against reality" (PR, p. 317). When I speak, I do not use just the "single gradation mark" that corresponds to the proposition spoken, but I apply the entire scale. When I say that something is blue, I am also saying that it is not red, not yellow, not green, etc. I simultaneously apply the whole color scale, a whole system of propositions. (This fundamental holistic insight remains with Wittgenstein until the end of his life, for in *On Certainty*, one cannot deny the existence, e.g., of one hand without denying everything in one's *Weltbild*.) The *Tractatus* is therefore wrong in concluding "that every inference depended on the form of a tautology . . . [and] believing that elementary propositions had to be independent of [externally related to] one another: from the fact that one state of affairs obtained you couldn't infer another did not" (PR, p. 317).

At this point it is instructive to compare Wittgenstein with Brand Blanshard, who is the century's most celebrated defender of the doctrine of internal relations. I choose as the source for Blanshard's views the published papers of a symposium on internal relations held at Smith College in 1967. This discussion is particularly significant because one of the respondents is Alice Ambrose, one of Wittgenstein's students in the 1930s. Ambrose criticizes Blanshard from a Wittgensteinian perspective, and it is clear that Blanshard sees Wittgenstein as the enemy of not only the doctrine of internal relations but of philosophy as a whole. One quip is especially revealing: "But philosophers, in spite of Wittgenstein's contempt for them, are not usually as far gone as that."[23] We will see that Blanshard is not as far from Wittgenstein as he and his critics believe.

Blanshard would therefore have been surprised to find Wittgenstein talking about internal relations so favorably, and Ambrose surely must have heard some of this in the lectures she attended. Let us first see if Wittgenstein and Blanshard are defining internal relations in the same way. Both agree that an internal relation is a necessary relation: "It is given in the terms involved, in the nature of proposition and fact" (L 1, p. 9, cf. pp. 57, 81). But even Blanshard's critics agree with this definition, and Wittgenstein's idea of necessity is much different from Blanshard's.

Wittgenstein again follows traditional formulations when he maintains that there is an internal relation between the strokes of a hand and the points of a pentagram, but an external relation between two sacks of potatoes with the same number of potatoes; or, the shape of any colored patch is externally related to the patch, but the shape of any geometrical figure is internally related to the figure (LFM, pp. 73, 78). This shows that Wittgenstein is not as radical as Blanshard, who insists that all relations are internal. Typically, Wittgenstein supports the common-sense view which takes some properties as intrinsic and therefore internal as opposed to others which are accidental and therefore external. In a 1939 lecture, he remarked that the shape of the face of the oldest man in his class is external to that man—it is accidental and "satisfies empirical conditions"; but the shape of the heptacaideca-gon they had been discussing is internal to that figure—it is necessary and satisfies what Wittgenstein calls "grammatical" conditions (LFM, p. 78).

The critics have no problem with internal relations among ideal ob-jects, e.g., "two is greater than one." For them the source of the confu-sion comes when this "ideal internality," as H. Malmgren calls it, is applied "to the realm of concrete, particular objects."[24] In 1939, Wittgenstein acknowledged that one might think that internal relations "lie in the essence of things," but that would be incorrect. Apparently, Wittgenstein wishes to remain within the confines of "ideal internality": "An internal relation is never a relation between two objects, but you might call it a relation between two concepts. And a sentence asserting an internal relation between two objects . . . is not describing objects but constructing concepts" (LFM, p. 73).

With a statement like this, conventionalist critics of internal relations may very well reclaim Wittgenstein as supporting their side of the de-bate. But we must keep in mind that for Wittgenstein all conceptual construction has its origin not in the mind, but in the worldly *Praxis* of language-games and forms of life. ("The person who cannot play this game does not have *this* concept" [OCo, p. 31].) When Wittgenstein claims that the relation between sense-data and physical objects is not causal but internal ("a necessary relation," L 1, p. 81), he names the locus of the internal relation: language itself. Wittgenstein believes that sense-data are grammatical fictions, because new concepts like this mis-takenly lead us to believe in new "objects" (PI, §401). Therefore, sense-data and physical objects are obviously internally related in the new "sense-data" language-game.

For Wittgenstein, internal relations make up the very tissue of our lives. There is an internal relation between "expectation and fulfill-ment," between "proposition and fact," between "speech and action," between "the act of intending and the thing intended," and the locus of this "superstrong connection" is "the list of rules of the game, in the teaching of it, in the day-to-day practice of playing" (RFM, p. 40; cf. L 1, pp. 9, 110, 112; PR, p. 63f). As Karsten J. Struhl phrases it: "The *Investigations* takes language as something *imbedded* in the world through the actions of language users."[25] Even the orthodox Wittgensteinian Norman Malcolm reminds us that Wittgenstein is not interested in mere words and linguistic analysis, but "he is trying to get his reader to think of how the words are tied up with human life, with patterns of response, in thought and action."[26]

Therefore, Wittgenstein believes that internal relations are *in the world*—not exclusively in the mind or mere linguistic conventions, and not exclusively in things themselves. Although the following passage is obscure, it does relate to the internal relation between sense-data and physical objects, and does appear to support my interpretation:

> The color of the visual impression corresponds to the color of the object . . . the shape of the visual impression to the shape of the object . . . but what I perceive in the dawning of an aspect is not a property of the object, but an internal relation between it and other objects (PI, p. 212).

Compare this with Merleau-Ponty:

> To see is to enter a universe of beings which *display themselves* . . . every object is the mirror of all others. . . . I can therefore see an object in so far as objects form a system or a world, and in so far as each one treats the other round it as spectators of its hidden aspects which guarantee the permanence of those aspects by their presence (PP, p. 68).

The similarities between Merleau-Ponty and Wittgenstein with regard to holistic perception are no doubt partially due to the influence of Gestalt psychology on both thinkers. We have already documented Wittgenstein's link to the Gestaltists, and Merleau-Ponty explicitly acknowledges his debt to them. For example, "Perception is here understood as a reference to a whole which can be grasped, in principle, only through certain of its parts or aspects" (PrP, p. 16). When Wittgenstein criticizes Mach for his attempt to make a visual picture of the visual field (PR, p. 267), he is paralleling a constant theme in phenomenology: that any perceptual context will remain incorrigibly opaque and that no analysis or perception will ever exhaust the object of perception. Similarly, Wittgenstein believes that "it is clear that this lack of clarity is an internal property of visual space" (PR, p. 268).

The evidence that firmly secures my interpretation is the fact that Wittgenstein resurrects the synthetic *a priori*. ("What distinguishes language from a game . . . is its application to reality" [L 1, p. 12].) Therefore, it is no accident that statements about the synthetic *a priori* appear simultaneously with comments about internal relations. Many philosophers could easily accept internal relations if they were strictly conceptual and solely expressed in terms of analytic propositions. Bruce Aune, however, makes it clear in his reply to Blanshard that to hold that there are necessary relations in the world would require "a basic commitment to the synthetic *a priori*—a commitment, it is fair to say, which few of us share."[27] As we have seen above, Wittgenstein believes that all the colors are internally related to one another, and this system of relations is the foundation of the following synthetic *a priori* proposition: "Different colors cannot be in the same place in the visual field at the same time."

In his reply to Blanshard, W. E. Kennick quotes from the *Tractatus*— "Whatever we can describe at all could be other than it is" (5.634)—to support his case that Blanshard is wrong to argue that things and events are internally related. But this is just as misleading as A. J. Ayer, who appealed to the authority of Wittgenstein on the elimination of the synthetic *a priori*, right at the very time Wittgenstein was reviving the notion. The later Wittgenstein does believe that—within our own *Weltbild* of language-games and forms of life—there are certain facts which cannot be doubted, which cannot be otherwise, i.e. unless we want to give up our *Weltbild* completely.

Ironically, Wittgenstein is a far more consistent "idealist" than Blanshard himself. Recall Wittgenstein's statement that idealists are correct in maintaining that the distinction between mind and matter is within experience itself (L 1, p. 80). Both he and Blanshard hold that "reality" is mind-dependent, but Blanshard has no appreciation for the functions of one crucial "mental" product, *viz.* language itself: If the world is really mind-dependent, how can Blanshard be so confident when he states that "one cannot rearrange fact to suit one's linguistic preferences," or "how nature is put together does not depend on how we put our words together"?[28] Both Brouwer and Wittgenstein reject the dubious claims that causal laws are necessary because that is the way nature is (Blanshard) or because of some innate category in the mind (Kant), and urge us to remain content with the plain, non-speculative truth that causality is a "style of thinking" (L 1, p. 104), intimately connected with speaking a certain language and living in a specific culture.

The truth of idealism and the "linguistic turn" lies in Kant's correlation of the forms of judgment and the forms of reality and his strict agnosticism about the nature of things in themselves. Like Kant, Wittgenstein never denies the existence of an external world; we constitute the sense of the world but never the world itself. As we can never step outside of our language-games and forms of life, this middle ground between "mind" and "reality" must be the proper locus of not only internal relations but all philosophical issues as well. After all, Wittgenstein believes that "reality" *is* immediate experience (PG, p. 222).

It is evident that Blanshard is philosophizing from the standpoint of a pre-critical rationalism which held that logic correlates directly with reality, that grammar is based on traditional logic, and that human language can ultimately express the nature of reality. Blanshard's critics repeatedly focus on the fact that he cannot conceive of any alternative to the merely contingent except the logically necessary. But Wittgenstein believes that all necessity is "grammatical" and is not tied to formal logic, and that there is a distinction between logical propositions and grammatical propositions, the latter always being synthetic *a priori*. (See Chapter Eight.)

For Wittgenstein, that which is necessary depends upon the way in which we view the world. Wittgenstein's constructivism contrasts strikingly with Blanshard's dogmatic rationalism. Finally, although Blanshard would agree that internal relations do complicate philosophical problems, he never gives up the idea of the ultimate clarity, comprehensiveness, and intelligibility of the philosophical vision. For Wittgenstein and the existential phenomenologists, internal relations do characterize the world and make it intelligible. But the world still remains incorrigibly vague and immune to the probings of traditional philosophical methods, be they Bruce Aune's "analytic" or Brand Blanshard's "speculative."

5. Phenomenology

Phenomenology is grammar.

–Wittgenstein (213, p. 437)

So in philosophy all that is not gas is grammar.

–Wittgenstein (L 1, p. 112)

Essence is expressed by grammar.

–Wittgenstein (PI, §371)

Philosophy as the custodian of grammar can in fact grasp the essence of the world, only not in the propositions of language, but in the rules for this language which exclude nonsensical combinations of signs.

–Wittgenstein (PR, p. 85)

Isn't the theory of harmony at least in part phenomenology and therefore grammar?

–Wittgenstein (PR, p. 53)

Phenomenological analysis (as e.g. Goethe would have it) is analysis of concepts and can neither agree with nor contradict physics.

–Wittgenstein (OCo, p. 16)

Thus phenomenology would be the grammar for the description of those facts upon which physics erects its theories.

–Wittgenstein (PR, p. 51)

So, for me, Wittgenstein is a phenomenologist pure and simple.

–Gerd Brand (EW, p. xxv)

WITTGENSTEIN'S USE OF THE TERM "PHENOMENOLOGY"

We have seen that Wittgenstein's support of internal relations and the synthetic *a priori* sets him off decidedly from the Vienna Circle and English philosophy at that time. It really should come as no surprise to discover that at this same time Wittgenstein started doing phenomenology, a discipline which is favorably inclined to both internal relations and the synthetic *a priori*. In the *Philosophical Remarks* Wittgenstein uses the noun "phenomenology" seven times (PR, pp. 51, 53, 88, 273). In conversations with Waismann and Schlick during the composition of the *Remarks,* he also uses the term (WK, pp. 63, 65, 101).

There is an entire chapter entitled "Phenomenology" in the Big Typescript of 1933. Here the terms "phenomenology" and "phenomenological language" are used in ways similar to passages published in the *Remarks* (213, pp. 437, 442=PR, 53, 467=PR, 267, 491). Here we also find the identification of phenomenology and grammar, one which is so important for Spiegelberg's thesis that Wittgenstein's phenomenology continued throughout all the later works as "grammar" (213, p. 437). In a typescript of 1930 he begins by observing that many think that physics is the "true phenomenology" because it is able to give the simplest representation (*Abbildung*) of our visual field. But this is incorrect, because physics deals with true and false sentences, while grammar as phenomenology deals with *Sinn* (208, p. 1; cf. 105, p. 3).

G. E. Moore's unpublished notes of Wittgenstein's lectures from this same period contain class material similar to the opening passages on phenomenology in the *Remarks*.[1] Most of Wittgenstein's remarks about phenomenology appear in connection with the problem of the blending of colors, the problem that, more than anything, convinced Wittgenstein that the *Tractatus* was flawed. In this particular lecture Wittgenstein draws the color octahedron on the blackboard and argues that the relationship of the colors is part of grammar, not psychology, and "there is such a color as greenish-blue" is a grammatical statement or a statement of phenomenology. Wittgenstein also mentioned three major disciplines that must be distinguished: logic, psychology, and phenomenology. This arrangement of disciplines throws light on an obscure statement about phenomenology much later in *On Color*. Here he calls phenomenology "something midway between science and logic" (OCo, p. 15). (Other uses of "phenomenology" or "phenomenological" in *On Color* are found on pp. 9, 16, and 49.)

In the *Philosophical Grammar*, which was edited from the Big Type-

script by Rush Rhees, the adjective "phenomenological" describes an essential distinction between a grammar in which "use" would be crucial
and a grammar in which it would not (PG, p. 215). Unpublished manuscript material again helps us clarify the use of terms here. In the latter
half of 1931 he wrote about an "essential difference" (*Wesensunterschied*)
between "logical" and "phenomenological" grammar, which later in the
work seems to coincide with the difference between an essential and
unessential grammar.[2] In the *Grammar* Wittgenstein speaks of a
"phenomenological" grammar, which, for example, in a chapter on the
grammar of colors, would set "out the rules for the use of color words";
and a "non-phenomenological" (or "logical") grammar, in which logical
constants would not be affected by use or experience in general (PG, p.
215). (This perhaps sheds some light on a statement from Moore's
notes: "In grammar some things are arbitrary, some not.") This distinction between a logical and phenomenological grammar will help us distinguish between logical and grammatical propositions in Chapter
Eight.

During the period 1929–1933, Wittgenstein uses the terms
"phenomenology" and "phenomenological" positively and without qualification, except for the fact that at one point ("however one cares to
name it" [208, p. 1; 105, p. 3]) he implies that the label does not mean
much. In *On Color*, however, he establishes some distance between what
he is doing and phenomenology: "Here the temptation to believe in a
phenomenology, something midway between science and logic, is very
great" (OCo, p. 15). In a letter to Spiegelberg, von Wright relates the
contents of some conversations he had with Wittgenstein which clarify
this statement somewhat. He told von Wright that he was reading
Goethe's *Farbenlehre* and that "what he was doing was of a kind some
philosophers call 'phenomenology.' "[3] But Wittgenstein did not want to
use this term, and von Wright speculates that it was primarily because
he saw his phenomenology as purely linguistic in orientation. Wittgenstein was apparently unaware of the fact that at least two major existential phenomenologists, Heidegger and Merleau-Ponty, stress the necessary role of language. We shall return to this topic of language in
Chapter Ten.

In some instances, Wittgenstein's use of the adjective "phenomenological" appears to indicate nothing more than an insistence upon a completely descriptive analysis of phenomena themselves.
This has led some observers to suppose that Wittgenstein's
phenomenology is nothing more than a version of the Viennese
phenomenalism of Ernst Mach. Mach even used the term "phe-

nomenology," and indicated that it comprises all the areas of physics.[4] When Wittgenstein mentions physics as phenomenology in the passage from TS 208 used above, he no doubt had Mach in mind; but significantly, it is a type of phenomenology which he explicitly rejects. Wittgenstein's transcendentalism and his method of directly experiencing essences (PR, p. 51) militate strongly against him accepting a Machian phenomenology. Wittgenstein is interested in the *logic* (the grammar, the essence) of a phenomena; therefore his philosophy is a transcendental phenomenology (a *logos* of *phenomena*) and not a mere phenomenalism based on physics.

In an unpublished work Barry Smith finds it significant that from the very beginning Wittgenstein called simple objects *"Gegenstände"* and not *"Elemente"* as did Mach and Avenarius. The introduction of *"Gegenstände"* as a technical, philosophical term was made by members of the Brentano school, including Meinong, Husserl, Stumpf, and Marty. Furthermore, Wittgenstein is critical of Mach throughout the middle period. Mach confuses the "physical" and the "phenomenological," because he believes that thought experiments reveal something factual, when actually they are grammatical investigations (PR, p. 52), and because he thought that one could make a visual picture of our visual field (PR, p. 267). As Janik and Toulmin state: "Mach's critique of mechanics . . . was based on a psychological theory *about* mechanical concepts. Hertz's critique of mechanics was far more penetrating than Mach's, because he was able to focus clearly upon the structure of these concepts as they are *used*."[5] We have already spoken of Hertz's probable influence on Wittgenstein in Chapter Two, and it is clear that Hertz's Kantianism and proto-phenomenology are in opposition to Mach's phenomenalism.

The main thrust of Wittgenstein's phenomenology is contained in the following passages:

> Physics wants to establish regularities, it does not look for what is possible. This is the reason why physics . . . does not offer a description of the phenomenological *Sachverhalte*. Phenomenology always deals only with possibility, i.e. the sense (*Sinn*), not with truth and falsehood (WK, p. 63).

> Physics differs from phenomenology in that it is concerned to establish laws. Phenomenology only establishes the possibilities. Thus phenomenology would be the grammar of the description of those facts on which physics builds its theories (PR, p. 51).

What sort of investigation is ours? Do I investigate the cases which I bring up according to their probability or factuality? No, I bring up only that which is possible by giving grammatical examples (213, p. 425).

These passages reveal Wittgenstein's phenomenological method as a transcendental method. He maintains a strict distinction between a science of facts and a science of essences, i.e., an investigation of the formal conditions that make the experience of facts possible. A phenomenalist of course would reject such a distinction along with any of the following talk of grasping essences: "The goal [is] grasping the essence of what is presented" (PR, p. 51) and "*essence* is expressed by grammar . . . grammar tells what kind of object anything is" (PI, §§371, 373).

SPENGLER'S "PHYSIOGNOMIC" METHOD

One of the principal assumptions of this study is that philosophies are not created in a vacuum, even if the philosopher disclaims all influences. We shall see that Wittgenstein was most likely influenced by some of the phenomenological schools of the time, perhaps even by Husserl himself. There is, however, another lead which has some significance, even if the Husserlian connection is more tenable. In *On Color*, a work inspired by Goethe's *Farbenlehre*, Wittgenstein speaks of phenomenological analysis as "Goethe would have it" (OCo, p. 16), and it is worthwhile to discuss briefly the implications of this remark. After all, Goethe told us: "Do not, I beg you, look for anything beyond phenomena, they are themselves their own lessons."[6]

The best formulation of a truly Goethian method is found in Spengler, who idolized Goethe just as most of the other *Lebensphilosophen* did. Spengler acknowledges that it was Goethe who gave him method, and he calls it a "physiognomic" method. This is an intuitive method, opposed to the dissection and causalism of scientific analysis, which "looks directly into the face" of historical events. Such a method requires great vision and what Goethe called an "exact percipient fancy," which, opposed to "the exact killing procedure of modern physics, . . . quietly lets itself be worked upon by the living" (DW I, p. 97). It is significant then that Finch calls Wittgenstein's philosophy a "physiognomic phenomenalism."[7]

Spengler claims that his physiognomic method is "detached from the objects considered," strictly descriptive, non-judgmental, and "free from prepossessions" (DW I, pp. 17, 25, 101). While Hegel's method was fully compromised by its commitment to progressivism, Spengler's "morphological point of view" holds that the 18th Century is no more important than the sixty centuries which preceded it (DW I, p. 17). Spengler forges his own Copernican revolution in the philosophy of history by criticizing modern historians who follow the "Ptolemaic" system and place the Greco-Roman culture firmly in the solar position. In contrast, no one culture occupies the central, privileged position in Spengler's "Copernican" approach (DW I, p. 18).

Spengler's method not only has its *epoché*, but an eidetic reduction as well. As we have seen in Chapter Three, Spengler's philosophy is a comparative morphology of cultures, and the basic forms (*eidē*) lie there "plain and immediate enough for one who has learned to see an *idea*" (DW I, p. 34). Husserl also believes that one has to learn to "see" phenomenologically; one has to be able to automatically bracket the causalism of the natural attitude and other theoretical impositions on immediate experience. The Goethian method is anchored in Goethe's concept of *Urphänomene* (DW I, p. 113), and the essences of all things and and events lie in *Urphänomene*. Behind every appearance the physiognomic method will find these primal phenomena: the vertebrate type, basic geological forms, etc. "To the spiritual eye of Goethe the idea of the prime plant was clearly visible in the form of every individual plant that happened to come up, or even that could possibly come up" (DW I, p. 105). With this *Wesenschau* Spengler would then be able "to separate the morphologically necessary from the accidental."

Recall that Wittgenstein terms his language-games *Urphänomene* and maintains that the grammar of language contains the *Darstellungsformen* of the necessary ways in which we speak and act. Furthermore, the Big Typescript gives firm support for connecting *Urphänomen* with Wittgenstein's phenomenology. In Section 96 of the chapter entitled "Phenomenology," Wittgenstein speaks of the experience of an *Urphänomen*, which is not reached by a superficial investigation of a physical or psychological phenomenon, but by an investigation which seeks "clarity in the grammar of the description of the primordial phenomenon (*die Klarheit in der Grammatik der Beschreibung des alten Phänomens*)" (213, p. 460). One of the problems in discussing Goethe's "phenomenology" is that, although he believes that *Urphänomene* are apprehended by a non-sensuous intuition, they are nonetheless hypothetical or even natural entities (e.g., the polarity of light and granite).[8] The *Phänomene* of Wittgenstein and Husserl are not like this at all.

Spengler even anticipates the body-ego of existential phenomenology. Apart from the superficial "inorganic, natural-law interdependence," there is "a *living* interdependence . . . [which] subsists within the world-picture, which radiates from nothing less than the whole man and not merely (as Kant thought) from the cognizing part of him" (DW I, p. 49). This sounds similar to descriptions of the intentional field, which we find in Merleau-Ponty, of vectors of intentionality reaching out to their respective intentional objects. Spengler also criticizes both realists and idealists for viewing the soul-world relation as one of cause and effect. In an intriguing anticipation of Heidegger's *Dasein*, Spengler proposes that "if, now, we designate the Soul . . . as the *possible* and the World on the other hand as the *actual*, . . . we see life as *the form in which the actualizing of the possible is accomplished*" (DW I, p. 54).

In Spengler we have a life-world phenomenology in everything but name. Even the existential phenomenologists would cringe at its rhapsodic and polemic strains, but all of the basic themes are present. They would agree with the position that philosophy does not deal with facts in causal relations, but with forms, essences, and structures. They all agree that some form of *epoché* is needed to get at these forms, and that some type of phenomenological "seeing" is required. Finally, Spengler joins with the existential phenomenologists in rejecting Husserl's transcendental ego.

GRAMMAR AND MAKING SENSE

Although we know that Wittgenstein read Spengler, and even acknowledged that he uses his method (220, p. 85), it is much more likely, particularly in the way in which Wittgenstein uses phenomenological terminology, that he was drawing on the early phenomenological tradition of Husserl and his disciples. It could have been this direct influence, as Barry Smith maintains, or something more indirect. Spiegelberg suggests that Wittgenstein could have taken the term from Rudolf Carnap, who uses the term and refers to Husserl in his *Der Logische Aufbau der Welt* of 1928. Anthony Kenny suggests that Wittgenstein's discovery of intentionality in the *Remarks* must have been influenced by Husserl.[9]

In his 1968 article, Spiegelberg tells of a meeting between J. N. Findlay and Wittgenstein in 1939. Findlay told Wittgenstein that he was working on Husserl's *Logical Investigations* (which he later translated) and Wittgenstein expressed astonishment that anyone was still interested in such an old text.[10] This comment certainly does not prove that Wittgenstein had read Husserl, but it is very likely that anyone reading as much Frege as he did would naturally turn to thinkers such as Husserl and Meinong. In his foreword to the Schlick-Waismann conversations, B. F. McGuinness indicates that there were discussions "about ideas of Husserl, Heidegger, and Weyl" (WK, p. 19). In the published conversations, Schlick asks a question about phenomenology and Wittgenstein knows enough to answer specifically using the name Husserl (WK, p. 67). At another point, Schlick makes reference to Husserl in a question, again presumably on the assumption that Wittgenstein knew something about him (WK, p. 78).

With its emphasis on pure description, and an apparent identification of descriptive psychology and phenomenology (PR, p. 273), Wittgenstein's phenomenology does initially have some strong affinities with the *Logical Investigations*. In the second edition of this book, Husserl rejects the identification of descriptive psychology and phenomenology, mainly because this psychology had been taken as a form of natural science (LI, pp. 261–2). If this was indeed the source of Wittgenstein's phenomenology, it is then possible that he had read Husserl's early phenomenology in terms of the first edition. An important clue in this connection is Wittgenstein's identification of phenomenology and epistemology (PR, pp. 88, 90). The phrases "epistemological criticism" and "epistemological investigations" occur frequently in the *Logical Investigations* and are closely connected with phenomenology (LI, p. 263). The only problem with this thesis is the fact that Wittgenstein definitely uses a phenomenological *epoché*, a concept which was not fully developed until Husserl's middle period.

This is still too speculative to establish any credible link between Wittgenstein and Husserl's phenomenology. The most promising connection is the concept of grammar, which they both share. Commentators have generally assumed that Wittgenstein got the term from his contemporaries at Cambridge, particularly I. A. Richards, who was using it extensively in the 1930s. Wittgenstein probably read Richards and Ogden's *The Meaning of Meaning*, in which grammar is defined as the "natural history of symbol systems." But Wittgenstein's grammar as a way of distinguishing between *Sinn* and *Unsinn* is not only different from Richards and Ogden's, but is used in the same way in the *Tractatus*. Therefore, if there was any borrowing, it must have come earlier. Furthermore, if the source was Husserl, then it must have been his early period, because Husserl did not use the term in the later works. Wittgenstein may have come to the concept of grammar through Anton Marty, a close associate of Brentano, rather than Husserl himself, who refers directly to Marty's work on grammar in the *Logical Investigations*. The Austrian philosopher Karl Bühler wrote a review of Marty's *Sprachphilosophie* of 1908, and Wittgenstein might have learned of Marty's grammar through Bühler, a Gestaltist who headed the Austrian school reform movement of which Wittgenstein was a part during the 1920s.

A number of commentators have spoken of this connection between Wittgenstein and Husserl on grammar. Max Black declares that there is a "striking parallel" between Husserl's "pure logico-grammatical doctrine of forms" and Wittgenstein's program in the *Tractatus*.[11] Barry Smith concurs: "Indeed there are conceptual and terminological parallels which are so close as to be hardly explicable except on the hypothesis that Wittgenstein had some access to the material [works of the phenomenologists] involved."[12] James L. Marsh also proposes that "such grammar, both in its distance from the givens of actual usage and its universality, seems to approximate the phenomenological notion of essence."[13]

In the *Tractatus* Wittgenstein equates "logical syntax" with "logical grammar" (3.325), and in a conversation with Moritz Schlick he maintains that the "can" in "red and green cannot be in the same place" is a "grammatical (logical) concept, and not an empirical one" (WK, p. 67). Von Wright's account of the Cambridge economist Piero Saffra's famous question to Wittgenstein about the "logical form" of a Neapolitan gesture differs from Malcolm's report. Von Wright claims that the question at issue was whether or not every proposition had a "grammar," and that Saffra asked Wittgenstein what the "grammar" of the gesture was.[14]

Both Husserl and Wittgenstein believe that there is a philosophical grammar more fundamental than traditional logic. It is similar to Kant's transcendental logic in that it is completely free from psychology and application to empirical content. When discussing the grammar of color, Wittgenstein concludes that there seems to be "a construction in logic which [does not] work by means of truth functions" (PR, p. 106). Husserl also speaks of grammar as the lowest sphere of logic where the "questions of truth, objectivity, objective possibility are not yet relevant" (LI, p. 526). As we have seen, Wittgenstein's phenomenology as grammar does not deal with truth or falsity, but with the possibility of sense: "What belongs to grammar are . . . the conditions necessary for the understanding of sense [of a proposition]" (PG, p. 88; cf. 213, p. 505). Sense, then, is anything that grammar allows.

Wittgenstein calls his grammar "a theory of logical types" (L 1, p. 13).

It is transcendental in the sense that it "is the expression of what is possible." It does not deal with the application of language, which is why, for the later Wittgenstein, the rules of grammar are arbitrary but their application is not. Grammar "shows the possibility of constructing true or false propositions, but not the truth or falsehood of any particular proposition" (L 1, p. 13). Therefore, grammar describes logical forms or types. In this same lecture, Wittgenstein articulates the point more exactly: the logical possibility of p depends on whether p has sense; if p has sense, then this shows that p is possible.

Ordinary grammar deals with the ways in which words are put together to make phrases and sentences. In their early periods, both Husserl and Wittgenstein reacted so strongly to psychologism that both of them maintained that the meanings to which words in ordinary language referred were objective entities (T, 3.203),[15] and that there were *a priori* laws that controlled their possible combinations. Just as the logical syntax (=grammar) of the *Tractatus* represents the possible configurations of objects (=meanings), Husserl's laws of grammar "provide pure logic with the *possible meaning-forms*" (LI, p. 492). These laws do not separate the true from the false; rather, they allow us first to distinguish combinations of meanings that make sense from those that are nonsense (*Unsinn*). Therefore, at the level of philosophical grammar, logical incompatibilities such as "a round square" are *grammatically* in order and represent unities of meaning. Only ungrammatical phrases such as "and king but" are *"unsinnig"* (LI, p. 517). But from the standpoint of "what is the case," a round square is an absurdity (*Widersinn*).

In the *Tractatus* Wittgenstein makes a similar distinction between *unsinnig* and *sinnlos*. "A round square" is not *unsinnig*, because it does not violate any rules of grammar; but it, like all contradictions (and tautologies, too), are *sinnlos* (Husserl's *widersinnig*) because it shows that it says nothing (T, 4.461). This same doctrine is found in the *Philosophical Grammar* of 1933. He argues that one can speak meaningfully (*sinnvoll*) of "bits of an apple," but not of "bits of the color red." While the latter phrase is *sinnlos*, it is not *unsinnig*. I can easily imagine what "bits of an apple" would be, whereas I cannot imagine what "bits of red" would be like. "Bits of red" is still grammatically correct, and "in spite of its senselessness (*Sinnlosigkeit*), [it] makes us think of a quite definite grammatical system" (PG, p. 126).

It is significant that Wittgenstein does not ultimately follow Frege on this matter. Frege would have said that "a round square" has *Sinn* but not *Bedeutung* (i.e., no reference). Early in the *Notebooks* he does appear

to be following Frege's lead, but as Anscombe editorializes in a footnote: ". . . there is a great contrast between his ideas at this stage of the
Notebooks and those of the *Tractatus,* where he denies that logical constants or sentences have *Bedeutung*" (NB, p. 15). Could it be that, since
the Tractarian use of grammar and *Sinn* is so much like Husserl's use, it
was during this period that Wittgenstein came into contact with Husserl's works, or works of his disciples? The evidence is only circumstan-
tial, but the influence is certainly possible nonetheless.

From 1929 onwards, Wittgenstein revises his views of grammar considerably. We can already see this change in the passage from the
Grammar cited above. Here he implies that even though the doctrine of
pure grammar would grant sense to "I'm cutting red into bits," this
point ultimately has no philosophical significance. What does now have
significance for Wittgenstein is the concept of "systems" of language,
language-games, which represent different linguistic worlds (PR, p.
178). Therefore, from the standpoint of a *particular* language, and this
is the only standpoint one can take for the later Wittgenstein, the proposition "I'm cutting red into bits" *is unsinnig* (PG, p. 126).

In the recently published lectures of 1930–32, we can see that
Wittgenstein had changed his mind as early as 1930. In the Lent Term
lectures of that year, he maintains that Lewis Carroll's nonsense
rhymes, though they are grammatically in order (they "can be analyzed
into subject and predicate and parts of speech"), they are nonetheless
what we all call them: nonsense. By the same token, to say that "This
book is tired" is also to speak nonsense (L 1, p. 33). In the Lent Term
lectures of 1931, his position is consistent: to say that a sound is red is
not false, but "it is nonsense—i.e. not language at all" (L 1, p. 47).

The *Philosophical Grammar* continues this basic change from the *Tractatus* and isolated sections of the middle works: language is *our* language, and the grammar it has is the grammar we speak of in philosophy. To put it in terms of Heidegger and Gadamer, the grammar of
cutting red into bits, tired books, and colored sound is outside our
"hermeneutical" circle, outside our particular language-games and
forms of life. By 1942 the Tractarian grammar is distant history; by this
time the sense of a mathematical proposition depends on human activity and application, and not on eternal, immutable grammatical rules
(RFM, pp. 115, 166). The universal *a priori* of pure grammar is completely replaced by the "relative" *a priori* of language-games. The strict
logical form of the *Tractatus* gives way to the fluid forms of life and language of the later works.

As a result of this development, Wittgenstein now calls the rules of grammar "arbitrary" and "conventional" (PG, pp. 184f, 190; PR, p. 53). That which is *sinnvoll, sinnlos, and unsinnig* corresponds to the *conventional* rules of the language-game being played (PR, p. 322). Meanings are no longer atemporal, ideal entities—meaning is *use*. Therefore, we have the possibility of parallel lines meeting being regarded as *sinnlos* in Euclidean geometry, but as *sinnvoll* in Riemannian geometry. The concept of indeterminate subatomic particles is *sinnlos* according to Newtonian mechanics, but *sinnvoll* for quantum mechanics. (I have added Riemannian geometry and quantum mechanics to the examples Wittgenstein uses.) From the standpoint of objective validity, each of these systems give "true" sentences.

All of this leads Wittgenstein to a form of *Weltanschauungsphilosophie*, which Husserl vigorously rejected in "Philosophy as a Rigorous Science" and continued to reject until his death. While Husserl's distinction between *Sinn* and *Unsinn* allows him to accept many different kinds of sense, he never would have embraced a pluralism of "truths." There are, of course, "everyday practical situational truths," but only one objective truth (K, p. 132), for Husserl's logic of truth, as Mikel Dufrenne states, "remains purely formal" (NA, p. 90). For Wittgenstein, however, there are, e.g., true statements in a Euclidean system that are false in another system (RFM, p. 50). As we have seen, what is true and false depends on one's *Weltbild* (OC, §94), or on an agreement in *Lebensformen* (PI, §241).

For Wittgenstein to state that the rules of grammar are arbitrary is not to say that we can change them at will—we must remain within our given *Weltbild* and *Lebensformen*. We remain because "grammatical rules are arbitrary, but their application is *not*" (L 1, p. 58, cf. p. 49). What "arbitrary" does mean is that there is no reason, no justification, why some propositions make sense and others do not. "There is no such thing as a justification and we ought simply to have said: *that's how we do it*" (RFM, p. 98). As Wittgenstein elaborates: "The language in which we might try to justify the rules of grammar of our language would have to have a grammar itself. No description of the world can justify the rules of grammar" (L 1, p. 44).

Because rules of sense are independent of objective validity, Husserl would definitely agree with Wittgenstein that those rules "cannot be justified by showing that their application makes a representation agree with reality" (PG, p. 186). (They have their agreement in a *Weltbild* or *Lebensformen*.) For Husserl (and the *Tractatus*), however, the rules of grammar will have their own *sui generis* justification, but for the later Wittgenstein, they have none and we can give none: "I must *begin* with the distinction between sense and nonsense. Nothing is possible prior to that. I can't give it a foundation" (PG, p. 126; OC, §559). This means that grammar as a pure logic of ideal meanings built on a strict distinction between *Sinn* and *Unsinn* is gone (and with it the distinction between *unsinnig* and *sinnlos* as Wittgenstein's use of these terms in the later works show). We begin in a world already interpreted by a language, where the bounds of "sense" are already set. This of course sounds very much like Heidegger, Merleau-Ponty, and the "new" hermeneutic.

SACHVERHALTE

There is an intimate connection between Husserl's philosophical grammar and the term *Sachverhalte*, because "meaning-things" (*Sachen*) such as "round squares" can be "related" (*verhalten*) to other meanings to form possible "states of affairs" (*Sachverhalte*). Smith is convinced that a case can be made for the hypothesis that Wittgenstein acquired the term from the Brentano-Stumpf-Husserl philosophical tradition. Smith argues that D. S. Shwayder is wrong in assuming that the word had "been fairly common currency in the speculations of German philosophers."[16] The fact is that Brentano's student, Carl Stumpf, coined it as a technical term, and that its first significant appearance in print was in the *Logical Investigations*. If Wittgenstein did not get it directly from the *Investigations*, he could have also read or heard of it from the most faithful followers of the early Husserl at the University of Munich. Smith points out that at Munich the logical grammar of the *Investigations* was expanded brilliantly by Alexander Pfänder, and the term *Sachverhalte* was refined in a way that made it superior to Meinong's "*Objecktiv*" and a match for the sophisticated Tractarian *Sachverhalte*.

Like Wittgenstein, Husserl distinguishes between *Sachverhalte* and *Tatsache*, i.e., between possible states of affairs and positive facts, those which are the case and can be sensibly perceived (LI, p. 611). Also similar to the Tractarian ontology is Husserl's distinction between simple objects that are named (e.g., knife-object) and the entire *Sachverhalte* that is judged (LI, p. 579; T, 4.031f). There is also the significant fact (at least for our present detective work) that Husserl and Wittgenstein use an alternative term, "*Sachlage*," synonymously with *Sachverhalte* (LI, p. 288; T, 4.031f). Furthermore, it is clear that there is a direct parallel between Husserl's "objective" and "non-objective" *Sachverhalte* (LI, pp. 623, 767) and Wittgenstein's "existing" and "non-existing" states of affairs.

The only problem with this theory of terminological origin is that some Wittgenstein scholars (like Max Black) agree with Ogden's translation of *Sachverhalte* as "atomic facts" thus precluding totally the interpretation that *Sachverhalte* could be conceived as *possible* facts. Space does not allow us to reopen this long debate on the meaning of *Sachverhalte* in the *Tractatus*. Wittgenstein continues to use the term during the period of 1929–1933 and I believe that here it is clear that its use is incompatible with Black's view. In the conversation with Schlick cited above, Wittgenstein states that physics does not describe phenomenological *Sachverhalte* and that it is the job of phenomenology to deal with *possibility* and *Sinn* (WK, p. 63). (Why does Wittgenstein qualify the term with "phenomenological"? Is it to show its origin in the phenomenologists?) If a *Sachverhalt* is always an actual fact, then it is very odd that Wittgenstein would have remarked: "How strange that one should be able to say that such and such a state of affairs is inconceivable" (PG, p. 130).

THE PHENOMENOLOGICAL *EPOCHÉ*

With his insistence that the language of science cannot be used to describe true phenomena, Wittgenstein has obviously accepted a type of phenomenological reduction similar to Husserl's *epoché*. John Hems maintains that there is only one serious element of phenomenology in Wittgenstein and that is the "*epoché*, and even then only in the negative sense that, like Husserl, Wittgenstein brackets existence."[17] Although Hems' article is misleading in several respects, principally that the *epoché* is the only phenomenological aspect of Wittgenstein's philosophy, he has nevertheless pointed out a significant link between Wittgenstein and phenomenology. Ricoeur insists that the *epoché* and the other phenomenological reductions that follow it are "the straight gate to phenomenology, without which it would be impossible."[18]

The *epoché* is the linchpin of phenomenology's strictly descriptive method. This is a method which Wittgenstein enthusiastically endorses—"We must do away with all *explanation*, and description alone must take its place"; and "philosophy *is* purely descriptive" (PI, §109; BB, p. 18)—and one which is religiously followed by all phenomenologists, including the later ones like Merleau-Ponty: "It is a matter of describing, not of explaining or analyzing. . . . The real has to be described, not constructed or formed" (PP, pp. viii, x).

Important passages that identify Wittgenstein's *epoché* are the following:

The worst philosophical errors always arise when we try to apply our ordinary—physical—language in the area of the immediately given. . . . All our forms of speech are taken from ordinary, physical language and cannot be used in epistemology or phenomenology without casting a distorting light on their objects. The very expression "I can perceive *x*" is itself taken from the idioms of physics, and *x* ought to be a physical object—e.g. a body—here. Things have already gone wrong if this expression is used in phenomenology, where *x* must refer to a datum (PR, p. 88).

Furthermore, it must be a theory in *pure* phenomenology in which mention is only made of what is actually perceptible and in which no hypothetical objects—waves, rods, cones and all that—occur (PR, p. 273).

Again it seems as if Wittgenstein has been reading some Husserl. In true phenomenological fashion, Wittgenstein refuses to deal with any hypothetical entities, either those from traditional metaphysics or from natural science. "There must not be anything hypothetical in our considerations" (PI, §109). Throughout the *Investigations* he attacks the notion of mental causes and events, and elsewhere he rejects the theory of subatomic particles (PR, p. 72; BB, pp. 45, 70). He concedes that hypothetical entities make explanation much easier, but a "phenomenological description" is inconceivably more complicated (PR, p. 286). The only legitimate data for Wittgenstein and the phenomenologists are the phenomena of immediate experience: "Psychology connects what is experienced (*das Erlebte*) with something physical, but we connect what is experienced with what is experienced (*Erlebtem*)" (OCo, p. 48). As Gerd Brand states: "Thus phenomenology aims to be a philosophy founded on experience and remaining in experience."[19]

In a discussion of intention in the *Grammar*, Wittgenstein concludes that the intentional object is not something that can be observed "from outside"—it does not exist in time and space. "The phenomena of doing [i.e. willing, thinking, etc.] *are* different from the phenomena of observing something like a reflex movement" (PG, pp. 143–4). Therefore, Hems is definitely wrong when he claims that "for Husserl the phenomena are outside nature, and hence (in complete contrast to Wittgenstein) he will maintain that they are also outside the sphere of causality. . . . Phenomena are immaculate of natural characteristics and . . . Husserl maintains that it is as absurd to seek for causal properties in the phenomenal sphere as in the mathematical sphere."[20]

If Wittgenstein's phenomena were within the natural world, then physicalistic language *could* describe them. But in the *Remarks* he states: "But how can physicalistic language describe the phenomenon?" (PR, p. 98); or "there appear to be simple colors. Simple as psychological phenomena. What I need is a psychological or phenomenological color theory, not a physical and equally not a physiological one" (PR, p. 273). That Wittgenstein strove to be as impartial about phenomena as Husserl can be seen in this passage:

> The words "seem," "error," etc., have a certain emotional overture which doesn't belong to the essence of the phenomena. . . . One could speak of a primary language as opposed to ours in so far as the former would not permit any way of expressing a preference for certain phenomena over others, it would have to be, so to speak, absolutely *impartial* (PR, p. 84).

During Wittgenstein's middle period it is clear that he maintained a phenomenological *epoché* as strict as Husserl's.

In a short article of early 1929, "Remarks on Logical Form," Wittgenstein indirectly introduces the phenomenological program of his middle period. Philosophy should be a "logical analysis of phenomena themselves," which would supply us with the "forms of space and time and with the manifold of spatial and temporal objects, with colors, and sounds, etc. . . . all of which we cannot seize by our ordinary means of expression" (RLF, pp. 163, 165). In the *Philosophical Remarks* a rejection of all natural hypotheses and theories affords Wittgenstein the access that he needs for a phenomenological description of time (Chapter V), space (Chapters VII and XX), and color (Chapters VIII and XXI). A phenomenology of time, as both Husserl and Heidegger discover in their own ways, is going to be radically different from the physics of time (PR, p. 83). Although not named as such in lectures of 1931, Wittgenstein outlines a phenomenology of sound in which there is a careful distinction between auditory and physical sounds (L 1, pp. 71–2).

A phenomenology of space will make the same discovery that Husserl and Merleau-Ponty make: *viz.*, perspectivism. Objective, physical space is obviously a construction based on subjective, visual (i.e., phenomenological) space (PR, p. 100). A phenomenology of space will also isolate space from its owner, from the sense organs, and from all physical theories of space. Therefore, phenomenological geometry will not be Euclidean (nor Riemannian, etc.) (PR, pp. 271–2); and "grammar will vary according to whether the reference is to the visual field or the Euclidean. Identity of length is entirely different in visual space and Euclidean space" (L 1, p. 90). Phenomenology is not interested in the validity of this or that theory, but in the general structures of experience as a whole.

In the *Remarks* there is no question that Wittgenstein has at least performed what the Husserl of the *Crisis* called the "first *epoché*," one which suspends the theories of the objective sciences and opens up a prescientific *Lebenswelt* (K, p. 139). Husserl and the Wittgenstein of the middle period agree that such a world has a general *a priori* structure that presents itself for immediate intuition (PR, p. 51). As Husserl states in the *Crisis*: "These categorical features of the *Lebenswelt* have the same names but are not concerned, so to speak, with the theoretical idealizations and the hypothetical substructions of the geometrician and the physicist" (K, p. 140).

Already in the middle period, however, we see Wittgenstein's growing commitment to pluralism and "logical multiplicity," instead of to pure logical unity. This is intimately connected with Wittgenstein's contextualism, which culminates in the later philosophy as the dictum that "meaning is use." Even though the phenomenology of the middle period is "purer" than the later, the separate "grammars" of color, sound, space, time, etc. would still set "out the rules for the use of color words" (PG, p. 215). Coupled with the concept of *Umgebung* in the later period, this means that all which is connected with a particular situation—culture, history, emotions, preferences—cannot be separated from the essence of the phenomena in question. For example, using the concept of *Umgebung*, Wittgenstein rejects the concept of simple colors (which he held in the *Remarks*) and thereby undermines the orthodox version of the eidetic reduction (cf. OCo, pp. 9, 46). These developments place the later Wittgenstein squarely within the camp of the existential phenomenologists.

Despite some ambiguity in the *Crisis*, we must assume that the *a priori* structure of the *Lebenswelt* does not change with historical and cultural variation. For Husserl the transcendental ego lives in time, but not in history. For the later Wittgenstein, however, it is clear that time is historical-cultural, and that the pure phenomenology of time which is implied in the middle period is rejected. Although we must assume that the earlier *epoché* is still in operation, it is now much more like the existential phenomenologists who recognized that even the first step in the phenomenological program could not be completed in the way Husserl envisioned, even given the revised *epoché* of the *Crisis*.

It might be quite feasible for us to completely bracket out theories of reality based on the principles of relativity or quantum mechanics, but it is impossible for us to disengage ourselves entirely from ordinary language and common-sense ontologies that are part of what Wittgenstein calls the very "weave of our lives." Each in their own way, Heidegger, Merleau-Ponty, and Wittgenstein declare that essence and fact are inextricably bound up in a *Dasein*-world, an embodied ego, or a form of life.

This does not mean that phenomenology ceases being reflective or critical; nor does it mean that it is reduced, as Ricoeur warns, "to a rhapsody of lived experiences . . . [baptizing] as 'phenomenology' any concern for the curiosities of human life. . . ."[21] As Merleau-Ponty phrases it: "It is true that we discover the unreflected. But the unreflected we go back to is not that which is prior to philosophy or prior to reflection. It is the unreflected which is understood and conquered by reflection" (PrP, p. 19). All of this does mean that philosophy must now learn to operate on "rough ground" (PI, §107). A "crystalline" pure logic, an ideal language, or pure *eidē* are no longer philosophy's goals. Even though we must leave language essentially as we find it, we are nevertheless still obligated to show that it has bewitched us on many issues: e.g., the separation of the mind and the body, the myth of mental processes and causes, and the notion that language is the clothing of thought. Each in their own ways Wittgenstein, Heidegger, and Merleau-Ponty, have shown that these notions, even though found frequently in ordinary language, do an injustice to lived experience. Appropriately, Richard Schmitt describes the phenomenological method as appealing to "what we actually do, think, or say," but at the same time "demythologizing common sense."[22]

Another aspect of Wittgenstein's phenomenology is also compatible with the existential phenomenologists: the rejection of Husserl's "egology," a doctrine that even orthodox Husserlians like Aron Gurwitsch have eschewed. Wittgenstein counts the ego as among those hypothetical entities that must be bracketed if a phenomenological investigation is to be successful. "It would be instructive to replace this way of speaking by another in which immediate experience would be represented without using the personal pronoun" (PR, p. 88). Heidegger too goes to great lengths to replace all previous concepts of the self with his new term *"Dasein,"* which attempts to indicate the presence of human Being in a non-substantial way.

Without affirming any form of phenomenalism, both Wittgenstein and Heidegger agree that the self is never presented to us in immediate experience. There is no "I think something" that stands over and against the world as an object of its thinking. The self must always be conceived existentially: "In saying 'I' *Dasein* expresses itself as Being-in-the-world" (SZ, pp. 318 321–22). Neither Heigger nor Wittgenstein need Kant's synthetic activity of consciousness, because experience as meaningful units (language-games, forms of life, existentials) is already given, already "laid-out" and interpreted (Heidegger's *Auslegung*). Both thinkers are primarily concerned with overcoming the subject-object split that has plagued philosophy for centuries.

To sum up, in the 1929–1933 period Wittgenstein thought that he could isolate completely the various phenomenal fields—e.g., his claim that "phenomenological language" will be able to isolate visual space and our experience of time (PR, p. 103), and his proposal that his "phenomenological grammar" will have separate chapters on color, sound, etc. (PG, p. 215). The phenomenological reduction of the later works, however, can only isolate the various lived-worlds (*Lebenswelten*) of language-games and forms of life. As early as in the *Grammar* of 1933 we have seen that Wittgenstein argues that he must begin with the distinction between *Sinn* and *Unsinn*; and for the later works this distinction is not found in any pure grammar, but is already given in various forms of life that are there and must be accepted. Therefore the evolution of Wittgenstein's phenomenology appears to follow the development of 20th Century phenomenology in general, from the more cognitive Husserlian form, with ambitious claims about the phenomenological reductions, to an existential phenomenology which is far less cognitive (and more committed to the *Lebenswelt*), and far less confident about the validity of a complete reduction.

WITTGENSTEIN'S *WESENSCHAU*

There are good grounds for proposing that Wittgenstein has a *Wesenschau* similar to the phenomenologists'. He never gives up the search for essences, for *"essence* is expressed in grammar" and "grammar tells what kind of object anything is" (PI, §§371, 373). But Wittgenstein's *Wesenschau* is one that is much closer to the existential phenomenologists. Just as Heidegger believes that there are no pure noises (SZ, p. 163; U K, p. 156), Wittgenstein argues that there are no pure colors. The eidetic reduction of the color red reaches its end in the shiny bright red of the football uniform, the woolly red of the carpet, and the rustic red of fall leaves. Like Heidegger, Wittgenstein recognizes the limits of the "hermeneutical circle," that fact and essence are inextricably bound in *Lebensformen*. In a direct criticism of Husserl,

Heidegger maintains that even the *Wesenschau* is grounded in existential *Verstehen* (SZ, p. 148). Both Heidegger and Wittgenstein agree that essences can be found in the grammar of our language and forms of our lives, but these essences cannot be *said*—i.e., articulated in a completed eidetic reduction—they can only be *shown*. Because the essence of language "lies open to view," one does not need any special method to see the "structure and function" of language, short of learning to view phenomena "synoptically" (PI, §92).

Let us therefore begin with the direct seeing (*übersehen*) involved in Wittgenstein's *Übersicht*, which as he explicitly states, gives us the grammar or essence of phenomena. It is a *Darstellungsform* that allows us to comprehend, as we cited Fogelin in Chapter Four, identity-in-difference. Said in another way, this means that an *Übersicht* allows us to bridge the gap between form and content, between subject and the world; in a word, it gives us the basis for a synthetic *a priori*. As we have argued, both Wittgenstein and Husserl inherit a Kantian transcendentalism, but contrary to Kant, who believed that intuition applied only to sensations, Husserl believes that we have direct intuitions of essences. The "seeing" of Wittgenstein's *Übersicht*, like Husserl's *Wesenschau*, is not merely something sensory, but also an intellectual intuition of form and essence. An *übersichtliche Darstellung* "produces that understanding which consists in 'seeing [formal] connections'" (PI, §122; RF, p. 69).

We can think of the *Wesenschau* of a cube in a way that demonstrates Wittgenstein's *Übersicht*. The intentional object of our perception is the cube in all of its formal connections, even though all of its elements are not perceived. One has an intuitive *Übersicht* of the cube in the same way that one can intuit the formal connections of the basic colors by presenting to oneself the color octahedron (PR, pp. 51–2). At the same time we do not want Wittgenstein to sound like what Merleau-Ponty calls an "intellectualist." As we shall see in Chapter Eight, Wittgenstein has much in common with the French phenomenologist Mikel Dufrenne, who prefers to reinterpret the *Wesenschau* in Bergsonian terms as "a fundamental openness to the object," which is "rooted in an 'interested' perception oriented . . . by an action . . ." (NA, p. 94).

In the *Remarks* Wittgenstein contends that one can pick out the redundant axiom in an axiomatic system by "seeing" and not by logical inference: "It's a matter of seeing, not of proving" (PR, p. 336). Recall the connection we established between *Übersicht* and internal relations in Chapter Four—an *Übersicht* grasps a grammatical system whole in all of its internal relations. In a 1931 lecture Wittgenstein said that in logical inference "the relation of following and similar relations are internal relations . . . [and] what justifies inference is seeing the internal relation" (L 1, p. 56). Back in 1929, when arguing for the synthetic character of arithmetic, he stated that "it is always only insight (*Einsicht*) into the internal relations of the structures and not some proposition or other or some logical consideration which tell us [that 7 + 5 = 12]" (PR, p. 127). Continuing on: "No investigation of concepts, only direct insight (*direkte Einsicht*) can tell us that 3 + 2 = 5 . . . the result . . . must be immediately visible (*unmittelbar sichtbar*)" (PR, p. 129).

We must stop at this point and attempt to get a better idea of what Wittgenstein means by *Einsicht*. This is especially crucial since Wittgenstein, in a correction to the typescript, expresses dissatisfaction with the phrase "*direkte Einsicht*." Additionally, in a 1939 lecture he appears to distance himself from the claim that "I see immediately that 2 + 2 = 4" (LFM, p. 173). John Findlay translates Husserl's *Einsicht* as "insight," but claims that it "more properly means 'intuition' " (LI, p. 38). In a letter to me Spiegelberg cautions against this interpretation, suggesting that one "try to get by on the ordinary sense of the word, which had for instance a major role in Wolfgang Kohler's Gestalt psychology known to Wittgenstein in the *Investigations*." Spiegelberg's point is well taken, for we now know, especially as a result of scholarship connecting Wittgenstein with the Austrian Gestaltist Karl Bühler, much more about the possible influence of Gestalt psychology on Wittgenstein.

Nevertheless, a case can be made for Wittgenstein using the term *Einsicht* in the technical sense of intuitionist mathematics. We have already cited Wittgenstein's uses of *Einsicht* and *Sehen* as contrasted with logical inference in a discussion that includes arguments against the formalist mathematician David Hilbert (PR, p. 336, cf., p. 198). More significant is the use of *Einsicht* in a discussion that involves direct reference to the founder of intuitionism, L. E. J. Brouwer. As we have seen in Chapter Three, Brouwer believed that all mathematical propositions were synthetic *a priori* and proposed that the genesis of the number system comes from an "*Urintuition*" of "two-oneness," which is the result of "the falling apart of moments of life into qualitatively different parts" (CW, I, p. 417). Although Hallett is definitely incorrect in contending that Wittgenstein follows Brouwer in his claim that intuition is needed at every step in a mathematical process,[23] there are important connections here nonetheless.

In the *Remarks* Wittgenstein refers directly to Brouwer's concept of undecidability; i.e., that some propositions are definitely true or false, but some are simply "undecidable." This, we will recall, was part of

Brouwer's attack on the law of the excluded middle. The discussion must be quoted at length:

> We might say, "a mathematical proposition is a pointer to an *Einsicht*." The assumption that no insight corresponded to it would reduce it to utter nonsense.
>
> We cannot *understand* the equation unless we recognize (*einsehen*) the connection between its two sides.
>
> Undecidability presupposes that there is, so to speak, a subterranean connection between the two sides; that the bridge *cannot* be made with symbols.
>
> A connection between symbols which exists but cannot be represented by symbolic transformations is a thought that cannot be thought. *If the connection is there, then it must be possible to see (einsehen) it* (my emphasis).
>
> For it *exists* in the same way as the connection between parts of visual space. It isn't a *casual* connection . . . (PR, p. 212).

This passage gives us a much better idea of what Wittgenstein means when he claims that we know the synthetic *a priori* proposition "3 + 2 = 5" by "direct insight," and it also strengthens the case that this insight is some form of intuition, at least in the tradition of intuitionist mathematics. Within the context of a discussion of Brouwer one could certainly be allowed the liberty of translating "*einsehen*" as "to intuit." Furthermore, this passage conforms nicely to the grammatical (=phenomenological) method of seeing formal, acausal connections.

A survey of Wittgenstein's use of the terms "*Einsicht*," "*Anschauung*," and "*Intuition*" shows, given an important qualification, surprising consistency throughout all of his works. In the *Tractatus* Wittgenstein claims that we can have *a priori* "insights" (*Einsichten*) about the forms of propositions, and he agrees that "intuition" (*Anschauung*) is needed for the solution of mathematical problems; and that both human activities ("the process of calculating") and "language itself provides this necessary intuition" (T, 6.34, 6.233). This conforms with what he says about the role of *Einsicht* in the *Remarks on the Foundations of Mathematics*. In the latter he identifies "*Intuition*" and "*unmittelbar Einsehen*" with regard to realizing the truth of a mathematical proposition (RFM, pp. 121, 123, 125). But at another point he seems to contradict himself when he states that "if you go on dividing 1:3, you must keep on getting 3 [is a] result . . . not known by intuition . . ." (RFM, p. 126). Upon closer scrutiny, however, it becomes clear that Wittgenstein is making a distinction between intuition as a psychological process and intuition as a *Phänomen*, i.e., a proper object of grammar or phenomenology. Here is the crucial point: "What interests me is not the immediate realization (*unmittelbar Einsehen*) of a truth, but the *Phänomen* of immediate realization. Not indeed as a special mental phenomenon (*Erscheinung*), but as one of human action" (RFM, p. 123). We therefore have a surprising agreement with the passage from the *Tractatus: viz.*, that intuition plays a role in mathematics through language and human action.

This distinction in *The Remarks on the Foundation of Mathematics* helps us understand why Wittgenstein is so critical of the role of intuition in the *Investigations*. At §213 he states that "intuition is an unnecessary shuffle," and at §186 he laughs at his interlocutor when the latter suggests that "a new *Einsicht—Intuition—*is needed at every step to carry out the '+n' correctly." But in each of these cases it is clear that the intuition that Wittgenstein is rejecting is a *psychological* process, i.e., it is a mental act, "an inner voice" that we must obey. We therefore must not conclude that the later Wittgenstein has given up the search for essences; rather, we must see that these essences are not found by the process of some mental act (like the Husserlian *Wesenschau*), but discovered openly in the grammar of our language and in human actions (cf. LFM, pp. 30, 82, 238). Husserl remains firmly convinced that a good phenomenologist will never encounter contradictory essential intuitions (cf. LI, p. 769). But for Wittgenstein the essence (=grammar) of colors can just as well be *dargestellt* by a double-cone instead of an octahedron (PR, p. 278). Furthermore, an *Übersicht* is a *Weltanschauung*, and grammar is a function of various views of the world. Again we see Wittgenstein holding a type of *Weltanschauungsphilosophie*, a philosophy of which Husserl was probably more appreciative in his later period, but a philosophy that simply was not phenomenology.

This then may be the key to the "puzzle" of Wittgenstein's phenomenology, and the reason why he stopped using the term in a positive way after 1933. As we have seen, the middle works contain a phenomenological program similar in some respects to Husserl's: a strict *epoché* leading to separate grammars of color, sound, number, etc. and an emphasis on "direct insight" and "grasping the essence of what is presented." But a developing contextualism (already nascent at T, 6.233), coupled with an ultimate rejection of any theory of mental acts, turns Wittgenstein's phenomenology towards language-games and forms of life. If Wittgenstein knew first-hand of any phenomenology, it was probably the phenomenology of Husserl; therefore, his investigations could not carry that label. If we can place any weight on the Findlay-Wittgenstein conversation mentioned above, it appears as if by 1939 Husserl was "old hat," even though there is still the possibility that he had been of some influence earlier.

FREE FANCY AND FICTITIOUS NATURAL HISTORY

In the *Ideas* Husserl states that "the element which makes up the life of phenomenology as of all eidetical science is 'fiction' " (*Ideas*, §70). A *Wesenschau* can be based on the data of perception and memory, but the ultimate configuration of the essential as opposed to the inessential is the use of free variation and fancy. Because essences are ideal and not real, essential knowledge makes no assertions concerning the realm of facts. Therefore, fictions serve the purpose of phenomenology much better than perceptual data: "Free fancies assume a privileged position over against perceptions, and that even in the phenomenology of perception itself" (*Ideas*, §70).

While it is important for the natural scientist to "stick to the facts," the eidetic scientist, geometer, and phenomenologist must engage in controlled flights of fancy and enjoy that "freedom which opens up to him for the first time an entry into the spacious realms of essential possibility with their infinite horizons of essential knowledge" (*Ideas*, §70). Thus the use of free variation should be seen as an integral part of the general *epoché*, i.e., the bracketing of everything contingent, and everything that possibly could not be.

Richard Schmitt has observed that Husserl's method of imaginative variations is very close to the method of "counter-examples" so common in analytic philosophy in general.[24] We must disagree with Don Ihde's observation that a key difference between Wittgenstein and Husserl lies in "Husserl's evaluation of imaginative variations in contrast to Wittgenstein's deliberate exclusion of them in favor of using concrete objects. . . ."[25] Wittgenstein uses "fictitious natural histories" just as many times as concrete examples in his search for essences.

Wittgenstein does not use the phrase "fictitious natural history" until the *Investigations*, but we can already observe the same method in the *Remarks*. Wittgenstein's use of *Darstellungen* as models or pictures is an example. Using the color octahedron we can gain a synoptic view of the grammar of colors, and by switching to the double-cone model we are then able to double-check the essence of color for any stray contingency (PR, pp. 51–2, 278). The following passage is the clearest example of Wittgenstein's use of free variation: "Not only does epistemology

[=phenomenology, p. 88] pay no attention to the truth or falsity of genuine propositions, it's even a philosophical method of focusing on precisely those propositions whose content seems to us as physically impossible as can be imagined . . ." (PR, p. 90). With such a recipe for free variation, Wittgenstein's flights of fancy easily match Husserl's. One must admit, however, that it would be difficult to top Husserl's famous proof for the absoluteness of consciousness by imagining the destruction of everything except the *cogito* (*Ideas* §54). In the *Remarks* Wittgenstein approaches Husserl in imaginative efforts with his proposal that our idea of space would be *essentially* different if we were nothing but disembodied eye-balls (PR, pp. 100–2).

In the *Investigations* Wittgenstein states that he is "not doing natural science, nor yet natural history—since we can also invent fictitious natural history for our purposes" (PI, p. 230). If one did not know that Wittgenstein's purposes were essentially phenomenological in the 20th Century sense, one could easily misunderstand this statement. In order to get at the essence of rationality, for example, we would have to confront the fact that it is possible that there is a culture with a "more primitive logic" and a language that allowed double negations (PI, §554). Or we can easily show that there is no essential connection between emotions and their overt expression if we imagine a society in which there is "no expression of feeling *of any kind*" (Z, §383; cf. PI, §§142, 257). Like the later Husserl, Wittgenstein is involved in an investigation of the essential features of a *Lebenswelt*, a procedure which is aptly described by Aron Gurwitsch:

> Starting from any actual *Lebenswelt*, we may freely vary it in imagination and thus contrive varieties of possible *Lebenswelten* merely as possible, with regard to which the question of their historical actuality is immaterial. The objective of this procedure is to disclose what essentially and necessarily pertains to a *Lebenswelt* as such. . . .[26]

6. The Life-World

The world is not what I think, but what I live through.
                                                —*Merleau-Ponty (PP, p. xvi)*

The World and Life are one. . . . Life is the World.
                                                —*Wittgenstein (NB, p. 77)*

It seems that I neglect life. But not life physiologically understood but life as consciousness. And consciousness not physiologically understood, or understood from the outside, but consciousness as the very essence of experience, the appearance of the world, the world.
                                                —*Wittgenstein (PE, p. 297)*

The stream of life, or the stream of the world, flows on and our propositions are so to speak verified only at instants.
                                                —*Wittgenstein (PR, p. 81)*

It might be argued that [Merleau-Ponty's] concern with the life-world and the later Wittgenstein's interest in forms of life bear a great resemblance.
                                                —*Raymond Herbenick*[1]

The Philosophical Investigations *attempt the description of this* Sprachwelt *which is Wittgenstein's counterpart of Husserl's* Lebenswelt, *since language is a kind of living for the man who is speaking.*
                                                —*John Hems*[2]

I see in Wittgenstein an excellent representative of a phenomenology of the life-world.
                                                —*Gerd Brand (EW, p. xxv)*

117

THE *LEBENSWELT* IN HUSSERL'S *CRISIS*

Philip J. Bossert begins his excellent comparison of Nelson Goodman and Husserl with an illuminating etymology of the word "world." It comes from the Old German "*weralt*," where "*wer*" means "man" (as in "werwolf") and "*alt*" means "age" as in "the modern age." As Bossert sums up: "Literally, 'world' thus orginally meant 'the age of man' and was descriptive of the human mode or state of existence; the world was the life of man or the course of human life."³ In other words, the science of etymology, plus everyday usages such as "it is a new world for him," support the interpretation of "world" as a human "life-world."

Although Husserl used the term "*Lebenswelt*" as early as *Ideas I* of 1917, it was only during the last year of his active life that he developed the term as a fundamental phenomenological theme. In *Ideas III* Husserl admitted that he had not paid enough attention to the *Weltphänomen*, and the existence of the world had of course fallen outside the bracketing of the *epoché*. Although some commentators like Aron Gurwitsch insist that Husserl does not make any significant concessions to the growing trend toward existential phenomenology, others like Hans-Georg Gadamer believe that the later Husserl's commitment to the *Lebenswelt* is an implicit admission that Heidegger was correct in his focus on the *Dasein*-world.⁴ The *Crisis* then spells the end of a phenomenology based on the transcendental ego and the strict reductions. Gadamer even contends that Husserl ends up agreeing with Dilthey by realizing that the life-world must remain within the *epoché* otherwise one would kill the "life" of the subject.⁵ Whereas for the pre-*Crisis* Husserl the world was always a fact-world whose existence was contingent, the world of the *Crisis* is a lived world whose existence must be a necessary truth.

Gadamer believes that the transcendental solipsism of the *Cartesian Meditations* was a dead-end and forced Husserl to replace the transcendental ego with the anonymous intersubjectivity of the *Lebenswelt*.⁶ Robert Ehman is just as emphatic as Gadamer about this shift in Husserl's thought: "There is no more decisive move in contemporary phenomenological thought than that from transcendental subjectivity to the world as the horizon of phenomenological investigation." This has allowed later phenomenologists such as Merleau-Ponty and Heidegger "to correct the idealist bias of the Husserlian approach without returning to the naive ontological realism of the tradition."⁷

The *Lebenswelt* of Husserl's *Crisis* is the product of the passive synthesis of operative intentionality. The early Husserl's emphasis on act intentionality had allowed him to neglect this arena, a "realm of original self-evidences" (K, p. 127). It is the "only real world, the one that is actually given through perception, that is ever experienced and experiencable" (K, p. 49). Although there is some equivocation, the *Lebenswelt* is not a cultural-historical world, because any such world would depend on the common perceptual ground of the *Lebenswelt*. Cultural-historical worlds are the result of specific purposes and goals; that is, they are always thematic, while the *Lebenswelt* is the ground for all thematization. The basic structures of the *Lebenswelt* are always "that which is taken for granted" (*das Selbstverständliche*) (K, p. 123); and any achievement of a cultural-historical world always presupposes the *a priori Lebenswelt*—"the universe of what is intuitable in principle" (K, p. 127).

Husserl usually makes this important distinction clear by calling cultural-historical worlds "*Umwelten*" or "*Lebensumwelten*", which David Carr translates as "surrounding (life-) worlds." For example, Husserl speaks of the "relativity of the surrounding life-worlds of particular human beings, peoples, and periods as mere matters of fact" (K, p. 147, cf. pp. 272, 328, 369), unsuitable for transcendental phenomenology. The topic of true phenomenology is the constant and unchanging *Lebenswelt*, the total horizon of all possible experiences, which is the ground of validity for the vast variations and contingencies of culture and history. "The life-world constantly functions as subsoil" and "its manifold pre-logical validities act as ground for the logical ones, for theoretical truths" (K, p. 124), which have come into being in a modern culture where science and logic are models of truth. Husserl declares that the *a priori* life-world can never be thought of as plural (K, p. 143), for it is the universal horizon for the plurality of cultural worlds, and the condition for the possibility of the intercommunication among these worlds.

In keeping with most life-philosophers, Husserl agrees that the basic thrust of life itself is not teleological. Therefore the *a priori Lebenswelt* is devoid of specific purposes, whereas the cultural-historical sub-worlds are expressly built on them (K, p. 462g). The *Lebenswelt* is the "*Weltall*" which absorbs all particular worlds and grounds the "absolute objectivity . . . which is common to all" (PhP, pp. 598f). The cultural worlds are a specific merger of fact and essence, whereas the life-world itself is pure essence and thus is the only suitable topic of phenomenology proper. In short, the *Lebenswelt* proper is not a construct, while each *Umwelt* definitely is. Husserl is convinced, however, that historical investigations still play a role in such a phenomenology, as his own brilliant analyses of both Galileo and the origins of geometry in the *Crisis* clearly shows. The pre-*Crisis* Husserl had generally shied away from historical philosophy, but the *Lebenswelt* approach now legitimizes such philosophical endeavors.

In his last years it is evident that Husserl was searching for a phenomenological method that would be concrete and transcendental at the same time, without compromising the rigid requirements of the transcendental method. The most significant element in this move towards the concrete is the subtle substitution of intersubjectivity for the transcendental ego. In the *Crisis* Husserl explicitly speaks of a "universal intersubjective horizon" (K, p. 243) in which "each soul . . . stands in community with others which are intentionally interelated . . . [an] internally and essentially closed nexus . . . of intersubjectivity" (K, p. 238). The theme is constant and continuous: "A transcendental community of subjects [is] one which . . . has in itself and continues ever to create the world as intentional validity-correlate, in ever new forms and strata of cultural worlds" (K, p. 259, cf., pp. 175, 179). But at least once the monadology of the *Cartesian Meditations* re-appears when he reminds us of the complete solitude of the *epoché* and admits that it was "wrong, methodically, to jump immediately into transcendental intersubjectivity and to leap over the primal 'I,' the ego of my *epoché*, which can never lose its uniqueness and personal indeclinability" (K, p. 185).

ALFRED SCHÜTZ ON *LEBENSFORM* AND *SINNSTRUKTUR*

Husserl sketches the outlines of a life-world phenomenology in the *Crisis*, but it is Alfred Schütz, more than any other phenomenologist, who has been the "founding father" of this form of phenomenology. He has the almost exclusive distinction of being accepted by both orthodox and existential phenomenologists. Schütz was Viennese and did much of his principal work during the 1920s, although he did not start publishing until the 30s. There is no evidence whatever to suggest that Wittgenstein read anything of Schütz; besides, his works would have come too late to influence Wittgenstein during the crucial middle period. Schütz was strongly opposed to positivism and refused to read the *Tractatus*, which he considered to be, as Helmut Wagner told me in a letter, the Bible of the "Enemy."

In 1925 Schütz began a book entitled *Lebensform und Sinnstruktur*, which could have been an appropriate German title for Wittgenstein's *Investigations* or other later works. This typescript is as yet unpublished and the only scholar who has access to it, Helmut Wagner, explains that

Schütz's *Lebensformen* are meaning structures which are found in hierarchical arrangement: "The higher life forms are grounded in the lower ones, but the meaning of the lower forms depends on the meaning structures of the higher ones. . . . No life form is self-contained, no meaning structure explains itself."[8] Although Schütz's life forms are basically psychological ("pure duration," "the memory endowed," "the acting I") and are therefore quite different from Wittgenstein's, this hierarchical and interdependent model fits very well the various statements about *Lebensformen* in the later works. Indeed, this idea of what David Carr calls "phenomenological stratification" is a pervasive theme throughout all forms of phenomenology.

Schütz's concept of forms of life was strongly influenced by Henri Bergson, the French embodiment of life-philosophy. We have characterized life-philosophy as a sociological neo-Kantianism, and Schütz's phenomenological sociology is definitely in the tradition of life-philosophy. The translators of Schütz's *The Structures of the Life-World* describe Schütz's philosophy as a "sweeping and novel epistemology: a phenomenological account of knowledge as basically social," primarily because "we are always in situation and the situation is always socially conditioned" (SLW, p. xxix). For Schütz the *Lebenswelt* is above all the province of *Praxis*, of social action.

In an article entitled "A Wittgensteinian Sociology?" A. K. Saran proposes that the Wittgensteinian Peter Winch and Schütz agree that the task of sociology is the "elucidation of what is involved in certain forms of social life."[9] Wittgenstein and Schütz do share some key basic assumptions. Both hold to phenomenological description which is sharpened by the use of intermediate, hypothetical cases (SLW, p. 110; PI, §122). Both are aware of what is appropriate to empirical sociology and therefore disavow "historical-causal hypotheses" and concentrate on the "basic pre-suppositions for the constitution of social knowledge" (SLW, p. 262; RF, p. 69). Furthermore, both recognize the value and the limits of the implicit *epoché* in everyday life and ordinary language. Because of this similarity both thinkers do not have the traditional obsession for "justification," because grounds for what we do and say are simply in ordinary, "life-worldly" doing and saying.

By way of contrast, Wittgenstein would frown at Schütz's penchant for psychologizing—characterized generally by his choice of the *Lebensformen* mentioned above and specifically by his claim that knowledge of the Pythagorean theorem depends upon "whether I can 'more or less' repeat the polythetic steps of the derivation or not" (SLW, p. 121). Schütz contends that William James was limited by his "psychological perspective," but this criticism applies to Schütz as well. The psychological *Lebensformen* of "pure duration," "the acting I," etc. serve as the basis for a genetic account of meaning that Wittgenstein would definitely have rejected.

Although Wittgenstein would disagree with the details of Schütz's psychology of learning, he would definitely assent to the claim that our "stock knowledge" is built up "polythetically" in such a way that the steps cannot be traced empirically (SLW, p. 120). The concept of "stock knowledge," and the images which Schütz uses to develop this concept, bear striking similarities to Wittgenstein's ideas about knowledge in *On Certainty.* Both thinkers believe that knowledge acquisition has a definite and specific history and that all our knowledge, characterized as it is by a "situational relatedness," is profoundly affected by history and culture. In each philosopher the historicity of knowledge is described in terms of a river metaphor; our "stock knowledge" is the result of "the sedimentation of current experiences in meaning-structures, according to relevance and typicality" (SLW, p. 119).

Like Michael Polanyi's "tacit knowledge,"[10] "stock knowledge" does not begin as explicit scientific or theoretical thought (cf. SLW, p. 122), but as Gurwitsch phrases it, "loosely connected rules and maxims of behavior in typical situations, recipes for handling things of certain types so as to attain typical results."[11] In other words, the logical lines of the arena of this pre-reflective knowledge are, as Wittgenstein would put it, "blurred," or as Schütz says, "what is taken for granted does not form a closed, unequivocally articulated and clearly arranged province" (SLW, p. 9).

In *On Certainty* Wittgenstein proposes that the process of sedimentation will give us both "hard" and "soft" facts, some which are indubitable and solid and others which are easily washed away. As Schütz's phrases it: "My 'knowledge' that I can't be in two places at the same time can never be problematic; no lifewordly experience can gainsay it" (SLW, p. 102). Even errors like "whales are fish," if sufficiently grounded in lifeworldly experiences, are truths (SLW, p. 104). Our "stock knowledge" is made up of "sedimented group experience that has passed the test and which does not need to be examined by individuals as regards its validity" (SLW, p. 8). This sounds surprisingly much like Wittgenstein's claim that hard facts are *a priori* because "nothing in my picture of the world speaks in favor of the opposite" (OC, §93). Schütz continually encloses "knowledge" in scare quotation marks, and I suspect that he does this for the same reason as Wittgenstein: that "framework facts," as we shall call them, are so fundamental that they are pre-epistemological.

Schütz is very much cognizant of the "linguistic turn," and realizes that the turn to the life-world means a move towards linguistic phenomenology. Schütz sometimes psychologizes about the origin of language, something of which Wittgenstein would disapprove, when, e.g., he speaks of subjective experiences being objectified in language as a part of the social *a priori* (SLW, p. 235). He is closer to Wittgenstein's type of behaviorism when he talks about the pre-linguistic stage in which the child assimilates "gestures, facial expressions, and typical conduct" and the general "grammar-gestures of the current historical-cultural age" (SLW, pp. 248–9). Wittgenstein and Schütz would also agree on the "intersubjective constitution of signs" (SLW, p. 278) and the claim that "the categories are to a great extent socially objectivated, above all, in language, as a highly anonymous system of meaning" (SLW, p. 116).

To return finally to the idea of phenomenological stratification, we find that Schütz follows Husserl in delineating a multiplicity of sub-worlds as the various strata beneath the universal life-world. Each sub-world constitutes a "finite province of meaning" (*Sinngebiet*), each with its own style and, as Husserl phrases it, its own "particularized *a priori* forms" (K, p. 259). Elaborating on Husserl's observation that various cultural worlds have characteristic normative "styles" (K, p. 280), Schütz proposes that each "province of meaning" has its own style, a style of life which can overlap and complement others or contradict them and radically differ (cf. SLW, p. 156). A new province of meaning, like Wittgenstein's new language-game, may open up as a result of new technical language or new slang (SLW, p. 286), while other provinces may fade away from disuse, just like those language-games which become obsolete (SLW, p. 125).

Schütz's *Sinngebieten* also have instructive parallels with Wittgenstein's forms of life: there are those which are cognitive, religious, aesthetic, and that which is preferred depends on where the "accent of reality" is placed (SLW, p. 125). Furthermore, there is sometimes no simple conversion from one province to another, and a Kierkegaardian leap of faith is necessary to change from one style or form of life to another (SLW, p. 24). This is exactly Wittgenstein's point in *On Certainty* about taking on the views of certain primitive tribes. Schütz also observes that many jokes are based on the immediate juxtaposition of conflicting *Sinngebieten*. (E.g., my daughter asks me what the difference is between a well-dressed man and a tired dog, I fumble for an answer, and she triumphantly responds: the one wears a suit and the other just pants!) For the same reason, Wittgenstein asks us: "Why do we feel a grammatical joke to be *deep*?" (PI, §111).

Schütz's *Lebenswelt* and provinces of meaning compare favorably with Wittgenstein's *Weltbild* and forms of life with their linguistic expressions. In both Schütz and Wittgenstein the *Lebenswelt* is a concept in which nature and culture are merged: the *Lebenswelt* is where physical bodies are transformed into cultural objects, or persons whose physical movements are then meaningful acts, gestures, and communication (SLW, p. 5). In a major move away from Husserl, which means a move towards existential phenomenology and Wittgenstein, Schütz claims that the *Lebenswelt* can change: "The *Lebenswelt* is thus a reality which we modify through our acts and which, on the other hand, modifies our actions" (SLW, p. 6, cf. p. 3). This reminds one of Merleau-Ponty's image of centrifugal and centripetal forces operating within the field of human intentionality.

THE *LEBENSWELT* IN HEIDEGGER AND WITTGENSTEIN

In *Being and Time* Heidegger offers four definitions of *"Welt,"* the third of which becomes the basis of the *Dasein*-analysis. This definition is that " 'wherein' factical *Dasein* as such can be said to 'live' " (SZ, p. 65). The verb *"leben"* is in scare quotations presumably because Heidegger, true to his transcendental method, does not wish to consider life in a biological sense. A phenomenological view of life must see it as "a unique mode of Being" (SZ, p. 50, cf. pp. 10, 58). The world in which we live can also be seen as the public *"Wir-Welt"* or as "one's own closest (domestic) environment (*Umwelt*)" (SZ, p. 65). The translation of *Umwelt* as "environment" is misleading, especially in these days of a new ecological or biological sense (SZ, p. 58).

Heidegger's *Umwelt* and Wittgenstein's *Umgebung* immediately suggest a comparison. An analysis of the passages where *Umgebung* is used shows that Wittgenstein uses the term in a non-physical sense. Some examples from *On Color* are instructive: "A color 'shines' in its *Umgebung*." (Just as eyes only smile in a face)"; or "something is grey or white only in a particular *Umgebung*" (OCo, pp. 9, 46). Any optical physicist would be completely baffled by Wittgenstein's remarks here, but Wittgenstein warns us that he is doing a phenomenology, i.e. a grammar of colors and not a physics of colors. These examples seem to indicate that the scope of an *Umgebung* is much narrower than Heidegger's *Umwelt*. But Wittgenstein also uses *Umgebung* in a much broader sense as in "the institution of language and all of its *Umgebung*" (PI, §540), or as in his contention that interpretations change in "a wider *Umgebung*" (PI, §539). In fact, Wittgenstein implies that an *Umgebung* can be as broad as human life itself: "The surroundings give it its importance. And the word 'hope' refers to a phenomenon of human life" (PI, §583). Connecting the idea of surroundings to the idea of a life-world, Wittgenstein states that "If I imagine such a person I also imagine a reality, a world that surrounds him" (OC, §595).

In the preceding passage Wittgenstein is reiterating his central concept of internal relations, and we can now see that a world for Wittgenstein is an internally related system of signs, events, and things. Wittgenstein comments that "a system is, so to speak, a world," and "these five axioms and whatever derives from them are—so to speak—my whole world" (PR, pp. 178, 335). The semantic holism of an internally related system is also found in *On Certainty:* "When we first begin to *believe* anything, what we believe is not a single proposition, it is a whole system of propositions. (Light dawns gradually over the whole)" (OC, §141). I have already used the following quotation from Merleau-Ponty, but its re-emphasis here is appropriate: "I can . . . see an object insofar as objects form a system or a world . . ." (PP, p. 68).

Merleau-Ponty, as he admits many times, is working out of Heidegger's concept of Being-in-the-World, and such a world is a "relational totality" of "significance" (*Bedeutung*), a "system of [internal] relations" (SZ, p. 87). Heidegger realizes that he has invoked the specter of a strict rationalist view of relations (as always "something thought"), which he admits would dissolve the *Dasein*-world into "pure thinking"; but he, just like Wittgenstein, definitely does not have a rationalist view of internal relations. George F. Sefler phrases our main point aptly: "To be worldly is to be in a relation. . . . In a word, relationality is Heidegger's ontological [transcendental] ground within which things appear."[12] Sefler is also correct in claiming that for both Wittgenstein and Heidegger traditional predicates and properties give way to a system of relations, in which, for example, the meaning of a hammer is not given in terms of its necessary qualities but strictly in terms of its use in the world.[13] Recall this crucial statement from Wittgenstein: "What I perceive in the dawning of an aspect is not a property of the object, but an internal relation between it and other objects" (PI, p. 212).

Wittgenstein is just as cryptic as Heidegger in his use of the words "*Welt*" and "*Leben*." At the beginning of the *Tractatus* he seems to be choosing the scientific view of the world which Heidegger rejects as that "totality of entities which can be present-at-hand within the world" (SZ, p. 64). Wittgenstein states that the world is the totality of facts, not objects or states of affairs (T, 1.1). By the end of the book, however, this positivistic view of the world has been replaced by an identification of *Welt* and *Leben* (T, 5.621). We have proved in Chapter One that Wittgenstein definitely does not use "life" in a physical sense, but let us repeat the crucial passage: "Physiological life is of course not 'Life.' And neither is psychological life. Life is the world (NB, p. 77). As Husserl states: "The word *life* here does not have a physiological sense; it signifies purposeful life accomplishing spiritual products: in the broadest sense, creating culture in the unity of a historical development" (K, p. 270).

The *Philosophical Remarks* also contains similar statements about life and world. Section 47 begins with a description of what Heideggerians would call "existential space" as a way of Being-in-the-world. He describes a pre-reflective, pre-scientific way of being-in-the-world in which we take everything for granted—e.g., "we do not notice that we see space perspectively or that our visual field is in some sense blurred towards the edges." No doubts arise with respect to the way we perceive things, "since there is nothing that contrasts with the form of our world" (PR, p. 80). Wittgenstein continues to develop these ideas of world and life in a very unclear way. Like the life-philosophers, he seems to replace the traditional metaphysical concept of "reality" with "life" itself.

> This which we take as matter of course, *life*, is supposed to be something accidental, subordinate, while something that normally never comes into my head, reality! That is, what we neither can nor want to go beyond would not be the world (PR, p. 80).

This passage is as obscure as anything in Heidegger, but let us attempt an interpretation. First, it is clear that he rejects the metaphysics of the *Tractatus* where the sum total of reality is the world (2.063). He wants to argue that life itself is the given, and that no legitimate concept of the world can go beyond what we can experience in our lives. The discussion fades away with this final comment: "The stream of life, or the stream of the world, flows on and our propositions are so to speak verified only at instants" (PR, p. 81).

At this point we must stop and analyze one problem we introduced earlier, *viz.* the problem of Wittgenstein's solipsism and these passages about life and world. In order to keep our phenomenological parallel intact, let me begin with a remark by Quentin Lauer: "the 'world' of which [Husserl] speaks is still a world in consciousness (PRS, p. 67). In 1934–35 Wittgenstein maintained that life is "consciousness as the very essence of experience, the appearance of the world, the world" (PE, p. 297; cf. NB, p. 79). Five years earlier in the passages from the *Remarks* quoted above, the life-world is a *"Vorstellungswelt,"* a world of ideas (PR, p. 80). Evidently the ghost of Schopenhauer and a transcendental solipsism is still pervading some of this middle work. But this solipsism is one which Wittgenstein now believes he has overcome. The passage is obscure but the gist of it is clear:

> But here solipsism teaches us a lesson: . . . For if the *world* is idea it isn't any person's idea. (Solipsism stops short of saying this and says that it is my idea.) But then how could I say what the world is if the realm of ideas has no neighbor (PE, p. 297).

What Wittgenstein appears to be saying is this: any meaningful talk about my world presupposes an external, common world. Is this what Wittgenstein was trying to tell us from the beginning? For example, when he stated in 1916 that "Here we can see that solipsism [by means of the concept of the life-world] coincides with pure realism, if it is strictly thought out" (NB, p. 82). Both phenomenology and Wittgenstein have passed beyond the problem of realism vs. idealism.

A similar tension between solipsism and realism is found in Heidegger's concept of *Dasein*. Heidegger stresses heavily that the Being of *Dasein* is "in each case mine" (SZ, p. 41)—the famous doctrine of *"Jemeinigkeit"* which inspired the existentialist interpretation of *Being and Time*. But Heidegger believes, along with Wittgenstein, that it is impossible to separate the subject from the world: "In clarifying Being-in-the-world we have shown that a bare subject without a world never is . . . given" (SZ, p. 116). There is an instructive ambiguity in the German *"Da,"* which can mean both "Here" as well as "There." Therefore, *Dasein* is both my "Being-here-in-my-world" (solipsism) and my "Being-there-in-the-world" (realism) along with other people (*Mit-sein*). Interestingly enough, P. M. S. Hacker, in his explication of Wittgenstein's refutation of solipsism, offers a similar mode of explanation. The solipsistic "Here" must always be understood in terms of a common or public "There."[14] The Danish scholar, Jens Glebe-Møller, suggests that the concept of *Lebensform* assumes that "I" and "You" are always together in a common world to which we are all personally committed.[15] Karl-Otto Apel also proposes that Wittgenstein's insights about forms of life converge with Heidegger's solution to the problem of other minds and intersubjectivity. The "I," the "You," and the "Others" are all given "equiprimordially" by means of the existentials "With-Being" and "Being-in-the-world."[16] To return finally to Wittgenstein's original solipsistic-sounding comments, we must conclude that consciousness is never just mental but, first and foremost, it is worldly.

HEIDEGGER'S EXISTENTIALS AND WITTGENSTEIN'S FORMS OF LIFE[17]

Heidegger rejected the traditional theories of categories, both Aristotelian and Kantian, because they were based on an analysis of presence-at-hand (*Vorhandensein*), a derivative mode of Being. The traditional categories therefore cannot possibly be adequate for an understanding of human life; in fact, the use of the categories of substance, causality, and quantity in the behavioral sciences today does a great violence to what it is to be human. Heidegger's *Dasein*-analysis is therefore an attempt to derive new categories—he calls them *"Existenzialen"*—from *Dasein's* immediate experience in its *Lebenswelt* with other *Daseins* and things ready-at-hand (*Zuhandendes*).

Many critics reject the *Dasein*-analysis as pseudo-psychology, based on rather perverse introspection and expressed in unintelligible language. I make no brief for Heidegger's language and his obscure modes of expression. But I do wish to reiterate some essential points of Heidegger's phenomenological method. The *Dasein*-analysis does not investigate being human in terms of the psychical or the physical (SZ, p. 47). Heidegger agrees with Husserl and Scheler who hold "that the unity of the person must have a constitution essentially different from that required for the unity of things in nature" (SZ, p. 48). Heidegger's method is a "formal phenomenology of consciousness" that is primarily interested in the structure and meaning of human acts. "Hope" is a specific "existential," a mode of *Dasein's* Being, and Heidegger states that "what is decisive for the structure of hope as a *Phänomen*, is not so much the 'futural' character of that *to which* it relates itself [i.e. an empirical question], but rather the existential meaning of *hoping itself*" (SZ, p. 345). Therefore, what Heidegger would call a phenomenology of hope has significant parallels with a Wittgensteinian "grammar" of hope.

Heidegger's analysis is not introspective because he, like Wittgenstein, has rejected the post-Cartesian distinction between the "inner" and the "outer." Moods like hope, joy, sadness—subspecies of the general existential "state-of-mind"—"come neither from 'outside' nor from 'inside,' but arise out of Being-in-the-world"; and state-of-mind "is very remote from anything like coming across a psychical condition by [a] kind of apprehending" (SZ, p. 156). In his analysis of the existential "knowing," Heidegger seems to go through the same general steps that Wittgenstein does in the *Investigations*. First he convinces us that knowing cannot be grasped in terms of anything outside, any overt behavior. "Now, inasmuch as knowing belongs to [things we know] and is not some external characteristic, it must be 'inside' " (SZ, p. 60). But this is a complete dead-end, because if knowing is a knowing of the world, how can "this knowing subject come out of its inner 'sphere' into one which is 'other and external' " (SZ, p. 60)?

Therefore both thinkers begin their analyses in the *Lebenswelt* where there is no subject-object split and no distinction between the inner and the outer. These are assumptions that are a product of philosophical reflection, not anything given in our experience. This is the reason why the problems of skepticism, of the external world, and other minds, do not bother Wittgenstein nor Heidegger. For Heidegger Being-in-the-world means that one is always and already "outside" of what could be called the classic ego-centric predicament (SZ, pp. 162, 205).

Let us take a closer look at some of the specific existentials like hope, joy, anxiety, etc., all forms of *Dasein's* life. Like Wittgenstein's analysis of hope (PI, §583) which we cited in Chapter Four, Heidegger contends that fear and anxiety never " 'occur' just isolated in the 'stream of experience,' each of them determines an understanding or determines itself in terms of one" (SZ, p. 344). Recall that Wittgenstein argued that "hope" could not be isolated from its specific *Umgebung* and that our interpretation of hope would change with the slightest change in context. For Heidegger moods are more than just behavioral dispositions, they are existentials that are "disclosive," i.e. they reveal a certain form of life (SZ, p. 137). As we have seen, for Wittgenstein humor is not just a mood, but a *Weltanschauung*, and sadness is a "medium" or a "viewpoint" (VB, p. 147; PR, p. 90). In other words, these forms of life disclose a way of looking at things; they reveal something about a life-world.

Many commentators on *Being and Time* complain that we are never given a definite list of existentials and it is never clear what sort of interrelations they all ultimately have. The same criticism can be leveled at Wittgenstein and his enigmatic remarks about forms of life. In all fairness we must realize that both thinkers stressed the fragmentary nature of their analyses. In my interpretation of forms of life in Chapter One, I proposed that the relationship among the many forms of life could be seen in terms of four levels, ranging from the biological to the most formal *Weltbild*. This stratified model is strengthened by the fact that Wittgenstein says that there are "those forms of life which are primitive and those which rise out of them" (119, p. 148). Heidegger also gives evidence that allows us to see his existentials in a similar fashion. He claims that some of the existentials are more fundamental than others (SZ, p. 160), that state-of-mind is a species of more fundamental existentials, and that "knowing" is a "sub-species" of understanding (SZ, p. 153).

With these clues the hierarchical structure of the existentials should look like this: specific modes of *Dasein's* Being, like moods (hope, anxiety, joy, etc.), are subspecies of state-of-mind, which is in a necessary trinity with understanding and discourse, which in turn are species of the most comprehensive existential: Being-in-the-world. When we compare this with the hierarchy of forms of life, we discover two interesting points: (1) that Heidegger does not speak of *Dasein's* animal nature at all; and (2) that he does not explicitly describe the effect of various cultural styles, although this is certainly implied in his concept of *Umwelt*. He does talk of European *Dasein* and Oriental *Dasein*, which would mean that these represent two different cultural worlds or "houses of Being." And similar to Wittgenstein, Heidegger would insist that common existentials like hope, joy, etc. would find different expressions within these various cultural styles.

Just as in Wittgenstein, there are definitely some loose ends here. One of them is the concept of *Horizont*, which is central to Husserl's concept of *Lebenswelt*. The *Horizont* is the formal framework or "horizon" in which the appearance of person and things is possible (SZ, pp. 116, 365–66). Heidegger uses *Welt* in the sense of *Horizont* at least once: "The world itself is not an entity-within-the-world, and yet it is determinative for such entities that only in so far as 'there is' a world can they be encountered and show themselves" (SZ, p. 72). Wittgenstein is characteristically evasive in giving us a clear definition of *Weltbild*, but its functions seem to correspond to some of those of Heidegger's *Horizont*. Especially significant is the historicistic emphasis that we find in the *Weltbild* of *On Certainty*. A *Weltbild* is likened to a river whose banks tend to change with the flow of time. It is conceivable that "hard" propositions would become "fluid" and "fluid" ones become "hard" (OC, §96). Again we see Wittgenstein's preference for an "existential" phenomenology, for Husserl resisted the merging of temporality and his concept of *Lebenswelt*.

HEIDEGGER VS. WITTGENSTEIN

Even though we have established a number of significant links between Wittgenstein and phenomenology in general, and with Heidegger in particular, there remains an important difference between the
two in terms of the question of what philosophy can ultimately achieve.
Like many thinkers, both Heidegger and Wittgenstein are better in
criticism than in construction, but in comparison to Heidegger,
Wittgenstein does very little constructive philosophy. Ingvar Horgby is
correct in arguing that Wittgenstein generally remains within a
philosophical "*via negativa*," while Heidegger continues on in an effort
to express the "higher things."[18] H. R. Smart contends that the only
constructive parts of the *Investigations* are those dealing with forms of
life, and we have seen how evasive Wittgenstein is in giving much information about them. Heidegger is much more tempted to articulate
and systematize the forms of experience that he has discovered, while
Wittgenstein is much more inclined to let those forms simply show
themselves.

That Heidegger's phenomenology is much more constructive than
Wittgenstein's is most clearly seen in the fact that Heidegger attempted
to unify all of the existentials into one: care. Wittgenstein did not, and
definitely would not have, attempted any such systematic effort with his
forms of life. Heidegger also attempts to make general statements
about all forms of life, while Wittgenstein is content to investigate only
our own "cross strip," the life forms of our own *Weltbild*. In a sense,
Heidegger does not follow his own advice when he argues that there is
no such thing as a "simple primal ground" (SZ, p. 131). Furthermore,
his concept of equiprimordiality also implies a more modest
Wittgensteinian approach of simply assuming many equiprimordial
forms of existence. Heidegger made it clear in *Being and Time* that the
Dasein-analysis was only a propadeutic for a more comprehensive investigation of Being itself. This is obviously far from Wittgenstein's much
less ambitious phenomenological program.

Both existentials and forms of life are concepts that have a built-in
ambivalence that is troublesome for both thinkers, especially Wittgenstein. As we have seen, they refer at the same time to formal patterns
and to lived experience. There is a tension between the formal and
experiential dimensions that is never satisfactorily resolved. Heidegger
has fewer problems than Wittgenstein because his hierarchical structure of existentials is clearly more formal than Wittgenstein's, which in-

cludes the biological aspect of forms of life. The tension between the biological and the purely formal *Weltbild* is very great, and it points to some instructive differences between the two philosophers.

As we have seen, John Hunter was able to write an impressive defense of forms of life as non-cultural, "biological adaptations," primarily because of explicit statements about language-games being a "primitive form of behavior" (Z, §545), about comparing specific life forms with walking, eating, etc. (PI, §25), and about life forms being grounded in "instinct" and "something animal" (OC, §§359, 475). There is also much emphasis on learning language-games and learning skills that make life forms possible: "To understand a language means to be master of a technique" (PI, §199). What this evidence shows is that there is generally a much larger empirical component in forms of life than in the existentials.

It appears as if Heidegger is much more consistent in his phenomenological method and is, in a certain sense, much more orthodox in his Kantianism. In general his analysis remains at a formal level and does not deal at all with the instincts or biology. His existentials, just like Kant categories, are not learned, but are given. As Walter Biemel asserts: "In Heidegger's view existentials are structural moments that are not historically determined. . . . The question of how they are materialized concretely is indeed a historical issue."[19] On this point Wittgenstein is definitely a relativist: while Heidegger could not conceive of a human being who did not "care," Wittgenstein is able to conceive of all sorts of possibilities, including tribes that do not express feelings in any way. At the same time, however, Wittgenstein is definitely not a Darwinist: humans are unique beings and they will always relate to a human world in special ways that exclude other animals. Wittgenstein simply refuses to state, *a priori*, which ways, which forms of life, are necessary and which ones are not.

In contrast to Heidegger, Wittgenstein retains a strong perspectivism and pragmatism. Heidegger would have criticized Wittgenstein for the same reasons that he criticized Dilthey: neither pushed their life-philosophies beyond an ontic or quasi-transcendental level. (Although we have established that Wittgenstein claims to operate with a transcendental method, it is obvious that he does not consistently follow it out.) Both remain at the level of *Weltanschauungen*, relativistic cultural styles and orientations. Wittgenstein's phenomenology does not rise much above the level of a *Kulturphilosophie*.[20] Without firm transcendental and universal foundations, philosophy in this vein would be little more than a descriptive socio-biology.

In Wittgenstein's defense one could cite the following observations by Gadamer: "One look at the fields of investigation in ethnology or history informs us that spaces and times bear highly different life-worlds in which highly different things pass as undoubted self-evidence."[21] Although we shall see that Gadamer must reaffirm one universal life-world if he is to make his doctrine of *Horizontsverschmelzung* credible, Wittgenstein is not interested, nor does he believe in, the "fusion of horizons." This makes a general phenomenology of the life-world an unfortunate impossibility.

All of the above amounts to saying that Wittgenstein has collapsed the distinction between Husserl's universal *Lebenswelt* and the plurality of cultural *Umwelten*. The horizon or *Weltbild* is always thematized as this culture or that, and a common *a priori* basis is not to be found. Wittgenstein would take Husserl's claim of constant, unchanging validity to be a cultural product as well, just like all claims to universal validity in logic, science, or religion. Even though Heidegger has attempted to merge being and time, he still believes that the *a priori* structure of the existentials is invariant: all humans, if they are humans, will care, dread, live in time, and exist as beings-toward-death. Even Merleau-Ponty appears to be at odds with Wittgenstein on this crucial point: "All human acts and all human creations constitute a single drama, and in this sense we are all saved or lost together. Our life is essentially universal" (PrP, p. 10).

7. Behaviorism and Intentionality

"Are you not really a behaviorist in disguise? Aren't you at bottom saying that everything except human behavior is a fiction?"–If I do speak of a fiction, then it is a grammatical *fiction.*

–Wittgenstein (PI, §307)

"Is there then no mind, but only a body?" Answer: The word "mind" has meaning, i.e., it has a use in our language.

–Wittgenstein (BB, p. 69)

If behaviorism is correct, then it would be intelligible to say that a camera perceives.

–Wittgenstein (213, p. 462)

Behaviorism: "It seems to me as if I'm sad, my head is drooping so."

–Wittgenstein (213, p. 509)

[Wittgenstein] did indeed reject both Cartesianism and behaviorism in their entirety.

–John W. Cook[1]

If you exclude the element of intention from language, its whole function then collapses. What is essential to intention is the picture: the picture of what is intended.

–Wittgenstein (PR, p. 63)

But thought does pledge itself to exteriority in aiming at an exterior object. Here Wittgenstein rediscovers intentionality.

–John Hems[2]

WITTGENSTEIN'S REFERENCES TO BEHAVIORISM

Wittgenstein's *Philosophical Investigations* has been taken by many, especially with regard to the argument against private language, as an expression of some form of behaviorism. Commentators do not entirely agree about what this behaviorism should be called: Garth Hallett suggests that Wittgenstein is a "methodological" behaviorist, not a "substantive" one;[3] C. W. K. Mundell argues that the can best be seen as a "linguistic" behaviorist;[4] C. S. Chihara and J. A. Fodor are convinced that Wittgenstein's behaviorism is "strikingly similar" to C. L. Hull's "logical" behaviorism;[5] and W. F. Day and Bruce Waller both argue that there are many similarities between Wittgenstein and B. F. Skinner.[6]

In an otherwise helpful article comparing Wittgenstein and Husserl, John Hems concludes that the ultimate difference between the two is that Wittgenstein is a traditional behaviorist in the sense of functionalism and mechanism. There is simply no ground for Hems' incredible claims that because of Wittgenstein's engineering background, behaviorism's mechanism and stimulus-response models were "congenial" to him and, that he was interested in "preserving the methodological model of the physical sciences in all its doctrinal purity," and that he, therefore, allowed for "the dictatorship of the physical sciences."[7]

Traditional behaviorism, especially in its rejection of intentionality, has been taken as a principal antagonist of phenomenology. It is therefore important to counter these claims about Wittgenstein's behaviorism if the thesis of this study is to be maintained. In this chapter it will be argued that Wittgenstein cannot be called a behaviorist in any of the traditional senses that involve physicalism, reductionism, atomism, and external relations. He might, however, be called a "social" behaviorist, a term used to describe the positions of George Herbert Mead and Maurice Merleau-Ponty. Such a behaviorism differs radically from the classical form in that it is non-reductionist and assumes the concepts of intentionality, internal relations, and acausalism. I choose not to call it "linguistic" behaviorism because I have shown that Wittgenstein's "forms of life" (*Lebensformen*), which are social and cultural in nature, are more basic than language-games.

Other commentators have shown that those who take Wittgenstein as a behaviorist are incorrect,[8] but I believe that I am the first to propose such an argument in terms of the ideas of internal relations and intentionality. If these doctrines can be shown to apply to Wittgenstein, then there is no question that his opposition to traditional behaviorism is the strongest possible. I agree with John Cook, who maintains, as I quoted above, that Wittgenstein rejected "both Cartesianism and [classical] behaviorism in their entirety." Later in this chapter there is a discussion of Skinner's radical behaviorism, which is in some respects close to Wittgenstein's, but ultimately the two diverge significantly.

There are certainly passages in the later work that sound like behaviorism. The *Investigations* is a brilliant critique of introspectionism, and any other view that would take the existence of mental processes and events as the starting point for psychology or philosophy. Wittgenstein does not deny the existence of the mental, but appears to hold, like Hull, that the only way we can talk coherently about the mental is to link that talk with observable behavior in the world. Wittgenstein seems to formulate a defense of this view: "Here is the point of behaviorism. It isn't that they deny there are feelings. But they say our description of behavior *is* our description of feelings" (LC, p. 33). When he is accused of being a "behaviorist in disguise" at PI, §307, he does not deny the title, but clarifies his position. He believes that the principal problem with mental states is not that they are metaphysical ghosts, but that we use "grammatical fictions" in referring to them. In other words, he does not deny their existence, he simply insists that we cannot talk about them in the way introspectionists do.

"Linguistic" behaviorism seems to be an appropriate term for this view, because Wittgenstein states "all other descriptions are crude compared with a description of the gesture he made, the tone of voice with which he made it"; or as Smythies heard it: "Can I describe his feelings better than [by] imitating the way he said it?" (LC, p. 33). Elsewhere Wittgenstein elaborates: "Our language-game is an extension of primitive behavior. (For our *language-game* is behavior.) (Instinct)" (Z, §545). A more explicit formulation of linguistic behavior is the following: "It is misleading then to talk of thinking as a 'mental activity.' We may say that thinking is essentially the activity of operating with signs" (BB, p. 6). There is no "agent that thinks," like the hand when it is writing, or the mouth and larynx in speaking.

In the *Investigations* Wittgenstein argues persuasively that it is absurd to think that for every outward human action there is a corresponding mental activity that accompanies it. For example, it is absurd to assume that when an outfielder goes back to catch a fly-ball, the mind acts like a computer in such a way that each of his movements could be explained in terms of mental calculations that correspond exactly with running straight back, a quick turn to the left, and the precise raising

of the mitt in order to catch the ball. Some commentators have, therefore, claimed to have found the behaviorist concept of conditioned response in passages such as "I have been trained to react to this sign in a
particular way, and now I do so react to it;" or "following a rule is
analogous to obeying an order. We are trained to do so, we react to an
order in a particular way" (PI, §§198, 206).

Wittgenstein's strongest support for behaviorism appears in the
Philosophical Grammar:

> It could be said that it can't be decided by outward observation
> whether I am *reading* or merely producing sounds while a text runs
> before my eyes. But what is of interest to us in reading can't be
> essentially something *internal.* . . . Every such more or less be-
> haviorist account leaves one with the feeling that it is crude and
> heavy-handed, but this is misleading—we are tempted to look for a
> 'better' account, but there isn't one (PG, pp. 99–100).

In the Big Typescript, from which the *Grammar* was edited, we again
find positive use of the term "behaviorism": "If I make myself understandable to another in language, then it must be a case of understanding in the sense of behaviorism" (213, p. 49-).

If we consider the preceding quotations within the entire framework
of the later philosophy, with the assumptions of intentionality, internal
relations, and acausalism that I shall establish shortly, we must conclude
that, even though Wittgenstein does occasionally use the term "behaviorism" uncritically, he does not accept behaviorism as we commonly know it. In an unpublished typescript he states:

> But don't you say that everything we can express by the word
> "soul" can also be expressed somehow by means of words for the
> bodily? I don't say it. But even were it true—what would it indi-
> cate? The words, as well as the things we point to in explaining
> them, are only instruments, and now the question is how they are
> used (229, p. 322).

In the Big Typescript he makes positive as well as very negative comments about behaviorism: "If behaviorism is correct, then it would be
intelligible to say that a camera perceives" (213, p. 462).

In *Zettel* Wittgenstein argues that sadness is not reducible to sad behavior and there is no one set of conditions that would *cause* one to be sad (Z, §526). In the Big Typescript he directly pokes fun at this behavioristic account of sadness: "Behaviorism: 'It seems to me as if I'm sad, my head is drooping so' " (213, p. 509). This same comment is incorporated into the *Remarks* without the introductory term "behaviorism," and the tone of criticism loses some of its edge. The context of its location in the *Remarks*, where sadness is called a "medium" or "viewpoint" (*viz.*, a form of life), still makes it clear that he is critical of the strictly behavioristic account (PR, p. 90). Even more explicitly on a similar emotion, he states that "of course joy is not joyful behavior, nor yet a feeling round the corners of the mouth and the eyes. 'But joy surely designates an inward thing.' No. 'Joy designates nothing at all. Neither any inward nor any outward thing' " (Z, §487). This appears to be a complete disavowal of both behaviorism and introspectionism, an interpretation which is supported by the following from a 1939 lecture: "We want in philosophy to see the absurdities both of what the behaviorists say and of what their opponents say" (LFM, p. 111).

One of the greatest drawbacks of traditional behaviorists' accounts of human action is that they are unable to explain ironic behavior. If human intentions and feelings *are* their outward expression, then behaviorism will always give a consistently incorrect account of ironic behavior. This argument can work in both directions: one can pretend one is having a toothache without really having one, and one can have a toothache without outwardly expressing its presence. In 1931 Wittgenstein charged that "behaviorism must be able to distinguish between real toothache and simulated toothache. ... " (L 1, p. 46). Presumably it cannot, and therefore we must conclude "that the word 'toothache' had a meaning entirely independent of a behavior connected with toothache" (PE, p. 290). As we have seen, one of Wittgenstein's most striking examples of a "fictitious" natural history is the conception of a group of people brought up in such a way "as to give no expression of feeling *of any kind*" (Z, §383; cf. PI, §§142, 257).

Finally, although aspects of the private language argument seem to support behaviorism, one aspect of it raises serious problems for it. One of Wittgenstein's most important contributions is his discovery of the asymmetry between first person and third person accounts. There are public criteria for verifying the proposition "he is in pain," but none for verifying "I am in pain" (cf. BB, pp. 68–9). "Everyone's sense-data are private" is a "grammatical" proposition for Wittgenstein: this means that this third person statement is *a priori* and therefore cannot be falsified. But propositions such as "I know what I want" or "I know what I feel" are not judgments *a priori*; indeed, they are *Unsinn* (PI, p. 221). This claim may strike many, philosophers and laymen alike, as a non-sensical claim itself, because all of us go around making claims like these without ever feeling foolish. We must keep in mind, however, that for Wittgenstein, "making sense" is a grammatical matter, and that the most persuasive arguments in the *Investigations* are those which conclude that philosophical analyses of inner states that are based on first person reports are grammatically incorrect. Therefore, although it is not nonsense for the common person to use these locutions, it is *philosophical* nonsense to build a theoretical psychology on them.

WITTGENSTEIN VS. CLASSICAL BEHAVIORISM

Let us now attack the problem more systematically. Wittgenstein's philosophy is the very opposite of classical behaviorism because of the following points: (1) he does not accept the traditional definition of "behavior"; (2) he is not an atomist; (3) he is not a reductionist; and (4) he believes that the most important connections in human action are not causal. The fact that he also accepts internal relations and intentionality is basic to these four points, but I shall discuss this separately in the section entitled "Intentionality."

(1) Wittgenstein definitely rejects the behavioristic assumption that there is nothing beyond overt, physical behavior (or if we could observe them, the physiological processes of the body). In some cases Wittgenstein does allow (if the proviso about first person reports above is maintained) sensations and thoughts as criteria for behavior: in his example of "having a thought of a formula" in deciding how a person knows how to finish a series (PI, §179) and the example of reading (PI, §§159–60). Wittgenstein's claim that "A knows he is not reading, and has a sense of just this while pretending to read" suggests a solution to the behaviorist dilemma about ironic behavior. The difference between one who is really in pain and who who is just pretending is simply that the one who really is in pain has the sensation of pain. (But if this is what Wittgenstein means, it directly implies that he is violating his own rule about the nonsense of first person reports about internal states.) As we shall see later, it depends strictly on the situation and the specific use of words whether or not something can count as a criterion for

human action. We again see Wittgenstein's vitalism (or *Lebensphilosophie*) in his claim that "in every case what is meant by 'thought' is the *living* element in the sentence, without which it is dead, a mere succession of sounds or series of written shapes" (PG, p. 107).

John Cook argues persuasively that Wittgenstein rejects Hull's basic idea of behavior as "colorless movements."[9] This also means that he rejects the Cartesian idea of the body, an idea that is held by mentalists and materialists alike. Therefore, for Wittgenstein, behavior can never be something defined and reduced to the movements of a mechanical body. Cook correctly points out that the idea of a mechanical body is an abstraction, a scientific hypothesis. We certainly do not learn it as children. In fact, our common attitude toward others is decidedly anti-behavioristic and non-mechanical: "My attitude towards him is an attitude towards a soul" (PI, p. 178), and therefore, "to talk about a mechanics of the soul is slightly funny" (LC, p. 29).

(2) All behavioristic theories are atomistic in the sense that there exists a one-to-one correspondence between mental states and brain states for "molecular" behaviorists like Watson, or between mental states and overt actions for "molar" behaviorists like Skinner. For all traditional behaviorists there are these basic bits, these atoms, to which human behavior can be reduced. Not only does Wittgenstein reject all hypothetical entities at the micro-physical level (PR, p. 72; BB, p. 45), but in his holism and globalism he goes beyond the molar units of overt behavior. We have already discussed Wittgenstein's holism in Chapter Four, and this has been frequently overlooked by many commentators, especially those who wish to associate him closely with positivist and behavioristic modes of thought.

(3) Intimately related to Wittgenstein's rejection of any form of atomism is his rejection of any form of reductionism. Wittgenstein sees the scientific method as a source of great temptation for philosophers, because it leads them to want to reduce everything to the smallest possible number or base. "I want to say here that it can never be our job to reduce anything to anything . . ." (BB, p. 18). For example, a wish cannot be reduced to either the linguistic expression of the wish or a correlated conceptual event; likewise, it cannot be reduced to a physiological state or an outward event or gesture. In his remarks on mathematics he strongly implies that the main problem with behaviorism is its reductionism and the reductionist's glib remark: "But surely, all we have here is . . ." (RFM, p. 63). We must "survey" (*übersehen*) the whole use of

mathematical propositions and get a "wider look around" with regard to the mathematical *Umgebung* (RFM, p. 54).

Wittgenstein argues that emotions and other intentional activities like understanding, knowing, expecting, hoping cannot be reduced to mental processes or sensations, let alone to behavioral configurations. "Love is not a feeling. Love is put to the test, pain not. One does not say: 'That was not true pain, or it would not have gone off so quickly' " (Z, §504). If I understand the Danish language, when and how does that understanding take place? Only when I hear or read Danish? (No) All the time? (That doesn't sound right either, because do I understand Danish in my sleep?) One could object that there was surely a definite time at which I did not understand any Danish at all, but this can be countered by the fact that we can always understand even the strangest foreign language through gestures, cognates, and the general *Umgebung*. Also note the contrast between pinpointing the time of beginning to understand a foreign language with the beginning of a sharp pain due to a knife stab.

The same type of thought experiment done with understanding above could be done with hoping, intending, knowing, etc. These activities, unlike sensations, are not locatable in time and space: "To 'know' something is not one clear-cut physical event. . . . [It] has no temporal structure" (L 1, p. 94). "One no more feels sorrow in one's body than one feels seeing in one's eyes" (Z, §494). Or: "Intention is neither an emotion, a mood, nor yet a sensation or image. It is not a state of consciousness. It does not have genuine duration" (Z, §45). If I am hoping, and then begin to whistle a tune, I don't stop hoping during my whistling (Z, §46); and, the nature of intending is such that it cannot be disturbed, and therefore it cannot be a state of mind (Z, §50). Therefore, it would be most appropriate to call these activities, like Wittgenstein does, *forms* of life and not *facts* of life.

Wittgenstein makes it clear that these *Lebensformen* are unique to human beings, for animals, as we have seen, cannot be sincere or hope (PI, p. 229), because only those who have mastered language, itself a complicated *Lebensform*, can hope (PI, p. 174). Therefore, Wittgenstein precludes the celebrated behaviorist reduction of human behavior to animal behavior. He rejects outright the assumption that there are universal laws governing all behavior, both human and non-human. Recalling Wittgenstein's commitment to Spengler's idea of cultural isolation, one could also say, given the vast variety of language-games and forms of life with different rules, that human behavior itself is not governed by universal, predictable laws.

(4) Wittgenstein's position that forms and not facts are the defining framework for human action clearly reveals his acausalism (and his Kantianism). When he claims that certain psychological phenomena may have no physiological correlates, or that memory need not be "stored" mechanically in the nervous system, he is very distant from the causalism of classical behaviorism. "Why should there not be a psychological regularity to which *no* physiological regularity corresponds? If this upsets our concept of causality then it is high time it was upset" (Z, §610). Psychological regularities like hoping, praying, and pretending are not *caused* by other things or empirical conditions, but are *constituted* within a general social-linguistic framework.

When Wittgenstein insists that "if you give a causal reason, then it is not a real reason" (L 1, p. 105), he is giving firm support to a whole generation of action theorists, like Peter Winch, who separate "reasons" and "causes" in their acausalistic interpretation of human behavior. Wittgenstein's acausalism is pervasive and emphatic: "We are not in the realm of causal explanations, and every such explanation sounds trivial for our purposes" (PG, p. 105). We have seen that Wittgenstein rejects all *Entwicklungshypothesen* and replaces them with his own *übersichtliche Darstellungen*. The former seek causal laws and explanations, while the latter show formal similarities and connections. In his remarks on mathematics in 1942 he stated that to consider a proof *übersichtlich* is to hold that "causality plays no role: and that we have grasped the use of the proposition as a whole" (RFM, pp. 125, 115).

The full force of Wittgenstein's acausalism and emphasis on *Umgebung* is summed up beautifully by Dennis O'Brien:

> The noise "Go left" does not have meaning like a conditioned reflex—a causal connection between a sound fact and a behavioral fact—but because it is seen as a move in a game. We say that a command has meaning, not because it determines any behavior or state of affairs, but because the person who understands it fits into a game. . . . If noises become commands by causal association, then commands must always be infallibly obeyed, as in any causal process. . . .[10]

As Wittgenstein states: "An intention is embedded in its situation in human customs and institutions" (PI, §337). In other words, human behavior is meaningful only within an "intentional field" (the *Umgebung* of language-games and forms of life) in which causalistic, mechanistic models fail completely. The following passage not only supports our immediate point but expresses again Wittgenstein's idea of a life-world:

If we imagine the expression of a wish as the wish, it is rather as if we were led by a train of thought to imagine something like a network of lines spread over the earth, and living beings who moved only along the lines ... the whole network to which the sentence belongs (PG, p. 149).

Such a network the phenomenologists call "operative" *(fungierende)* intentionality.

SKINNER'S RADICAL BEHAVIORISM

A critic might respond that I have concentrated too much on "Watsonian" behaviorism and not enough on more sophisticated views like B. F. Skinner's. Willard F. Day argues that there are at least ten significant parallels between Skinner and Wittgenstein, and that it might even be more appropriate to call Skinner a phenomenologist and not a behaviorist. Day contends that both thinkers react against logical positivism: they oppose its "explanatory fictions" and emphasize description rather than hypothesis or theory. Day recognizes the strong pragmatic instincts in both, claiming that Skinner has his own version of Wittgenstein's concept of meaning as use. While both reject the private language theory, they do not believe that all talk about mental states is meaningless, for they do use introspective data in a strictly prescribed fashion.[11] If Day is correct, this means that Skinner would agree with Wittgenstein's criticism of classical behaviorism: "To deny the mental process would mean to deny the remembering ..." (PI, §306). But the meaning of "mental" for both is not interpreted introspectively, but concretely in the way we use language and our bodies.

Day did not have the advantage of Skinner's most recent book, *About Behaviorism,* in which his thesis finds further support. Here Skinner states that "operant behavior is the very field of intention and purpose" (AB, p. 55), a view that sounds very much like the *Lebenswelt* of existential phenomenology and Wittgenstein's *Weltbild.* Because of such views, Skinner, the existential phenomenologists, and Wittgenstein can argue that self-knowledge is "worldly" and social in origin. As Skinner states: "It is only when a person's private world becomes important to others that it is made important to him" (AB, p. 31). In his article on Wittgenstein and behaviorism, D. A. Begelman contends that Wittgenstein has turned the argument from analogy on its head: "It is the concept of self-knowledge which is parasitic on the notion of knowledge of others."[12]

Skinner argues that earlier behaviorists were wrong in claiming great explanatory power in reflexes and instincts (AB, p. 34). Like Wittgenstein, Skinner believes that all we can do is *describe* this behavior as simply "what we all do." Birds build nests not because they have a nest-building instinct, but because that is the way in which this species' behavior has evolved. But Skinner's example reveals a significant difference between him and Wittgenstein: Skinner's Darwinism.[13] Skinner assumes that there is a natural continuum between animal and human life and appears to agree with Watson's statement that "man is an animal different from other animals only in the types of behavior he displays."[14] As we have shown above, Wittgenstein believes that it is impossible for animals to participate in human life-forms, because he believes, with the existential phenomenologists, that a human life-world is qualitatively different from the natural world. Skinner accepts only one world, the world of the natural sciences.

Skinner rejects much of the phony causalism of introspectionism and early behaviorism. He agrees with Wittgenstein that, even though feelings of anger do usually precede angry and violent behavior, this does not mean that these feelings are the cause of the behavior. He is equally critical of many behaviorists and epiphenomenalists who claim that firing neurons and other physiological activity are the causes of our behavior. Nonetheless, Skinner, in opposition to Wittgenstein, is still a causalist. Skinner's unabashed Darwinism is again evident when he accepts natural selection as his central causal principle (AB, p. 36). As Skinner states: "We seek 'causes' of behavior which have an acceptable scientific status and which, with luck will be susceptible to measurement and manipulation."[15] At this point the break with Wittgenstein is clean and significant: Wittgenstein believes that philosophy has no use for causal theories like natural selection and other *Entwicklungshypothesen*. One might attempt to mitigate the difference here by maintaining that Skinner is doing a philosophy of psychology and Wittgenstein is always doing a "philosophy of philosophy." But if we consider Wittgenstein's work on the foundation of mathematics, we must conclude that *Entwicklungshypothesen* are not even permitted in the philosophy of science.

Skinner replaces "methodological" behaviorism, which took its cues from logical positivism and its strict distinction between the private and the public, with his "radical" behaviorism. This is a behaviorism which allows mental states a qualified role in developing a comprehensive view of human action. Like Wittgenstein and the existential phenomenologists, Skinner dissolves the Cartesian distinction between the inner and the outer, one preserved by both introspectionists and methodological behaviorists alike. But the qualified use of mental states in both Wittgenstein and Skinner is done for very different reasons. For the former the reasons are the grammatical insights discussed above; but the latter "questions the nature of the object observed and the reliability of the observations" (AB, pp. 16–17). I believe that this is only a disguised form of saying that mental states are private and therefore not proper scientific data. If this is true, then the major distinction between methodological and radical behaviorism falls.

Day is correct in claiming that both Wittgenstein and Skinner reject the dualism of experience and reality—another way of saying that they merge the inner and the outer. What Day overlooks, however, is the fact that ultimately Wittgenstein chooses experience (his *Lebensphilosophie*) and Skinner chooses reality. It is clear that radical behaviorism is still a physicalism: its aim is "an analysis both of seeing and of seeing that one sees in purely physical terms" (AB, p. 216). Contrast this with Wittgenstein: "Psychology connects what is experienced with something physical, but we connect what is experienced with what is experienced" (OCo, p. 48). As we have seen, Wittgenstein's formulation of the phenomenological *epoché* is explicitly opposed to physicalism. Hems is obviously wrong: it is Skinner, not Wittgenstein, who maintains the "dictatorship of the physical sciences" and shares their goal of prediction and control.

Skinner claims that he is not a reductionist, but this claim becomes dubious upon closer comparison with Wittgenstein's transcendental phenomenology. Skinner argues that his behaviorism is not reductionistic, because it, unlike physiological psychology, "does not move from one dimensional system to another. It simply provides an alternative account of the same facts. It does not *reduce* feelings to bodily states; it simply argues that bodily states are and always have been what are felt" (AB, p. 241). Skinner is correct only if his principal assumption is sound: that all there are are facts. If the human organism is nothing but a biological system, then the "behavioristic position is . . . nothing more than that" (AB, p. 4). But if the transcendental method of Wittgenstein and phenomenology is sound, then there are *forms* of life in addition to facts of life, and any theory that dissolves these transcendental forms into a mere association of facts is reductionistic. The contrast between Wittgenstein and Skinner is especially clear on this point if we compare the latter's view of language in *Verbal Behavior* with the former's account of language.

When Skinner says that "behavior . . . is under the control of a current setting" (AB, p. 207), he appears to be very close to Wittgenstein's concept of *Umgebung* and Heidegger's *Umwelt*. Skinner criticizes the view that a runner, whose heart is beating quickly before a race, is subjectively associating "the situation with the exertion which follows" (AB, p. 39). When Skinner states that it is "the environment, not the runner, that 'associates' the two features," he appears to be speaking very much like Merleau-Ponty in his critique of associationism, based as it is on Heidegger's concept of Being-in-the-world. But Skinner's "environmentalism" cannot possibly be the same because of his physicalism and reductionism. For Skinner the environment is still the world described by the causalism of natural science, and not the qualitatively different life-world of Wittgenstein, Heidegger, and Merleau-Ponty.

Finally, this also means that Skinner's description of operant behavior as the "field of intention and purpose" cannot be equivalent to the intentional field founded on the "operative" intentionality of phenomenology. Just as Darwinism replaced "antecedent design" with "subsequent selection by contingencies of survival," Skinner replaces "antecedent intention or plan" with "subsequent selection contingencies of reinforcement" (AB, p. 224). Skinner's associationism, something Wittgenstein categorically rejects, is clearly revealed in these formulations. Therefore, it is difficult to understand why this view does not, counter to Skinner's claim, explain purpose and intention away. Furthermore, Skinner seems to have broken his vow to give some qualified role to mental states.

In existential phenomenology the emphasis on operative intentionality is an attempt to balance the excessive subjectivism of Husserl, who concentrated on the "act" intentionality of a transcendental ego. Merleau-Ponty describes this in terms of the "centrifugal forces" of the subject meeting the "centripetal forces" of the world (PP, p. 436). In Wittgenstein, operative intentionality is the meeting place of the conventionalism of language-games and forms of life on the subjective side with "what nature has to say" (Z, §364) on the objective side. (These images should not be construed as resurrecting the Cartesian inner and outer.) True to classical behaviorism, Skinner's explanation of purpose and intention eliminates completely the subjective pole; and as a Darwinist he simply ought to be more honest in the elimination of intentionality.

Therefore, we must conclude that Wittgenstein's formalism, acausalism, and transcendentalism mean that he must join the camp of structuralism and phenomenology—views that Skinner eschews in *About Behaviorism*. Day's dramatic claim that Skinner is really a phenomenologist is simply misguided, mainly because he somehow takes Ernst Mach as a proto-phenomenologist. But Mach is a phenomenalist, one, like Skinner, who concentrates on phenomena alone and misses the transcendental *logos* of true phenomenology *(phenomenon + logos)*. As we have seen, Wittgenstein develops his own phenomenology on the basis of a criticism of Mach, and a Machian phenomenalist, just like Skinner, cannot do proper justice to intentionality.

INTENTIONALITY

In Chapter III of the *Philosophical Remarks* there is remarkable discussions on internal relations and intentionality—remarkable in the sense that those positivists who knew Wittgenstein's *Tractatus* and were searching him out for his opinions in the years 1928–1930 would have found his comments here very disturbing. He argues that Russell, Ogden, and Richards were wrong in their account of intentional activities like expectation, primarily because of their doctrine of external relations and their elimination of intention from the function of language. "If you exclude the element of intention from language, its whole function then collapses" (PR, p. 63). In fact, the phenomenologists' doctrine of intentionality can be seen in Wittgenstein's formulation of the concept of the intentional object: "What is essential to intention is the picture: the picture of what is intended" (PR, p. 63). In other words, there is an internal relation between the intention and the intentional object. In 1937–38 Wittgenstein argued that there is a "super strong connection . . . between the act of intending and the thing intended" and that this connection is not an empirical one (RFM, p. 40; cf. PI, §197).

According to Wittgenstein's concept of intentionality, an account of any intention can suffice with just two elements, "the thought and the fact, whereas for Russell, there are three, i.e. thought, fact, and a third event which, if it occurs, is just recognition" (PR, p. 63). This third element is the causal connection, e.g., the sensation that an expectation is fulfilled, and this "causal connection between speech and action is an external relation, whereas we need an internal one" (PR, p. 64). The absurdity of the Russellian theory, which on this point is virtually identical with behaviorism (there is an obvious indirect reference to Pavlov on p. 70), is shown in the following thought experiments Wittgenstein offers:

> If I give someone an order and I am happy with what he then does, then he has carried out my order. (If I wanted to eat an apple, and someone punched me in the stomach, taking away my appetite, then it was this punch that I originally wanted) (PR, p. 64).

What if someone played chess and, when he was mated, said "Look, I've won, for *that* is the goal I was aiming at"? We would say that such a man simply wasn't trying to play chess, but another game, whereas Russell would have to say that if anyone plays with the pieces and is satisfied with the outcome, then he has won at chess (PR, p. 65).

Phenomenology teaches us that intentionality is "directedness" (*Richtung*) towards an object. Like the phenomenologists, and unlike the behaviorists, Wittgenstein believes that "it isn't any remarkable feature of the sensation which explains the directionality of meaning (*die Richtung der Meinung*)" (PG, p. 156). An intentional act is different from a sensation: it has a "direction" (PG, p. 143), because one always "takes pleasure *in something*, which does not mean that this something produces a sensation in us" (Z, §507); or "the language-game 'I am afraid' already contains the object" (Z, §489). Therefore, the intentional object is not a fact, nor need it be correlated with a fact. For. example, "the thought that 'p' is the case doesn't presuppose that it is the case . . ." (PG, p. 142). Or, how can I think of Mr. Smith when he is not present? He is indeed an object of my thought. Signalling an important turn in his thought, Wittgenstein tells us "I am here using the expression 'object of our thought' in a way different from that in which I have used it before. I mean now a thing I am thinking *about* . . ." (BB, p. 38). This to me is a clear-cut formulation of the phenomenological doctrine of intentionality.

In the recently published lectures of 1930−32 there is extensive material that parallels the discussion on intentionality in the *Remarks*. Wittgenstein believes that there is an internal relation between propositions and facts, whereas Russell believes there is an external relation. This, as we have seen, forces Russell to add a third component between an expectation and its fulfillment, but Wittgenstein shows that this leads to an infinite regress of intermediate components. "Russell treats wish (expectation) and hunger as if they were on the same level. But several things will satisfy my hunger, my wish (expectation) can only be fulfilled by something definite" (L 1, p. 9). A wish carries its own fulfillment with it as a definite intentional object internally related to the wish. If there is any "third thing" like "recognition" then it is simply "seeing the internal relation" between them (PR, p. 63); e.g., in playing crotchets "we *see* the [general] rule between playing and score" (L 1, p. 40). "The rule of projection is expressed in projecting, the intention in intending. The internal relation is only there if both things related are there" (L 1, p. 32).

In these 1930 lectures the phenomenological notion of intentional object is pervasive: "If one expects a green patch on the blackboard, then there must be a 'green' constituent in the expectation . . ." (L 1, p. 33). In a similar passage we can obtain a traditional phenomenological reading by making some simple word substitutions: "If we say that expectation and fulfillment have a constituent [=*eidos*] in common, we are making a grammatical [=phenomenological] statement" (L 1, p. 36). The answer to Wittgenstein's question in the *Investigations*—"How was it possible for thought to deal with the very object itself" (§428)—is clear: thought already contains its object as an intentional object. Gerd Brand paraphrases Wittgenstein aptly: "When I intend something I find myself immediately related to what I intend. Moreover, what is intended, or wished for, or expected, in no way needs to be present (EW, p. 27).

Russell and earlier theorists had separated the inner intentions from their outer objects, thereby establishing the "two-world" mythology that has perpetuated the ego-centric predicament. With the doctrine of intentionality, Wittgenstein and the phenomenologists have overcome this duality of the inner and the outer and now intentions are truly "in the world." The world, as we have seen, is a life-world, a "network of lines spread over the earth, and living beings who move only along the lines" (PG, p. 149). Therefore, intentionality and Wittgenstein's *Umgebung*, as Fredrick Stoutland indicates, are intimately connected: "Directedness . . . is a 'global' phenomenon inseparable from the surroundings—past, future, social, institutional—in which an activity takes place."[16] Russell and others pretend that they can step outside of this complex intentional field and nicely separate the various components, but this, according to Wittgenstein, destroys the "life" of the life-world (PG, p. 146). Again, Brand's paraphrase of this passage from the *Grammar* is beautifully done:

> If, for example, in a brightly illuminated cinema we let the film unroll slowly picture by picture, then we would have something like isolated, dead processes, which indeed present images but mean or intend nothing. If the light is extinguished and the film proceeds and we let ourselves be absorbed by it, then we live in it, then we have a picture of what liveliness of meaning means as opposed to dead processes (EW, p. 25).

This not only shows Wittgenstein's idea of a holistic intentional field, but also shows his strong life-philosophy which we have been emphasizing all along.

Therefore, Hems is definitely correct when he claims that Wittgenstein has "rediscovered" intentionality, but seems to be quite confused and inconsistent with regard to what kind it is. He contends that it is "thoroughly psychological," but then goes on to "prove" this by quoting "An intention is embedded in its situation in human customs and institutions" (PI, §337). He further contradicts himself by maintaining that for Wittgenstein "all intention is subject to objective conditions."[17] Although he does concede that Wittgenstein's idea of intentionality coincides with the phenomenologists' in that "thought does pledge itself to exteriority in aiming at an exterior object," he observes that the fundamental difference between Husserl and Wittgenstein is that the former believed in mental acts and also held that there was an internal relation between intention and fulfillment. We have already shown that Wittgenstein explicitly maintained this doctrine of internal relations in the middle works, and there is no sign that he gave up this idea in the later works.

As we have seen, Wittgenstein does not deny the existence of mental acts; rather, he holds that we cannot talk coherently about them unless this discourse is within a specific linguistic-cultural world. "It is in language that an expectation and its fulfillment make contact" (PI, §445). The role of language here is crucial, for while I cannot point to a nonexistent object, I can always express the object in language: " 'To mean him' means, say, 'to talk of him.' Not: to point to him. And if I talk *of him*, of course there is a connection between my talk and him, but this connection resides in the application of the talk, not in an act of pointing" (Z, §24). Don Ihde cannot find an intentionality of conscious acts in Wittgenstein, but he does locate the function of intentionality in language itself.[18] For Husserl the acts of meaning-intending are objectified in inner-perception (a realm, Wittgenstein believes, of which we are unable to speak), but similar acts for existential phenomenologists are objectified in a *Lebenswelt*. Merleau-Ponty and Heidegger do not give up act intentionality completely, but it is always practical and not pure as it was in Husserl.

For Wittgenstein, the internal relation between intention and fulfillment is not established in the mind, but in the *Praxis* of language-games and forms of life. As we have seen earlier, he explicitly names the locus of the "super strong" connection between intentional acts and their objects: "In the list of rules of the game, in the teaching of it, in the day-to-day practice of playing" (RFM, p. 40). Or, later in the same book Wittgenstein states that he is interested in the "phenomenon" (*Phänomen*) of the immediate realization of a mathematical truth, but not "as a special mental phenomenon (*Erscheinung*), but as one of human action" (p. 123). Hems is surprisingly correct when he states that Wittgenstein, "rather than subscrib[ing] to a *consciousness* or *ego*, . . . attributes to behavior itself the structure and powers proper to the intentional life . . . thus he does not deny consciousness but conscious processes are not 'interior.' They exhibit themselves."[19] They show themselves in a *Lebenswelt* of language-games and forms of life.

SOCIAL BEHAVIORISM

With so much skepticism about the autonomy of private mental states, and so much emphasis on human action in the world, it would be unwise to hold that Wittgenstein is not a behaviorist in any sense. As he states: "Pleasure does at any rate go with a facial expression" (Z, §508); or, "I am asking: What is the characteristic demeanor of human beings who 'realize' something 'immediately' . . ." (RFM, p. 123); or, he explicates the expressions "I expect he is coming" and "He is coming" strictly in terms of overt behavior and happenings (PI, §444). But, as we have argued above, none of this necessarily leads us to behaviorism in the classical, or even the Skinnerian, sense. One does not have to be an associationist, atomist, reductionist, or causalist to be a behaviorist. The most appropriate label for Wittgenstein's behaviorism is "social," but only if we keep in mind the fact that he does not ever intend to give a genetic explanation of behavior in terms of what people have learned in their social experiences. As we have emphasized, Wittgenstein is interested in pre-given forms of life, not facts of life.

The behaviorism of George Herbert Mead and Maurice Merleau-Ponty are good examples of this type of social behaviorism. Their emphasis is the same as Wittgenstein's: rules, reasons, and intentions (instead of causes), which have their primary locus in socio-linguistic activities. Undoubtedly, there is something going on inside the head, but discourse about this arena is not admissable for the existential phenomenology that these thinkers develop. As Wittgenstein states: "The subject—we want to say—does not drop out of the experience, but is so much involved in it that the experience cannot be described" (PG, p. 156). This sounds very much like Heidegger's doctrine of *Dasein* and the general dissolution of the Cartesian inner and outer that we discussed earlier. ("Here there is no outside or inside" [PG, p. 156].) Hannah Pitkin characterizes this position aptly when she claims that Wittgenstein has combined both phenomenology and behaviorism: there is the co-existence of intentionality and observation, because in-

tentionality is found in the intentional field of a public *Lebenswelt*.[20]
Anger is neither merely what I *feel* when I am angry nor merely what I
do when I am angry, but a fusion of the inner and outer in a *Lebensform*,
or as Heidegger would say, in an *Existenzial*.

Hems is again wrong when he attempts to contrast Merleau-Ponty's
view of intentionality and behavior with Wittgenstein's. As we have
pointed out above, there is no sense at all in Hems' claim that Wittgenstein's concept of intentionality is "thoroughly psychological." I believe
that I have proved conclusively that basic intentionality for Wittgenstein is very much like the phenomenologists' operative intentionality, which comes to be stressed more and more in the later
phenomenologists, especially Heidegger and Merleau-Ponty. This
operative intentionality is essentially non-psychological and pre-
reflective, as it is found hidden in the intentional field of a *Lebenswelt*.
As Merleau-Ponty states: "We found beneath intentionality related to
acts, or thetic intentionality, another kind which is the condition of the
former's possibility: namely an operative intentionality already at work
before any positing or any judgment . . ."; or more succinctly: "The
world is not what I think, but what I live through" (PP, pp. 429, xvi-
xvii).

Therefore, both Wittgenstein and Merleau-Ponty agree in general
terms on a social behaviorism that rests on the doctrine of internal relations and intentionality and rejects reductionism and atomism. Like
Wittgenstein, Merleau-Ponty believes that "behavior is constituted of relations," and that it cannot be reduced to the atoms of things-in-
themselves or conceived as items of inner perception. "Behavior is not a
thing, but neither is it an idea. . . . Behavior is a form" (SB, p. 127).
Such a position coincides beautifully with Wittgenstein's fundamental
idea of behavior as "fixed regularities of doing," as forms of life, because "what has to be accepted, the given is—so one could say—*forms of
life*" (PI, p. 226).

8. The A Priori

Wittgenstein's main interest was always the a priori.

–Garth Hallett[1]

But if it is a priori, *that means that it is a form of account which is very convincing to us.*

–Wittgenstein (PI, §158)

The avowal of adherence to a form of expression, if it is formulated in the guise of a proposition dealing with objects *(instead of signs) must be "*a priori.*"*

–Wittgenstein (Z, §442)

What I said earlier about the nature of arithmetical equations and about an equation's not being replaceable by a tautology explains–I believe–what Kant means when he insists that $7 + 5 = 12$ *is not an analytic proposition, but synthetic* a priori.

–Wittgenstein (PR, p. 129; PG, p. 404)

Distinctions between the a priori *and the empirical, between form and content, [must] be done away with....Every factual truth is a rational truth and vice versa.*

–Merleau-Ponty (PP, pp. 222, 394)

This is why our first task will be to delogicize the a priori, *putting its feet back on earth; we shall discover that it is immanent in experience when objective, and borne by the concrete subject when subjective.*

–Mikel Dufrenne (NA, p. 55)

THE RESURRECTION OF THE SYNTHETIC *A PRIORI*

Major traditions in 20th Century philosophy, first pragmatism and phenomenology and then Anglo-American philosophy since the last world war, have called into question the time-honored distinction between the *a priori* truths of analytic judgments and the empirical truths of synthetic judgments. Using the "conceptual pragmatism" of C. I. Lewis, Arthur Pap develops his own version of a "material *a priori*" in his *The "A Priori" in Physical Theory*. His phrases "functional *a priori*" and "contextual *a priori*" can also be used to describe parallel developments that we shall investigate shortly in Wittgenstein and Merleau-Ponty. Compare Pap's "A proposition which is *a priori* in one context of inquiry may be *a posteriori* in another context"[2] with Wittgenstein's comment: "The same proposition may get treated at one time as something to test by experience, at another as a rule of testing" (OC, §98; OCo, p. 6).

Among the analytic philosophers we find Willard Quine strongly criticizing the traditional distinction in his "Two Dogmas of Empiricism." His principal point is one that we shall see both Wittgenstein and Merleau-Ponty stressing: that even the truth of analytical statements is contextual and depends on behavioral and cultural factors.[3] More recently there has been Saul Kripke, who, in a similar rejection of the formal *a priori*, argues that one can discover essences empirically, and that there exist both contingent truths *a priori* like "the standard meter is 39.37 inches long" and necessary truths *a posteriori* like "heat is the motion of molecules."[4]

Although Husserl insists on a strict distinction between *Wesen* and *Tatsache*, his later theory of constitution and his doctrine of the "material *a priori*" seem to betray his outward allegiance to the traditional distinction. (But at least the material *a priori* never becomes a factual *a priori* as it does in Merleau-Ponty and Wittgenstein.) Heidegger's view of the *a priori* is especially significant for later developments in phenomenology: "To disclose the *a priori* is not to make an aprioristic construction," but involves returning to *Dasein's* everydayness and "Being-in-the-world" (SZ, p. 50fn). Merleau-Ponty follows Heidegger's lead in a radical way with his phenomenological program in which the "distinctions between the *a priori* and the empirical . . . have been done away with . . ." and where "every factual truth is a rational truth and vice versa" (PP, pp. 222, 394). Mikel Dufrenne who sees important parallels between Husserl and Wittgenstein,[5] follows Merleau-Ponty in the French phenomenological tradition in this radical formulation of the issue. In his *The Notion of the "A Priori"* he proposes that while the *a priori* is "the condition for the objectivity of the *a posteriori*, . . . the *a posteriori* appears as the condition for the legitimacy of the *a priori*" (NA, p. 10).

One of the best explanations why the traditional analytic-synthetic distinction no longer works is given by the Danish analytic philosopher, Peter Zinkernagel, in his book *Conditions for Description*.[6] He argues that the analytic-synthetic distinction creates a problematic bifurcation in our knowledge between empty analytic statements, which do not deal with reality, and probablistic empirical statements of the sciences, which are not enough to justify true objective knowledge of the world—i.e., knowledge that cannot be meaningfully denied. Zinkernagel attempts to solve this dilemma by showing that there are conditions for description besides formal logic. In contrast to Kripke, who grounds his "material" logic in the theoretical propositions of the sciences, Zinkernagel finds the basis for such a logic in the linguistic rules of ordinary language. This is essentially a Wittgensteinian project, although Zinkernagel does not follow some of his radical conclusions, and offers a good critique of the idea that grammatical rules are analogous to rules of a game.

Wittgenstein has been called the father of both logical empiricism, which represented the last strong-hold of the traditional distinction, and of ordinary language philosophy, which has generally been critical of the distinction. At the end of his article "Is There A Factual *A Priori*?", written in 1930 against Husserl's doctrine of the material *a priori*, Moritz Schlick calls on the authority of Wittgenstein to drive the final nail into the coffin of the synthetic *a priori*.[7] This has to be one of the most ironic moments in the history of 20th Century philosophy, because Wittgenstein, during the year of the publication of Schlick's article, had finished the manuscript which was published in 1964 as the *Philosophische Bemerkungen*. Here, as we have seen, he uses the term "phenomenology" to describe his methodology, claims that we can have "direct insight" of essences (PR, p. 129), and explicitly refers to Kant in a resurrection of the synthetic *a priori* (PR, p. 129; cf. PG, p. 404).

There is, however, a serious inconsistency in Wittgenstein's approach to the synthetic *a priori* during this period. In December 1929, right at the time he was privately writing about Kant's synthetic *a priori* in a favorable light, he had some conversations with Schlick. He asked Wittgenstein's opinion of a philosopher who holds that propositions of phenomenology are synthetic *a priori*. Wittgenstein answered that such propositions are not possible and also recognized that it was Husserl who held such a view (WK, pp. 67–8). Schlick was perhaps prompted to ask this question for two reasons: (1) he himself had been carrying on a heated polemic against Husserl on the question of the synthetic *a priori*; and (2) on the same day he had heard (undoubtedly to his surprise) Wittgenstein use the term "phenomenology" without any qualification and in a way that was completely compatible with Husserl's use (WK, p. 63).

This is a deep mystery, because we know enough about Wittgenstein's personality to assume that he would never engage in duplicity and give an answer simply to please his questioner. Wittgenstein was definitely not one to ingratiate himself with any person, especially the members of the Vienna Circle, for whom he had little respect. One might propose that the solution lies in the fact that in his conversation with Schlick he is talking about the grammar of color, which is analytic, while other grammars, such as that of number, are synthetic. While it is difficult to find Wittgenstein claiming "this applies in all cases," I believe it is safe to assume that all grammatical propositions are synthetic *a priori*. In 1939 he told his class that the very proposition he discussed with Schlick, "A patch cannot be at the same time both red and green," is synthetic *a priori* (LFM, p. 232).

Wittgenstein's surprising acceptance of a synthetic *a priori* is at odds with his forceful rejection of the concept in the *Tractatus*. Here mathematical propositions are tautologies, i.e. analytic truths that show nothing about the world. In the *Remarks*, Wittgenstein changes his mind on this significant question by proving that an arithmetical equation cannot be replaced by a tautology and that it therefore represents a synthetic *a priori* truth (PR, p. 129). This represents a significant departure from the traditions of Frege and Russell, not to mention his positivistic contemporaries. Although the other phenomenologists and the pragmatists were about the only ones in general agreement with Wittgenstein at this time, it is important to note that Husserl disagreed with him on the question of arithmetic. For example, Husserl chides Kant for not seeing that arithmetic is a part of an analytic logic under which all mathematics (except of course geometry) could be subsumed.[8] But Wittgenstein is convinced that arithmetical truths are *about something*, and that their *a priori* synthetic character is clearly seen "in the unpredictable occurrence of the prime numbers" which obviously is "not discoverable by an analysis of the concept of a prime number" (RFM, pp. 125–6; PR, p. 218).

THE MATERIAL *A PRIORI*

The claim that one can directly experience essences is one of the basic assumptions of all phenomenology. We have shown in Chapter Five that Wittgenstein has a *Wesenschau* like the phenomenologists. Traditional philosophy had assumed that the *a priori*, including the Kantian synthetic *a priori*, was purely formal and therefore unexperienceable. For Kant, any proposition which referred only to the content of experience could not possibly be *a priori*. As we have seen, Husserl rejects Kant's theory of essence and insists that form and content can be intuited together. While keeping a formal, analytic *a priori* for the "regions" of logic, mathematics, and grammar, Husserl extends the *a priori* into "material regions," which then would give a firm apodictic ground for the various sciences.

At least in *Experience and Judgment* (§85), and definitely in the *Crisis* (§36), Husserl maintains that the formal regions are derived from the universal life-world *a priori*, which is presumably the all-inclusive horizon for the material regions. For Husserl this is the only way true (i.e. essential) knowledge can be possible, and the doctrine of the material *a priori* is the only way in which logic can have any application to the world. As Gerd Brand states:

> The formal *a priori* can neither be verified nor falsified, its congruity with experience, with reality, of which it is meant to be the condition, is external and postulated. The concrete *a priori* is verified by recognizing with evidence . . . that it is the fundamental structure of experience which penetrates everyday experience.[9]

In holding that there were *a priori* forms of sensibility, Kant had inadvertently left open the possibility of the synthetic *a priori* becoming truly material. The pure forms of time and space are actually material essences in so far as they are not justified by the logic of the transcendental deduction. Kant's form-matter distinction is still present in Husserl, but the Kantian relation between matter and form, as George J. Seidel explains, "might be termed vertical, the matter subsumed under the form. . . . For Husserl the relation between form and matter would have to be termed horizontal, that is, intentional."[10] As Dufrenne expresses it, Kant conceived of form as a "seal of logic being impressed onto an empirical" intuition (NA, p. 56); but Husserl, as Seidel aptly phrases it, has "turned Kant on his side": the vertical subsumption of matter under form gives way to the horizontal relation of intention-ality as *noesis* and *noema*. As Dufrenne states: "Perception . . . exempts me from the necessity of subsumption, precisely because it gives me the concept in intuition" (NA, p. 86).

Later phenomenologists have enthusiastically exploited Husserl's concept of the material *a priori*, expanding it into areas where Husserl perhaps would have hesitated. The leader among these thinkers is Mikel Dufrenne, who contends that "everyone possesses a certain natural geometry, but not everyone is capable of grasping the sense of the tragic, a mythical form, or a moral value" (NA, p. 48). Dufrenne, with his strong interest in aesthetics, moves the material *a priori* into the affective realm where essences are felt rather than thought. "It seems," Dufrenne remarks, "that we have at least discovered the real *a priori*, which [is] not only anterior to experience, but founds it, and [does so] more solidly than the formal *a priori*" (NA, p. 75), which is empty and separated from the world.

There are some significant parallels with Wittgenstein to be noted here. The idea of non-overlapping regions of sense would be compati-ble with Wittgenstein's strong perspectivism, but the basic similarity is the concept of the material *a priori* as affective. The principal locus of the *a priori* in Wittgenstein is forms of life, and these—even a theoreti-cal *Lebensform*—are thoroughly affective. When Dufrenne claims that we immediately encounter concrete meanings in the world which ap-pear as "countenances" (*physionomies*) rather than analytical relations, we have at least discovered a clue to a cryptic statement in the *Investiga-tions*: "Meaning is a physiognomy" (PI, §568). This is Wittgenstein's ma-terial *a priori*; and although its aim is not as ambitious as Husserl's, nor does it use his type of *Wesenschau*, there is a common methodological ground that is significant for comparative philosophy and the history of phenomenology.

Another crucial implication of Husserl's material *a priori* is the as-sumption that *every* actual and possible object has an *eidos*, including "hair" and "mud" (*Ideas*, §2), as Husserl implicitly resolves the eidetic difficulties of the young Socrates in the *Parmenides* (130c). Dufrenne phrases it this way: "A *quid* may always be converted into an idea, and eidetic intuition is always possible" (NA, p. 76). This is a general axiom of all phenomenology, as it evinces itself in Heidegger's doctrine that every entity has its own unique Being, just as every Tractarian object must have some logical form. This fundamental premise continues in the later works as all entire material and affective regions are opened up for grammatical (=phenomenological) investigation. For Wittgenstein, everything we talk about must have a grammar, and a sense must always be given anteriorly to the spoken words.

Gerd Brand, to whom I am much indebted on the topic of the material *a priori*, observes that the principal reason for Husserl's doctrine was a firm belief in the givenness of sense. Sense is not the product of a human mind meeting a senseless world of atomic particles, sense data, or Kantian empirical intuitions. Form and content are never separated except in abstraction. Brand states that the "givenness of sense shows itself by the fact that a meaningful given cannot be experienced by the intermediary of other givens, only of the experience itself."[11] Brand briefly mentions that Wittgenstein's "showing of sense" is very similar, but he gives no justification for this connection. Even in the *Tractatus* there are no objects that do not have a *Bedeutung* (indeed, simple objects *are* meanings), and in the later works the givenness of sense is found in language-games and forms of life, the ultimate and indivisible units of sense. They cannot be explained, nor can they in turn explain anything in terms of a theory—they simply must be accepted as given.

Let us now return to Heidegger's only direct reference to Husserl's material *a priori*: "But to disclose the *a priori* is not to make an aprioristic construction. Edmund Husserl has not only enabled us to understand once more the meaning of any genuine philosophical empiricism, he has also given us the necessary tools" (SZ, p. 50 fn). He goes on to conclude that the starting point for proper *a priori* research lies in *Dasein's* everydayness. There is a puzzling passage in Wittgenstein's "Remarks on Logical Form" which Spiegelberg contends shows serious confusion in Wittgenstein's concept of phenomenology. He states that "the logical analysis of the phenomena themselves [must be] in a certain sense *a posteriori*" (RFL, p. 163). Spiegelberg believes that this is inconsistent with the phenomenological program of the *Remarks* in which he explicitly states that it is an *a priori* investigation.

But within the context of the doctrine of the material *a priori*, Wittgenstein is simply agreeing with Husserl that the search for the *a priori* must begin in experience, and that "aprioristic" constructions or conjectures are not the proper starting point. As Garth Hallet affirms in his commentary on the *Investigations*: "Paradoxical as it may sound, the study of the *a priori* must be thoroughly *a posteriori*."[12] This empirical approach to the *a priori* must be what Wittgenstein came to when he was puzzled by "what kind of proposition is that, that blending in white removes the coloredness for the color," and was tempted "to believe in a phenomenology, something midway between science and logic . . ." (OCo, p. 15).

Brand observes that the doctrine of the concrete *a priori* leads to "novel" relations between it and the *a posteriori*, including concepts of "relative apodicticity" and the possibility that the *a priori* can be falsified.[13] Logical empiricists like Schlick and Carnap were utterly shocked by such possibilities and constantly warned (Schlick unwittingly using Wittgenstein as an expert witness in the attack!) against such a confusion of logical and empirical questions. But Husserl, Wittgenstein, the pragmatists—plus some leading contemporary analytic philosophers like Strawson, Quine, and Hare—have realized that such an unorthodox move is necessary if logic is to have any meaningful relationship with the world.

Within the context of the foregoing, there is certainly a lot to be said for Robert Sokolowski's claim that "in this matter of material logic, Husserl's constitutional studies have much in common with . . . Wittgenstein's theory of language-games, regions of discourse, which have an internal logic specific to themselves. . . ."[14] Although both of them move rather hesitatingly and unclearly towards a *Weltontologie* (see Wittgenstein's *Weltbild*, OC, §93), both obviously feel more at home with the particular or regional analysis. (Both of them find phenomenological analysis so incredibly difficult that they, especially Wittgenstein, simply do not feel comfortable at a more general level.) For Husserl, synthetic *a priori* truths have their necessity limited to certain regions of meaning, and Wittgenstein would certainly have been sympathetic to Husserl's claim that "every regional essence determines '*synthetic*' *essential truths* . . . [which] are not mere specifications of formal-ontological truths" (*Ideas*, §16).

The best example of Wittgenstein's regional methodology combined with a material logic is found in the *Grammar*, where he proposes that phenomenology (=grammar) is very different from traditional logic. In a book on phenomenology there would be separate chapters on the grammar of color, number, sound, etc., each setting out the unique rules for using color words, number words, etc. While these grammatical rules would be discovered *in experience*, the rules for the use of logical constants like "not," "or," etc., "would not be the kind that are discovered by experience, but the generality of a supreme rule of the game admitting of no appeal" (PG, p. 215). Wittgenstein would therefore divide philosophy into a non-phenomenological "Analytic" and a phenomenological "Synthetic."

If we follow out the implication of one of Dufrenne's criticisms of Husserl (NA, p. 92), we must apply the same distinction to Husserl as well. When Husserl introduces his pure grammar in the beginning of the *Logical Investigations*, he observes that the elementary forms of liaison, i.e. the logical constants, cannot by themselves be found as concrete examples. But if an eidetic reduction always requires such an example, and if the products of the reductions are the only admissible data for genuine phenomenology, then the analysis of logical constants and pure grammar in general, cannot be a legitimate part of phenomenology. This means that these formal essences are not true aprioris, but only abstractions that are derived from their being used in the sentences of actual human speech. For Wittgenstein there is no such thing as a pure, formal meaning, because meaning is always use.

The preceding conclusion allows us to emphasize once again an important difference between Wittgenstein and Husserl. We do not find much about grammar in Husserl's work after the *Investigations*, but we assume that he did not change his mind about an essential point: that his grammar must be conceived in terms of the *grammaire générale et raisonée* of the classical rationalists (LI, p. 525; cf. FTL, pp. 72–74, 100f). Such a grammar would be a part of an *analytic* logic along the lines of Leibniz's universal *mathesis* and would attempt to remedy the mixing of the logical and the empirical which the rationalists had done. In other words, the basic *a priori* of speech for Husserl is not synthetic, but a self-justifying analytic. Although some believe that the rules for the logical syntax (=grammar) of the *Tractatus* could possibly be synthetic,[15] there is no question that the *a priori* of the later grammar is synthetic, with the exception, as we have seen above, of the grammar of logical constants. Instead of locating grammar in a realm of pure logic, the later Wittgenstein locates it in a material logic, and this becomes the basis for his phenomenology in a far-reaching domain between logic and science.

CONSTITUTION AND THE *A PRIORI*

This decided shift towards a material logic appears ironic for two philosophers who take such a strong stand against psychologism and insist on a firm distinction between *Wesen* and *Tatsache*. Husserl believes it was contradictory for Kant to hold that synethetic *a priori* propositions are universal and necessary and yet dependent upon the functioning of a *factual* subject for their validity. While it is true that Kant psychologizes the *a priori*, Husserl, while at the same time maintaining the *a priori* as an objective *eidos*, began as early as 1907 to develop the concept in terms of a *constituting* subject. Indeed, the later Husserl goes as far as to say that the *a priori* is a "transcendental achievement" (EB,

p. 88), or that the *a priori* of history is "related to the being of mankind
. . ." (K, p. 349). Kern has done a masterful job in proving that Husserl,
while of course avoiding Kant's disastrous "faculty" psychology and
formal *a priori*, definitely returns to an *a priori* of Kantian descent; i.e.
one connected with the subjective *Bedingungen der Möglichkeit der Erfahrung* and at variance with the eidetic *a priori* available through imaginative variation.[16]

It might seem as if Husserl has passed from one extreme to the other
with regard to the *a priori*. In the very early work we find that essences
are completely objective, and in the later work we discover that the *a
priori* is fully constituted by human agency. It appears as if Wittgenstein
has experienced a similar journey from the *Tractatus* to the *Investigations*, i.e. if we clarify beforehand that human agency is seen not in
terms of some mental activity but in terms of linguistic rules and forms
of life. That Wittgenstein is an adherent of the constitution theory is
abundantly clear from his middle and later works: "It is grammatical
rules that determine meaning (constitute [*konstituieren*] it)" (PG, p. 184;
cf. 213, p. 233); and if something "is *a priori*, that means that it is a
form of account (*Darstellungsform*) that is very convincing to us" (PI,
§158). "It is not the property of an object that is ever 'essential,' but
rather the mark of a concept" (RFM, p. 23). "So it depends wholly on
our grammar what will be called possible and what not, i.e. what that
grammar permits" (PG, p. 127). We must also recall Wittgenstein's vigorous self-criticism of the Tractarian picture theory: "One thinks that
one is tracing the outline of the thing's nature over and over again, and
one is merely tracing round the frame through which we look at it" (PI,
§114).

If we have all along been correct in assuming that phenomenology
has gone beyond realism and idealism in its affirmation of an internal
relation between the self and world, these extremes of objective and
subjective *a priori* are simply symptoms of the Cartesian antitheses of
the inner and the outer. Therefore, it is more correct to say that essences are found *in the world*, a world which has subjective as well as
objective dimensions. Again it is Dufrenne who has thought out the details of this approach to the *a priori*. Dufrenne believes that we must
give empiricism its due without destroying the discoveries of the
Copernican revolution and the transcendental method. For example, a
person born blind could never experience colors in the world, and even
if they somehow were able to think or dream "in color," they would not
use color words in the same way that sighted persons do. Using
Wittgenstein's idiom, nature does have something to say and there is

definitely a biological basis to forms of life. The fact that color-blind people cannot learn the language-game of normal colors is not due to something cultural but something physiological (OCo, §112).

Dufrenne suggests that an excessive emphasis on constitution, with its latent idealism, can damage a legitimate theory of the *a priori* as badly as any realist or associationist. Warning of the dangers of a "transcendental demiurge," Dufrenne proposes that the "idealism involved in the notion of constitution can be avoided by defining the *a priori* as the immediate for which there is no empirical genesis or learning process" (NA, p. 53). We must at all costs avoid a genetic account of the *a priori* from both the subjective and objective poles—"We must refuse the reduction of logic to chronology" (NA, p. 53). The true *a priori* is that which has no genesis, for although it is inextricably bound up with time, it is nonetheless fundamentally atemporal.

The parallels with Wittgenstein are again instructive. Dufrenne mentions the fact that Gestalt psychology has played a leading role in convincing us of the givenness of sense—that, contrary to associationism, sensations are always already ordered. Thomas Langan expresses the Gestaltist contribution succinctly: "This was their notion that the synthesizing forms of our experience are not ideas but corporeal aprioris."[17] It is certainly not too speculative to assume that Wittgenstein's own exposure to this mode of thought fortified his own belief on this point. In addition, we have repeatedly seen Wittgenstein's strong aversion to *Entwicklungshypothesen*, and we have stressed the fact that even though forms of life depend of biology they are not to be explained in terms of our animal nature or in terms of a psychology of learning.[18] While it is possible that some cultures will lack, or eventually discard, forms of life and certain language-games, *Lebensformen*, strictly speaking, do not change. The form of certainty may take on a decidedly different hue in Islamic culture as opposed to American culture, but the form remains the same. This is one way of saying that one can be a cultural relativist without being a historicist.

Although Dufrenne is unusually critical of Heidegger, he still appears to have assumed the latter's claim that *Dasein* and its world are equiprimordial. Heidegger's idea is clearly present when Dufrenne introduces his basic foil against both realism and idealism: *viz.* the "consubstantiality of man and world" (NA, p. 45). This basic accord of subjects and objects is an irreducible fact—as irreducible as the givenness of sense, which can only be shown, lived, or witnessed. When Dufrenne begins referring favorably to pre-critical giants like Spinoza, one fears that he has given empiricism, in the form of naturalism, too much its due. If Dufrenne's translator, Edward S. Casey, is correct in his interpretation that Being itself is nothing but the beings of the world, and that Dufrenne prefers "Nature" to Being, then Dufrenne has not at all been successful in establishing "an empiricism of the transcendental." For Heidegger at least, the ontological difference between Being and beings is the fundamental insight of the transcendental method.

ORDINARY CERTAINTY

With Wittgenstein's rejection of the formal *a priori* there is a concomitant disavowal of the concepts of formal certainty and necessity. Michael Sukale argues that Heidegger must hold that the proposition "a (*Dasein*-) world is" is a necessary truth, synthetic *a priori*.[19] Traditionally of course such a proposition was definitely taken as contingent. With his concept of "grammatical" propositions, Wittgenstein has also expanded considerably the arena of "necessary" truths. There are some propositions which we never question because "nothing in our *Weltbild* speaks in favor of the opposite" (OC, §93). Wittgenstein calls these privileged propositions "grammatical" or "hard." The concept of necessity has been broadened dramatically, because Wittgenstein's "ordinary" certainty has now replaced the "super" certainty of post-Cartesian philosophy, a philosophy that ultimately ruined itself in skepticism because of the unrealistic demands of its method. Grammatical propositions are therefore synthetic and *a priori*, since ordinary certainty is the ground of their necessity. Examples of such propositions in *On Certainty* are "the external world exists," "I have two hands," "my name is N. N.," "that is a tree," etc. Since Wittgenstein recognizes a plurality of linguistic worlds, these propositions, while necessary, are not necessarily univeral. For example, it is possible to conceive of a society whose members have no names.

It is worthwhile to discuss briefly Wittgenstein's change in Kant's definition of the *a priori* as spontaneous, necessary, and universal. The order of these characteristics is important for Kant because necessity arises from the unified spontaneous action of all transcendental egos and therefore this necessity must imply universality. Wittgenstein also believes that necessity arises from spontaneous human action, but replaces the idea of the transcendental ego with an intersubjective *Lebenswelt*. All of the existential phenomenologists do this, and one in particular, Mikel Dufrenne, diverges from Wittgenstein on one important point. In contrast to Wittgenstein, Dufrenne retains the universality of the *a priori* and bases it in the perceptual uniformity of a universal *Lebenswelt* (NA, pp. 60–61). I believe most other existential phenomenologists would agree with Dufrenne, but Wittgenstein, the most radical of them, refuses to speak in terms of a universal life-world, and speaks only of a variety of cultural worlds.

In their deformalization of the *a priori* both Dufrenne and Wittgenstein agree that Kant is wrong in deriving the universality of the *a priori* from logical necessity. But in contrast to Dufrenne, who then derives necessity from perceptual universality, Wittgenstein bases necessity on *Darstellungsformen* which we would never think of doubting, but could be doubted or be non-existent in another culture. For him that which is necessary is simply that which is always *used* and *used* without hesitation. At the same time, however, Wittgenstein does strongly imply that there are limits to constitutive spontaneity, *viz.* "what nature has to say."

One of the interesting aspects of the concept of Husserl's material *a priori* is that it was not originally expressed in terms of a general *Weltontologie*, but in terms of regional ontologies which would have their own set of *a priori* principles (*Ideas*, §16). (Here is an *a priori*, like Wittgenstein's, which is necessary but *not* universal. It is puzzling why Dufrenne did not follow out these implications of the *Ideas*.) Furthermore, as Sukale points out in the article cited above, Husserl for the most part uses the term "world" in such a way that the proposition "the world exists" would definitely be contingent (especially in the context of the thought experiment of the *cogito* surviving the destruction of the world). But we have already seen that the later Husserl tends to replace the transcendental ego with the concepts of *Lebenswelt* and intersubjectivity. This means that the later Husserl does have a *Weltontologie* and the concept of *Weltgewissheit* (K, p. 407g) now indicates that the *Lebenswelt* and consciousness itself are necessarily related. This means that the proposition "the (life-) world exists" is now a necessary one (cf. K, p. 110). The *Lebenswelt* is "simply there, unbroken existing in pure ontic certainty (undoubted)"; or "in advance there is the world, even pregiven and undoubted in ontic certainty and self-verification" (K, pp. 172, 187).

Husserl does not go as far as Wittgenstein in declaring the proposition "there is a tree" a necessary truth (cf. K, p. 236), because Husserl's material *a priori* is not a *factual a priori*. In addition to this significant difference, there is a minor one to note here. In contrast to Wittgenstein, who draws many of his grammatical propositions from empirical propositions, Husserl is more concerned to show that many analytic propositions are synthetic. For example, while "all unmarried males are unmarried" is analytic, "all bachelors are unmarried" is synthetic, along with "every tone has a pitch," and "a red spot cannot at the same time be green."[20] This last example is one which Wittgenstein uses many times as a grammatical, i.e. synthetic *a priori*, proposition.

Husserl appears to anticipate Wittgenstein's radical insight in *On Certainty* that the basis for "ordinary" certainty is pre-epistemological:

> This knowing, as horizon certainty, is not something learned, not knowledge which was once actual and merely sunk back to become part of the background; . . . it is already presupposed in order that we can seek to know what we do not know (K, p. 374).

Grammatical propositions are not really beliefs, but the *grounds* for believing this or that. The "existence of the earth" is a "hard" fact which is "the starting-point of belief for me" (OC, §205). Henry LeRoy Finch phrases it aptly: "Making sense is not based upon knowing, but rather knowing itself must make sense."[21] Michael Polanyi's "tacit" knowledge also converges nicely with Husserl and Wittgenstein on this point.

As their philosophies developed, both Husserl and Wittgenstein came to see that the intuitive bases for many non-trivial *a priori* judgments could never be fully adequate. Although Husserl throughout his entire career demanded a clarity and exactness that the later Wittgenstein found impossible or or unnecessary to achieve (cf. PI, §107), he nonetheless rejected Cartesian super-certainty and its ideal in the mathematical sciences. We have already quoted his observation that some concepts are essentially inexact and therefore cannot lend themselves to a method based on mathematics (*Ideas*, §74). The later Husserl therefore speaks of "ordinary" certainty, the *"schlicte Erfahrungsgewissheit"* of the *Crisis*: "The *naïve obviousness* of the certainty of the world, the certainty in which we live . . . the certainty of the *everyday* world . . ." (K, pp. 105, 96, cf., p. 142). The major difference between Husserlian *epoché* and Cartesian doubt is seen in this passage: "One cannot arbitrarily and unhesitatingly modalize a validity: one cannot transform certainty into doubt or negation, or pleasure into displeasure. . . . But one can unhesitatingly abstain from any validity, that is, one can put its performance out of play for certain particular purposes" (K, p. 237).

MERLEAU-PONTY ON THE *A PRIORI*

Even though Wittgenstein argues that many former empirical propositions will now, according to his criteria, become "grammatical" propositions, he still maintains a strict distinction between them: those propositions whose denial is readily conceivable, and those whose nature is such that "we can't imagine the opposite" (PI, §251). These grammatical propositions are synthetic *a priori* judgments and they concern essences (RFM, pp. 125–6). In *Zettel* he gives a succinct view of his "dynamic" theory of synthetic *a priori* propositions:

> The avowal of adherence to a form of expression, if it is formulated in the guise of a proposition dealing with *objects* (instead of signs) must be "*a priori*." For its opposite will really be unthinkable, inasmuch as there corresponds to it a form of thought, a form of expression, that we have excluded (Z, §442, cf. §444).

Wittgenstein therefore emphasizes the distinction between the *a priori* and the empirical in the strongest possible terms: the formal connections of grammar are not causal or experiential, but are "much stricter and harder, so rigid even, that the one thing somehow already *is* the other . . ." (RFM, p. 40). Wittgenstein contends that despite the apparent similarity, there is a "*fundamental* difference" between grammatical and empirical propositions: the former are based on following rules and their truth can only be "shown" and lived, while the latter are not based on rules and can be "believed," and therefore falsified (RFM, p. 32).

Wittgenstein's attempts to preserve a modified distinction between the *a priori* and the empirical initially seem quite distant from Merleau-Ponty's efforts to eliminate the distinction entirely. But Harrison Hall, to whom I am heavily indebted on this topic, qualifies Merleau-Ponty's statements on the *a priori* such that their implications are not as outrageous and are more plausible. Merleau-Ponty's declaration that "every factual truth is a rational truth and vice versa" must be seen in relation to another assumption, *viz.* "that the relation of reason to fact . . . is this two-way relationship that phenomenology has called '*Fundierung*' . . ." (PP, p. 394). With this clue Hall is able to transform the first implausible claim into something more reasonable: "Factual truth is the foundation of rational truth, and rational truth is founded upon factual truth."[22]

In arguing for the second part of this thesis, Merleau-Ponty takes the example of the geometrical proposition: "The sum of the angles of a triangle equals two right angles." He claims that this statement cannot be analytic, because the definition of triangularity does not include the properties named in the predicate. Merleau-Ponty believes that this statement has an obvious empirical basis, because, as Hall phrases it, "the actual discovery of validation ('re-discovery') of the theorem is as much perceptual as conceptual in nature and has a logic of its own."[23]

In addition, the theorem has a definite contingent nature due to the fact that Euclidean geometry is now recognized as only one among several alternatives in describing the nature of space. As Merleau-Ponty states: "Once launched and committed to a certain set of thoughts, Euclidean space, for example . . . I discover evident truths, but these are not unchallengeable, since perhaps this space [is] not the only one possible" (PP, p. 396). All truths have this element of contingency and facticity, because all truth acquisition has a history in which human agency and perception play an important role.

Merleau-Ponty is not as convincing when he turns to prove the first part of his bold thesis: that every factual truth is the foundation of a rational truth. First he offers the trivial point that even a falsehood has an eternal existence: "It is true that a false thought, no less than a true one, possesses this sort of eternity: if I am mistaken at this moment, it is forever true that I am mistaken" (PP, p. 393). Merleau-Ponty reformulates this argument somewhat when he claims that truths can be built out of past errors: "For there is not one of my actions, not one of even my fallacious thoughts, once it is adhered to, which has not been directed towards a value or a truth" (PP, p. 393). Neither of these arguments, no matter how striking or clever, makes factual truths into the *a priori* truths we know from tradition. If we use Wittgenstein's criterion of "Can we conceive of the opposite?" on these examples, it is obvious that they fail the test.

Hall salvages the main force of Merleau-Ponty's position by drawing out a significant implication from his theory of perception. Normal perception is based on certain assumptions and expectations which would be unthinkable to deny, e.g. that we have a body, that we live on an earth which has had a long history, and that our world is governed by certain laws, both causal and logical. These assumptions and expectations constitute "optimal perceptual beliefs" that do have the same character as traditional *a priori* propositions. Given Merleau-Ponty's close affinity to Heidegger, especially the former's explicit use of the latter's concept of "Being-in-the-world," he too would believe that "the world exists" is a necessary truth, especially since he speaks of the "self-evidence" of the world (PP, p. 397).

Such beliefs do indeed fulfill Wittgenstein's criterion of undeniability. Denying these beliefs would involve a total restructuring of our present *Weltanschauung*: they are "necessary" truths for *our* world. At this point one could object to Hall's argument by reminding us that Merleau-Ponty's full claim is that *every* fact, not just those connected with these comprehensive beliefs, is the foundation for a rational truth.

But for Merleau-Ponty's holistic methodology, there is no such thing as an isolated fact unconnected with general, unassailable truths. One cannot deny the existence of a single fact without denying the fabric of the whole. As Merleau-Ponty states: "There is significance, something and not nothing, there is an indefinite train of concordant experiences, to which this ash-tray in its permanence testifies . . ." (PP, p. 397). We have of course discovered a similar holism in the later Wittgenstein.

THE FUNCTIONAL *A PRIORI*

If we now take a closer look at Wittgenstein's concept of grammatical propositions, we can begin to see that there is not as much distance between him and Merleau-Ponty as we first assumed. Although Wittgenstein does maintain a distinction between grammatical and empirical propositions, it is important to be clear about the reasons for and origins of this distinction. Wittgenstein holds that a grammatical proposition can never be false, but it can be useless (RFM, p. 98). This word "use" is the key to understanding the role and function of grammatical propositions. For example, the grammatical proposition "there are 60 seconds in a minute" can never be false, but it certainly can be useless in a culture in which time is not measured (RFM, p. 173). (The words "second" and "minute" would then have no meaning.) And if for some reason we decided to change to a 40-second minute, the proposition "there are 60 seconds in a minute" does not become false—we have simply changed the rule and are now playing a different game.

Wittgenstein's grammatical propositions therefore fulfill an essential criterion of classic *a priori* truths: they do not depend on the empirical facts that they describe. As Wittgenstein states: "The mathematical proposition [as grammatical proposition] is only supposed to supply a framework for a description"; or "there is no doubt at all that *in certain language-games* mathematical propositions play the part of rules of description, as opposed to descriptive propositions" (RFM, pp. 160, 163). But in some situations, mathematical propositions will not always function in an *a priori* capacity. For example, the proposition "Every shape has size" might be synthetic *a priori*, but it always depends on how "shape" and "size" are used in language; or generally, "some propositions are *a priori* in visual space but in physical space empirical" (L 1, pp. 70, 77). For example, in visual space $2 + 2 = 4$ is synthetic *a priori*, but in physical space one is dealing with physical objects, therefore it is "an hypothesis and needs verification" (L 1, p. 77).

The reason we cannot negate a grammatical proposition is due to its function and use and not due to any unchangeable essence in things or innate categories in the mind. With regard to mathematical propositions, Wittgenstein contends that "something is an axiom, not because we accept it as extremely probable, nay certain, but because we assign it a particular function, and one that conflicts with that of an empirical proposition" (RFM, p. 114). But with non-mathematical propositions it is usually not a single person or group of persons that assigns the function, for that function is already built into what Wittgenstein calls our *Weltbild* or *Weltanschauung*. To accept a proposition as unshakable *already* assumes that it is being used as a grammatical rule, that it is already built into the language-game in which the proposition is found.

It is within the context of mathematics that Wittgenstein has the most to say about grammatical propositions. And it is here that we can see a parallel between Merleau-Ponty and Wittgenstein's rejection of the analytic character of mathematical propositions. In 1942 he affirmed that mathematical propositions are synthetic *a priori* and that their truth is "not to be got out of their concepts by means of some kind of analysis" but is determined by synthesis (RFM, p. 126). For Wittgenstein mathematics *works* with numbers and figures; its essence is not on some ethereal plane, but it is found in application and use. He believes that it was wrong for philosophers not to have seen that the foundation of arithmetic involves "saying something about its application" (PR, p. 130; cf. LFM, p. 46). Wittgenstein would definitely agree with Merleau-Ponty that proving theorems in geometry involves the construction of figures, and therefore perception plays an essential role. We *see* the results in mathematics, we don't arrive at them solely by logical inference (PR, p. 129; RFM, pp. 121, 123, 125).

Neither Wittgenstein nor Merleau-Ponty would wish to deny that there are conceptual components in the proving of mathematical theorems. Like Wittgenstein, Merleau-Ponty readily recognizes the operation of a *"Darstellungsfunktion"* or "categorial" activity, but he denies that this must commit us to any form of "intellectualism" (PP, p. 190). Wittgenstein also believes that "the limit of the empirical—is *concept-formation*" (RFM, p. 121), and concept-formation is governed by the *Darstellungsformen* of grammar. Therefore, since all mathematical propositions involve the following of rules, they cannot be merely empirical, but grammatical.

Although Merleau-Ponty gives the initial impression that mathematical propositions are simply empirical ones in disguise, a much more coherent interpretation must hold that Merleau-Ponty thought mathematical propositions to be more like the traditional synthetic *a priori*. His emphasis on "verbal schema" and "*Darstellungsfunktion*" leads us to conclude that Merleau-Ponty must also distinguish between empirical and grammatical propositions. This *Darstellungsfunktion* is "at the core of subjectivity, a total project or a logic of the world which empirical perceptions endow with specific form, but to which they cannot give rise" (PP, p. 405). This is clear Kantian language and firm evidence for our proposed distinction between the empirical and the *a priori*. For Merleau-Ponty this reciprocal relation of reason and fact is embedded synthetically in a *Lebenswelt* which has a "sedimented" history. As William Lawhead explains Merleau-Ponty's linguistic phenomenology: "The verbal schema [grammar] of the spoken word is not a static *a priori*, but develops through a process of sedimentation."[24] Wittgenstein concurs: "*Darstellung* is dynamic, not static" (PG, p. 100).

If grammatical propositions have their ground in "*Gebrauch*" (a word that can be translated as "custom" as well as "use"), then it is clear that grammar is intimately connected with human agency and culture. Since the use of words can change and new uses can come into being, grammar itself must have a genesis and a history. (A new mathematical proof can "change the grammar of our language" [RFM, p. 79].) Therefore, while the truth of grammatical propositions is independent of the specific empirical facts which their terms describe, it is not independent of the general power of human constitution. "The rule *qua* rule is detached, it stands as it were alone in its glory, although what gives it importance are the facts of daily experience" (RFM, p. 160, cf. p. 159).

Therefore grammar is created and stored in the memory of the linguistic community. It is also possible to conceive of a plurality of linguistic systems or language-games which represent different linguistic worlds and cultures (PR, p. 178; BB, p. 134). Already as early as 1929, Wittgenstein recognized the possibility that there might not be a universal grammar common to all. One of the most important mistakes in the *Tractatus* was that he did not realize that the knowledge of any color presupposes the entire color system. If, for example, I saw nothing but red all my life, would I have the same concept of color as others who have experienced colors normally? There are two possibilities: either I am part of the normal grammatical system and therefore know all the colors, even though I have experienced only red; or, I know only "red," but have thereby cut myself off from normal discourse and use color concepts in an entirely different way than others (WK, pp. 88–89). Friedrich Waismann has pointed out that the English language uses color words exclusively as adjectives, but German, Russian, and Italian use them as verbs as well. As E. K. Specht states: "Now, in rendering color phenomena by verbs we assimilate them more closely to the phenomena of lustre, and in doing so we alter not only our manner of speaking but out entire way of apprehending color."[25] This discussion throws important light on an otherwise cryptic statement in the *Remarks*, which we have already used: "And you could almost say that someone could hope in German and fear in English or vice versa" (PR, p. 69).

Wittgenstein's claim that grammatical propositions have their basis in use is intimately connected with his definition of meaning as use. For example, if the meaning of the word "cube" lies either in a mental cube or in a physical one, then it is admissable that the proposition "the cube has twelve edges" is analytic; i.e. twelve edges (physical or mental) are contained in the meaning. But if the meaning of the word "cube" is its use, then any proposition in which the word is used must be synthetic. For Wittgenstein all concept formation is temporal and synthetic in character. This means that the Tractarian doctrine of self-contained, objective meanings is replaced by an "environmental" or "contextual" doctrine of meaning in which *Umgebung* and *Umstände* play a leading role. Therefore, the classical example of the analytic *a priori*, "All bachelors are unmarried males," must now be regarded as synthetic, because the meaning of the word "bachelor" is dependent on a specific linguistic-cultural world in which institutions like marriage exist and where the meanings of words are constituted within various forms of life. Therefore, the idea of analyticity is evidently eliminated in the later Wittgenstein, because the universal logic in which some concepts are subsumed under others (like "bachelors" under "unmaried males") is broken by the pluralism and radical contextualism of language-games and forms of life. If we are to speak of analyticity at all, we must now qualify it as a "functional analyticity."[26]

FRAMEWORK FACTS

We are now in a better position to see how Wittgenstein can accept Merleau-Ponty's reformulated claim that "factual truth is the foundation of rational truth, and rational truth is founded upon factual truth." The reason we take some propositions to be unassailable is due both to certain facts of nature and to certain historical-cultural facts, including human functions and needs (cf. RFM, p. 23). To reiterate Merleau-Ponty's main point: only after we have committed ourselves to a certain framework do we then begin to discover evident truths (PP, p.

396). Wittgenstein's cryptic discussion of *Weltbild* in *On Certainty* contains the most striking parallels to Merleau-Ponty's general position on the *a priori*. A *Weltbild* is a tacit font of shared understanding, which is not a hypothesis invented by any single person, but a pre-epistemological framework that we all take on as we enter the life-world. "Hard" propositions, such as "The world exists and has had a long history," "My name is N. N.," and "This is a tree" are *a priori*, for we never question them and would be called insane if we did (cf. OC, §467).

One is initially inclined to assume that the arena of Wittgenstein's "hard" propositions is coextensive with his grammatical propositions. But this proves to be a mistake, and also reveals some possible confusion in Wittgenstein's thinking. Wittgenstein uses the term "grammatical proposition" only once in *On Certainty* (§58) and generally speaks of *empirical* propositions that have the privileged position as "hard," because of the role that they play in our *Weltbild*. In the *Remarks* these are described simply as "remarkable and interesting facts" that support "completely general propositions of great importance," like "I have only *one* body. That my sensations never reach out beyond this body . . ." (PR, p. 86). He continues by contending that such a proposition is completely different from one like "I cannot remember the future," which "says nothing, and, like its opposite, is something inconceivable." Under the Tractarian distinction between *Sinn* and *Unsinn*, this proposition and its opposite still would have sense, but now Wittgenstein, as we have seen before, appears to have changed his mind. "I can remember the future" makes no sense for our linguistic system. This is not the way we use the verb "remember"—its grammar (=use) is clear: remembering refers only to the past.[27] Therefore, "hard" propositions, like "I have only one body" are *not grammatical* propositions because their truth is not directly bound to grammatical rules.

This example of never being able to remember the future reveals a troublesome equivocation in the middle period which can be phrased as two questions: Are there grammatical rules of usage which can never be broken? Is there a possible life-world in which one could remember the future? There is indeed scattered evidence in the middle works that Wittgenstein is not ready to completely relativize the *a priori*. We have already discussed the key passage in the *Grammar* where grammatical rules for the use of color, number, and sound words would be discovered *in experience* (and thereby subject to a relative *a priori*), but the rules for the use of logical constants like "not," "or," etc. "would not be the kind that [are] discovered by experience, but the generality of a supreme rule of the game admitting of no appeal" (PG, p. 215). We have already surmised that Wittgenstein might not only exempt the logical constants from grammatical (=phenomenological) investigation, but may also exclude them as *a priori* because for him all aprioris are material, worldly. But, along with grammatical and "hard" propositions, he does speak of logical propositions in *On Certainty* (§§319, 401) and he considers them all *a priori*—"there is no such thing as doubt" in these cases (OC, §58).

Although the texts appear to be confused about the relationship among these three types of propositions, I would like to offer an interpretative schema which attempts to reconcile Wittgenstein's views. The following diagram is an *übersichtliche Darstellung* of the Wittgensteinian *a priori*.

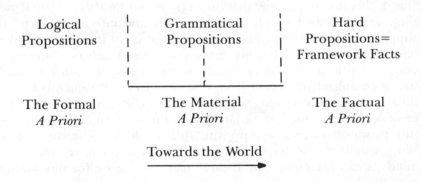

There is a real possibility that, since we have argued that there is ultimately no formal *a priori* for Wittgenstein (except as abstract), the first division on the left merges with grammatical propositions. I have left it separate in order to do full justice to all the texts, and to allow for the opportunity to discuss why Wittgenstein would choose to distinguish between logical and grammatical propositions. In other words, I wish to take Wittgenstein at his word when he states that there are "rules of the game" which are unaffected by use and are so general as to admit of no appeal (PG, p. 215). These rules could be those of syntactical connection that would forever ban "king and but" from making sense, but allow the contradiction "Jesus is both man and God" as perfectly good sense for a Christian life-world. One could also include here obvious tautologies, such as "all unmarried males are unmarried," yet agree with Husserl and Wittgenstein that "all unmarried males are bachelors" would be a grammatical proposition. The only problem here is that Husserl thinks the former proposition is analytic, and we have argued that Wittgenstein has probably eliminated analyticity along with the pure, formal *a priori*. This means of course that the left-hand category again collapses into grammatical propositions.

Grammatical propositions are "half-way," so to speak, between the formal and factual *a priori*, which is compatible with Wittgenstein's proposal that grammar as phenomenology might be a discipline between logic and science, between the purely formal and the purely factual (OCo, p. 15). One might propose that logical propositions contain the rules of grammatical connection, while grammatical propositions express the rules of grammatical usage. While logical propositions define the outer limits of sense, grammatical propositions are fully within the world of sense. Because of their trademark of explicitly involving basic rules, they are more formal than hard propositions, but because they do relate directly to the world, they are material as well. For example, while basic syntactical rules exclude "60 there minute a in" from the world of sense, "there are 60 seconds in a minute" is definitely a grammatical proposition, along with "one must play solitaire with one's self." If I want to say "there are 40 seconds in a minute" or "please play solitaire with me," I may initially get some blank responses, but if I am an absolute despot, I could easily decree that any rules could be changed at my whim. With such propositions I have not left the world of sense; indeed, the two new propositions I have decreed are not even false—I have just changed the rules of the game.

As we have seen, hard propositions, or "framework facts" as Finch calls them, are decidedly different from grammatical propositions in that they do not deal explicitly with rules. No grammatical rules are being broken when I say that I have no name, or that a tree is not a tree, but explicit rules of usage for the verb "remember" are being broken when I claim that I can remember the future. Unlike grammatical propositions, hard propositions have the outward form of empirical propositions, but because of their privileged status as indubitable, they are completely different from them. Empirical propositions are expressions of beliefs that are judged true or false within the framework of *a priori* propositions. The latter are neither true nor false, but are the transcendental conditions for the validity of all empirical propositions (cf. L 1, p. 13). As Finch affirms: "They do not agree or disagree with reality; they constitute *what we mean by reality*."[28]

Although Wittgenstein describes them as if they had a formal dimension—they are "norms for description" or they give "our way of looking at things . . . their form" (OC, §§167, 211)—framework facts constitute a fully factual *a priori*. Nature does have much to say in hard propositions like "every human being has two parents," but it does not seem to play any role in choosing the conventions of how one divides up time or how one plays and names card games. As Wittgenstein points out, there are some interesting exceptions (ones that prove the rule) among hard propositions. Although Christians accept the framework fact that all humans have two parents, they nonetheless continue to affirm Jesus' full humanity. Or if I am an Austrian count with ten middle names, it may be false that I know my own name. The pervasive empirical component in framework facts is revealed by Wittgenstein's comment that "if one of my names were used only very rarely, then it might happen that I did not know it. It goes without saying that I know my name, only because, like anyone else, I use it over and over again" (OC, §568).

Therefore, while grammatical propositions definitely represent a material *a priori*, they are not factual aprioris because they are independent from contingent matters of fact. Framework facts, however, are *necessary* facts, but paradoxically, necessary facts which may have a few exceptions, or as Brand indicated above, may be outright falsified. For example, if a rare disease killed all males in the world but only caused a genetic mutation in females that allowed virgin conceptions, then it would become necessarily true that human beings have only one parent.

Many of Wittgenstein's hard propositions have a striking resemblance to Merleau-Ponty's "optimal perceptual beliefs." The denial of such beliefs would involve conceiving of an entirely different world and culture, but it would not involve violating any basic grammatical rules. Whereas no amount of cultural change would presumably enable us to conceive of being able to remember the future, the transition from an ordinary empirical proposition to a hard one is the direct result of human agency. "It is clear that our empirical propositions do not all have the same status, since one can lay down such a proposition and turn it from an empirical proposition into a norm of description" (OC, §167). Since this preceding passage relates framework facts to a *Weltbild*, one could call them "world-view" facts, just as Hall calls the objects of Merleau-Ponty's optimal beliefs "global" or "world" facts, as opposed to local or isolated facts. "The *a priori* is the fact understood, made explicit, and followed through into all the consequences of its latent logic; the *a posteriori* is the isolated and implicit fact" (PP, p. 221).

Although Wittgenstein emphasizes the tacit nature of framework facts, he does agree with Merleau-Ponty that global facts are "necessary to this world" (PP, p. 221).

Merleau-Ponty also discusses Kant in his reformulation of the meaning of the *a priori* (PP, pp. 220–2). He shows that Kant's rational truths have a foundation in factual truths in the sense that the Kantian *a priori* is based on a factual subject that constitutes the meaning of phenomena. In this way Kant has proved that the *a priori* is not knowable "outside of our horizon of facticity," and that therefore there cannot be any ultimate distinction between it and the empirical. Facts that appeared to Kant as "empirical oddities" now play a central role as global facts, as bona fide *a priori* truths. It has been left to latter-day Kantians, first the *Lebensphilosophen* and then the existential phenomenologists, to complete and radicalize Kant's program: to historicize and relativize the *a priori* and to show that reason and fact converge irretrievably in a *Lebenswelt*. In such a view we give up the traditional goal of "plenary objectivity" and concede that not all perspectives are compossible, and that we must content with a plurality of linguistic-cultural worlds.

Before closing this section let us document the preceding claim that the life-philosophers prepared the stage for the relative, factual *a priori* of the existential phenomenologists and Wittgenstein. Wittgenstein believes that whether a proposition is *a priori* or not depends on our point of view, and Weingartner, writing about Georg Simmel's account of form and content, claims that "looked at in one way, an event is merely a fleeting phase in an individual's career; but regarded in another, that same event is something logical, . . . 'something that is in principle fully definite and definable.' "[29]

Conceding that "there are doubtless certain characters of very wide-ranging validity which are (seemingly at any rate) independent of the culture and the century to which the cognizing individual may belong," Oswald Spengler nonetheless rejects the sharp distinction drawn traditionally between the *a priori* and the empirical (DW I, p. 60). Spengler therefore subjects Kant's *a priori* to the flow of history and declares that there are obviously various degrees of universal validity. There are "particular necessities" which characterize some cultures and not others, and these cultures have their own "styles of knowing" that condition the *a priori*. Furthermore, some traditional aprioris are in only approximate agreement with lived experience, and the scope of Euclidean geometry is especially narrow: *viz.* its limits are the small expanse of a drawing board (DW I, p. 68).

THE "CORPOREAL" *A PRIORI* AND FORMS OF LIFE

Although we have established some solid parallels between Wittgenstein and Merleau-Ponty on the *a priori*, some might object to the ultimate value of such a comparison in view of more fundamental differences between the two thinkers. A critic might, for example, even concede that Wittgenstein's phenomenological method does have some surprising similarities with the continental variety, but then contend that Wittgenstein's exclusive emphasis on grammar and linguistic analysis is not found in Heidegger or Merleau-Ponty. In this connection the critic could also point out a related difference: Merleau-Ponty's heavy emphasis on perception and the body, themes very little discussed in Wittgenstein's writings. We shall discuss the topic of linguistic phenomenology in Chapter Ten, but we can now simply reiterate a thesis already proposed in Chapter Three: In Wittgenstein *Lebensphilosophie* ultimately takes precedence over any narrow, analytic *Sprachphilosophie*. This has the result of reducing considerably the initial contrast between Wittgenstein and existential phenomenology.

It is true that Wittgenstein does not deal much with the philosophical problems of perception and the body. He does, however, seem to come very close to Merleau-Ponty's theory of the soul as a "body image" when he suggests that "the human body is the best picture of the human soul" (PI, p. 178). As we saw in Chapter Seven, John Cook has argued persuasively that Wittgenstein, like Merleau-Ponty, has given up the post-Cartesian concept of a senseless, mechanical body. Wittgenstein's spatialization and embodiment of the ego is seen clearly in this passage: " 'I' clearly refers to my body, for *I* am in this room; and 'I' is essentially something that is in a place, and in a place belonging to the same space as the one the other bodies are in too" (PR, p. 86). In the *Investigations* he contends that it is absurd to say that a body has pain, and it is much more intelligible to say that it is the "I in my hand" that feels pain rather than the isolated hand itself (PI, §286). This is Merleau-Ponty's "body-ego," and we must therefore assume that Wittgenstein would not reject Dufrenne's "corporeal" *a priori*. Such an *a priori*

> constitutes a style of life for a species in a certain environment [and comprises a] sort of pre-language, an original orientation of the body as still not speaking—an orientation by which consciousness becomes sensitive to certain experiences that language can later render explicit, but that do not refer to any particular and namable objects . . . (NA, p. 159).

Dufrenne's "style of life" phraseology, as well as his emphasis on the body, are drawn from his fellow Frenchman Merleau-Ponty. The latter uses "style of life" in a way that makes it an equivalent to Wittgenstein's "form of life." In the same way that Wittgenstein's *Weltbild* is the more comprehensive form of life, Merleau-Ponty says that the *Lebenswelt* is the "universal style shared by all perceptual beings" (PrP, p. 6). Wittgenstein would have especially appreciated Merleau-Ponty's contention that when I make myself understood to another, my words do not work by initiating correlative representations in the mind of the other. Rather, "what I communicate with primarily is not 'representations' or thought, but a speaking [embodied] subject, with a certain style of being . . ." (PP, p. 183). The following passage sums up our argument:

> Thought and objective language [are] two manifestations of that fundamental activity whereby man projects toward a "world". . . . If we go back to concrete descriptions we notice that the categorial activity [i.e. *Darstellungsfunktion*], before being a thought or a form of knowledge, is a certain manner of relating oneself to the world, and correspondingly, a style or shape of experience (PP, p. 191).

Similarly, Wittgenstein believes that to imagine a language presupposes a cultural style (e.g. a caste system, BB, p. 134) and "to imagine a language means to imagine a form of life" (PI, §19).

Therefore, Merleau-Ponty can now join Heidegger and Wittgenstein in a phenomenology of forms of life. These life-forms are the locus of the material *a priori* based on the expansion of the Kantian-Husserlian model, which is functional, relative and corporeal. "If there is one world," as Harrison Hall so elegantly states, "and if the world of reason and the world of fact are capable of forming together a single fabric,"[30] then a self-contained, self-justifying, formal *a priori* cannot be maintained. If this is so, then the correct relation between the *a priori* and the empirical must be along the lines that Wittgenstein and Merleau-Ponty have indicated.

9. Rationality

Life comes first: logic is no more than one of its products.
                              —John Passmore on James and Bergson[1]

Logic must be included among the sciences overthrown in overthrowing all science.
                              —Husserl (CM, p. 7)

If language is to be a means of communication there must be agreement not only in definitions but also (queer as this may sound) in judgments. This seems to abolish logic, but does not do so.
                              —Wittgenstein (PI, §242)

The laws of logic, e.g. excluded middle and contradiction, are arbitrary. This statement is a bit repulsive but nevertheless true.
                              —Wittgenstein (L 3, p. 71)

I need hardly say that where the law of the excluded middle doesn't apply, no other law of logic applies either. . . .
                              —Wittgenstein (PR, p. 176)

I should like to show that one tends to have an altogether wrong idea of logic and the role it plays; and a wrong idea of the truth of logic.
                              —Wittgenstein (LFM, p. 181)

The idea of "logic" itself disintegrates in the turbulence of a more original questioning.
                              —Heidegger (WM, p. 107)

Reason does not provide its own justifications; all justifications lead back to purposes.
                              —Nietzsche[2]

183

THE REVOLT AGAINST SELF-SUFFICIENT LOGIC

The preceding epigrams may puzzle or even offend those not familiar with the philosophical methods of the persons involved. Obviously
none of these thinkers (except for perhaps Nietzsche) wish to abolish
logic, but all are convinced that philosophy's job is quite different from
the tasks of traditional logic or science. In phenomenology all traditional forms of logic and demonstration in general fall to the *epoché*
(cf. K, p. 181). Husserl rejects false, naturalistic epistemologies, and the
"idolization of a logic that does not understand itself" (K, p. 189). The
idea of a self-sufficient logic, independent of the universal life-world *a
priori*, is an illusion (K, p. 141). As logic becomes more and more
sophisticated, it further alienates itself from philosophy proper. As
Lothar Ely phrases it: "Logic is no longer an integral component of
man's act of living (*Lebensvollzug*) and is consequently no longer preserved in an universal and binding language."[3] Combining Husserl and
Wittgenstein, Ely states that "logic is a language-game" that "refers back
to the everyday world"; and, in what appears to be a Wittgensteinian
critique of Husserl, Ely chides the latter for still retaining the concept
of pure mathematical and logical structures within the life-world *a priori*.

We have seen that both Husserl and Wittgenstein believe that
grammar is more fundamental than traditional logic, and that before
questions of truth or falsity there are the more basic questions of *Sinn*
and *Unsinn*. Wittgenstein believes that the famous Tractarian truth
tables are passé, and that there is no way one can make the laws of logic
self-evident by symbolization (LFM, p. 177). Traditional concepts of logical necessity have ignored the "role of thinking and inferring in our
life" (RFM, p. 34). In the *Philosophical Remarks* he charges that "mathematics is ridden through and through with the pernicious idioms of set
theory, and that "it is nonsensical to classify in philosophy and logic"
(PR, p. 211; L 1, p. 11). The following passage from 1942–3 is crucial
to Wittgenstein's critique of logic:

> "Mathematical logic" has completely deformed the thinking of
> mathematicians and of philosophers, by setting up a superficial in-
> terpretation of the forms of our everyday language as an analysis
> of the structures of facts. Of course in this it has only continued to
> build on the Aristotelian logic (RFM, p. 156).

H. R. Smart claims that "Wittgenstein's way of doing philosophy is,
among other things, a vigorous revolt against the excessive pretentions
of symbolic or mathematical logic;"[4] and Peter French contends that

"the use which Wittgenstein puts the term 'logical' in *On Certainty* probably strikes one as an extension at best, maybe even a perversion, of that found in standard textbooks on the subject."[5]

At the same time that Wittgenstein was beginning to generate his own attack on modern logic, Heidegger delivered his famous inaugural address at the University of Freiburg in which he enigmatically revealed that "the idea of 'logic' itself disintegrates in the turbulence of a more original questioning" (WM, p. 107). As Thomas Fay explains in his book *Heidegger: The Critique of Logic,* Heidegger's intent was not to abolish logic, but simply to show that traditional logic was inadequate, not incorrect. Fay shows that Heidegger, like Wittgenstein, was especially critical of mathematical logic, which, as Fay states, "is anything but logic. It is merely mathematics applied to propositional forms."[6] It is only a superficial exercise in the empty forms of conceptual connection and has little to do with life or with objects in the world. Although Heidegger believes that Kant's transcendental logic was a step in the right direction, Kant's idea of Being as "pure position" (KTS, *passim*) and his preservation of the dominance of mathematics prevented him from discovering the true *logos* behind all rational thinking. For Heidegger there can be no logic without the primordial *logos*.

LOGOS AND "BROAD" REASON

The etymology of *logos*, the Greek word behind our "reason" and "logic," offers an instructive guideline for the rest of the discussion in this chapter. The following analysis has been inspired by Heidegger, but goes somewhat beyond what he has done in his own works. The Greek *logos* is the verbal noun of *lego*, which, if we follow the one root $\sqrt{leg}$, means "to gather," "to collect", "to pick up," "to put together," and later "to speak or say." Is this not, figuratively speaking, the way in which one goes about any rational endeavor? We collect a great field of individual facts and thoughts and put them together in an orderly way. Heidegger believes that every time we use the copula we are representing a synthetic act (SZ, p. 160).

Heidegger expresses this etymology somewhat more poetically, but the meaning is the same. He emphasizes the meaning "to lay," even though this meaning comes from another root $\sqrt{lech}$ (as in *lechos*, the marital couch) and not $\sqrt{leg}$, the actual root for *logos*. Heidegger contends that *lego* in its "meaning of 'saying' and 'speaking' can only be understood if it is considered in the light of its most proper meaning as 'laying' and 'gathering' " (VA, p. 223). The pre-Socratics, according to

Heidegger, understood *logos* to be the "Being of a being" (VA, p. 228), that which made a thing what it is. Heidegger therefore implies that the pre-Socratics had an inkling of the transcendental function of Being as the condition for the possibility of experience. Stressing the meaning "putting together," Heidegger proposes that *logos* is Being as primoridal "collectedness" (*Versammlung*) (VA, p. 216); it is that which makes everything hang together and intelligible.

These original meanings of *lego* are the basis for the construction of "broad" reason. In light of our etymological exercise above, it is significant that Leibniz gave the name "Combination" to what he considered to be the most important discipline: "real logic" or "metaphysics."[7] This type of logic was synthetic (i.e., putting together) and not analytic (i.e., taking apart). Kant also believed that synthesis, rather than analysis was the first step in knowledge (KRV, p. 111), and Husserl follows Kant in maintaining that synthesis is "a mode of combination exclusively peculiar to consciousness (CM, p. 39). Wittgenstein's concept of a synoptic view is also synthetic in character. He believes that philosophers have totally misunderstood the nature of a mathematical proof: a proof is an *Übersicht* and "exhibits a fact of synthesis to us" (RFM, p. 75).

This analytic-synthetic distinction will be the first basis for distinguishing "broad" reason from "strict" reason. Strict reason is the reason of formal logic, the traditional Aristotelian logic which Leibniz thought was derivative from his "real logic" or the "art of discovery." In our definition of broad reason we intend to go somewhat beyond Leibniz. Leibniz assumed the principle of non-contradiction as an integral part of his "real logic," but the original meanings above do not dictate that the *logos* must follow such a principle. The pre-Socratic philosophers did not always use the principle and were thoroughly criticized by Aristotle (esp. Heraclitus and Anaxagoras) for this deficiency. In Aristotle's logic we have the beginnings of strict reason, and significantly enough, he called it "Analytics."

The "Logos Christology" of the book of *John* is an instructive example of a broad understanding of a "logic" of the world that ignores the principle of non-contradiction. In the English translations of *John*, Christ is referred to as the "Word." The original Greek term here, significantly enough, is *logos*. *John* opens with these lines: "In the beginning was the *logos*, and the *logos* was with God, and the *logos* was God." In other words, God is the author of the logic of the world, and his son is the expression of this logic. Christ is the one who orders the world; he is the one who "puts it together," gives it meaning, and re-

deems humankind. As Paul states: "For in him all things were created
. . . and in him all things hold together" (*Col.* 1:16−17).

With the rise of modern science and mathematics, the words "reason" and "logic" took on, almost exclusively, the strict sense. The Latin
ratio, the translation of the Greek *logos*, became strict mathematical
"ratio." Contrary to the broad and figurative Greek roots, modern *logos*
became the rigorous deductions of formal logic and mathematics. Logic
and reason were closely tied to incontrovertible proofs, syllogisms, and
other forms of exact demonstration. To strict reason the Incarnation is
just as absurd as a round square and involves making the same type of
category mistake.

Let us define the concept of broad reason in more detail. At the most
fundamental level it deals with the order of the human mind and the
order of the world. Humans are "rational" because they are able to
"put the world together" (*lego*) in a certain way, a way that makes
"sense" to them. An individual does not have to be able to do a
mathematical proof or construct a syllogism in order to be rational in
the broad sense. According to Husserl and Wittgenstein, all one has to
do to make sense is to put word-meanings together in grammatical
order and communicate them to another person.

Broad reason then would obviously include mythological constructions, for this is still the predominant way in which individuals put their
world together. Therefore, the broad notion of reason bridges the gap
between *mythos* and *logos*. In myth we see the "passive" interpretation of
logos: the world and its order are already laid out by God or one of his
agents, or simply just there. Humans then are exhorted to conform to
this pre-established order, and to celebrate this union through ritual
and magic. These individuals then do not actively put the world together, but passively submit to a *fait accompli*. As Leibniz states: "Human combination can only imitate and imperfectly reproduce divine
Combination."[8]

The "active" interpretation of reason is a modern phenomenon, the
best example being modern artists in literature and the fine arts. Artists
actively shape new "worlds," and new ways of looking at the world
often in reaction against a world view that has been given passively by
traditional institutions. The active view is also found, surprisingly
enough, in modern physics where, according to some views, the difference between a particle and a wave does not lie in "reality out there,"
but lies in the human perspective of the observer and in her presuppositions and instruments. Broad reason recognizes the role of one's "point
of view" (*Betrachtungsweise*) or one's *Weltanschauung*, and we have al-

ready seen how committed Wittgenstein was to a *Weltan-schauungsphilosophie*. In our non-conventionalist interpretation of Wittgenstein, however, we are forced to play down the active role of broad reason, because he does stress the fact that the world is given *for* us in institutions and traditions and not created *by* us through arbitrary conventions. This parallels Heidegger's concept of being thrown (*Geworfenheit*) into the *Dasein*-world.

A person's life-world is formed by broad reason (both passive and active). Strict reason is simply a derivative form of reason that has characterized philosophical movements both East and West (the Orient "discovered" logic at least a hundred years before Aristotle) which have attempted to dictate certain rules for "correct" thinking. The method of broad reason always remains *descriptive*, while strict reason has definitely been *prescriptive*, i.e. rules of thought that *ought* to be followed. As the respective methods of existential phenomenology and Wittgenstein are strictly descriptive, it is no surprise then that we find the concept of broad reason in their works. For both, philosophy's job is not to prescribe the ways in which the world ought to be, but to describe the world in terms of the ways in which it has actually made sense. If one wants to say that traditional logic only describes what we *can* do and therefore remains descriptive, Wittgenstein, as we shall see shortly, strongly disagrees. The laws of logic are prescriptive in the same ways as the laws of society.

There is obviously no advantage to broad reason if we are going to argue successfully about certain philosophical issues, but the concept of broad reason can become the basis for a new appreciation of non-Western cultures. Merleau-Ponty states that it was Hegel who

> started the attempt to explore the irrational and integrate it into an expanded reason which remains the task of our century. He is the inventor of that reason, broader than [Kantian] understanding [i.e., strict reason], which can respect the variety and singularity of individual consciousness, civilizations, ways of thinking, and historical contingency, but which nevertheless does not give up the attempt to master them in order to guide them to their own truth (SN, p. 63).

Some of Wittgenstein's most bitter criticism is found in his "Remarks on Frazer's *Golden Bough*." Here he berates Frazer for his use of strict reason and his failure to appreciate the values of the primitive life-worlds which he studies. Wittgenstein believes that language-games and forms of life, regardless of their content and internal consistence or coherence, are autonomous systems with their own sense and their own ways of distinguishing between truth and falsity. Recall that Wittgenstein believes that the true and the false depend upon one's *Weltbild* (OC, §94) or forms of life (PI, §241). As Wittgenstein told his class in 1932: "A style gives us satisfaction, but one style is not more rational than another" (L 1, p. 104).

Hegel claimed that his "dialectical" logic was far superior to traditional logic because he made reason subject to the conditions of history. The expression of reason is culturally conditioned, and if we are insightful enough (Hegel thought he was), we can discern the development of a universal mind (*logos* itself) throughout all of human history. Contradictions and brute, irrational fact are only appearances, because all will be reconciled in the universal mind. Although Heidegger, Merleau-Ponty, and Wittgenstein reject these specific Hegelian theses, they, along with the *Lebensphilosophen*, agree with Hegel that reason is subject to the conditions of history and society. As Heidegger puts it, "the 'logic' of the *logos* is rooted in the existential analytic of *Dasein*" (SZ, p. 160).

WITTGENSTEIN'S VIEWS ON REASON

I have made some rather controversial claims about Wittgenstein and I should now substantiate them. In a very instructive comparison between Wittgenstein and Ernst Cassirer, R. S. Rajan makes these comments with regard to Wittgenstein's view of logic:

> His conception of logic is essentially that of an evolving structure and pattern of developing uses, customs, criteria and standards. . . . What is distinctive of Wittgenstein is neither the abolition of logic, nor its absolute severance from the empirical conditions of developing inquiry, but its "temporalization". . . .[9]

Rajan points out that Cassirer (as well as other neo-Kantians including Husserl) did not agree with such a radical move as this. These thinkers maintained a strict distinction between the "context of discovery" and the "context of validation," and judged that historical change affected only the former. The significant exception among neo-Kantian philosophers were the *Lebensphilosophen*, whom we of course have connected with Wittgenstein.

Of all the traditional Wittgensteinians is only Peter Winch who is fully aware of Wittgenstein's radical views on logic and reason, but he is only half-aware of their relationship to continental developments. In

The Idea of a Social Science Winch argues that rationality has a thoroughly social basis: "The criteria of logic are not a direct gift of God, but arise out of, and are only intelligible in the context of ways of living or modes of social life."[10] Winch bases this conclusion on Wittgenstein's claim that agreement in judgments is derived from a pre-cognitive agreement in forms of life (PI, §§241–2). Winch states that "learning to infer is not just a matter of being taught about explicit logical relations between propositions; it is learning to *do* something" within the social context of forms of life.[11]

Wittgenstein believes that the laws of logic are like the laws of society. Stealing the neighbor's cow and contradicting one's self are certainly different violations, yet in both one gets into conflict with society only, and not with any ethereal realm of divine law or logic. Logical necessity is decidedly not like natural necessity: we are not physically restrained from saying "a round-square exists" as we are in attempting to high-jump twenty feet. Yet some people still insist that logical laws are more inexorable than natural laws. They persist in believing that the "hardness" of the logical "must" is somehow analogous to the impenetrability of a solid object (RFM, p. 110; cf. PG, p. 467). But the "obstructions" in logic are not at all physical (L 1, p. 92), and "the *must* corresponds to a track which I lay down in language" (RFM, p. 78). If we deny the laws of logic, we would simply upset the practical system which we have chosen to use. Such denial does not go against thought *per se* or nature in itself (cf. LFM, p. 235).

Therefore, Wittgenstein can claim that he has refuted Frege's claim that "it is impossible for human beings . . . to recognize an object as different from itself" by simply looking at his lamp and saying "This lamp is different from itself" (RFM, p. 41). As Wittgenstein remarks, "Nothing stirs," there is no Olympian god of logic who sends a thunderbolt to punish those who violate the laws of logic. Wittgenstein charges that Frege was wrong in saying that logical laws are super laws of nature, and trying to make logic into the "physics of the intellectual realm" (LFM, p. 172, cf. p. 230). The inexorability of logic lies in us and our forms of life. One of these specific life-forms is certainty, which Wittgenstein describes as a "matter of attitude" (OC, §404), or as a "manner (*Art und Weise*) of judging, and therefore of acting" (OC, §232). A. B. Levison sums up the point nicely: "These laws are not inexorable; rather, it is *we* who are inexorable in applying them—because we want them to do a job and because we see that in order to get the job done everyone has to do it by the same rules."[12]

In the Big Typescript Wittgenstein declares that Aristotelian logic is a language-game (213, p. 260), and in a later work, agrees that "the rules of logical inference are rules of the *language-game*" (RFM, p. 181). That language-games have an historical basis and therefore can change is evident in many passages: ". . . new language-games . . . come into existence, and others become obsolete and get forgotten" (PI, §23); they are always something "new, spontaneous, and specific" (PI, p. 224); "new ways of speaking" are a "new way of looking at things" (PI, §§400−1); "when language-games change, then there is a change in concepts, and with the concepts the meanings of words change" (OC, §65, cf. §63); and ". . . a language-game does change with time" (OC, §256).

If Aristotelian logic is a language-game, then it is just one of many ways of looking at the world, of making sense of it, and it is conceivable that more primitive "logics" can serve just as well without following Aristotle's laws of inference. With some difficulty we can conceive of a tribe with a "more primitive" logic in which negation and double negation are done in a way quite baffling to us but grammatically correct for them (PI, §554; cf. OC, §475). In our own culture it is easier to conceive of someone accepting the idea of a man-god in one context, but rejecting the idea of a round-square in another, while many would find the two concepts logically analogous.

If what belongs to a language-game belongs to logic (OC, §§256, 56, 628; RFM, p. 181), then there could be as many logics as there are language-games. Fritz Mauthner, a Viennese writer who probably influenced Wittgenstein considerably, believed that logic was based on a *Völkerpsychologie*, and Gershon Weiler is convinced that Wittgenstein's concept of truth, which tended towards the coherence theory, is "very much like that of Mauthner."[13] Like Wittgenstein, Mauthner believed that logic and grammar are historical products and that there would be as many logics as there were languages with different structures. He would have agreed with Wittgenstein's claim that "whether a thing is a blunder or not—it is blunder in a particular system . . . in a particular game" (LC, p. 56). The reason why we persist in believing that there is only one logic, i.e., the strict reason of traditional logic, is because of the dominance of this particular language-game in the history of Western thought. Indeed, each culture will insist that its way of putting the "world" together is the correct one, primarily because, as Mauthner put it, "it is against logic, against the feel of language, to construct a plural for the word logic."[14]

We must comment briefly on the relationship between Wittgenstein's holism and his views on logic. We have seen that one of the major points of disagreement between Wittgenstein and Brouwer is that the latter held that the rejection of the law of the excluded middle would have no effect on the operation of other laws. To the contrary, Wittgenstein maintains that "where the laws of the excluded middle doesn't apply, no other law of logic applies either . . . (Against Weyl and Brouwer)" (PR, p. 176). Wittgenstein told his students in 1932 that something is rational only within the entire system, which, we have seen, he equates with a life-world (L 1, p. 105). He also believes that the wrong conception of language would destroy the "*whole* of logic and everything that goes with it, and doesn't just create some merely local disturbance" (PR, p. 63). Nine years later he expressed the same theme: if people make a minor change in linguistic use, then this "would entirely change their outlook on logic" (LFM, p. 193).

CONTRADICTION

Conceivably, a proponent of broad reason could provoke hostile questions like those Wittgenstein receives from his alter-ego interlocutors. Once he is asked, "Are you in favor of contradiction?" and Wittgenstein answers, "Not at all; any more than of soft rulers" (RFM, p. 171). The real reason we try not to contradict ourselves is the same reason we do not use soft rulers: it would not be *useful*. But, if there happens to be a contradiction in a mathematical system that has served us well, we should not reject the system, we should modify strict reason and our concept of certainty (RFM, p. 181, cf. p. 167). A similar situation can be observed in the intellectual system we call Christian theology. Some of the theological axioms or articles of faith contain obvious contradictions and absurdities (e.g., the man-god and redemption through blood sacrifice), but these belief systems serve millions of people very well. It is also interesting to note that once the articles of faith are accepted, then the inferences drawn from them, especially in theologies like Aquinas' or Barth's, are flawless and precisely presented. (There should be no surprise in the fact that fideism has been reborn in recent philosophical theology based on Wittgenstein. Interestingly enough, Mauthner believed that our faith in strict reason has the character of a theological faith.)

Again it appears as if Mauthner has been a major influence in Wittgenstein's thinking on reason and logic. Mauthner took the etymology of the word "contradiction" as seriously as we have taken the history of the word "reason." As the word clearly implies, a contradiction is a "talking-against" (*Dagegensprechen*) not necessarily a "being-against" (*Dagegensein*).[15] In fact, Mauthner believes that we should sometimes praise the thinker or poet who contradicts herself; bold thinking like this may lead to new discoveries or new aesthetic vistas. For example, there are Heisenberg's sub-atomic particles that appear to be in the same place at the same time; furthermore, the poem or painting which is too straight-forward or unambiguous is usually of little value. Similarly, the formal, logical (~ p. ~ p) is simply empty if it can play no role in significant discourse. Wittgenstein argues that this "crystalline purity of logic was of course, not a *result of investigation:* it was a requirement, [and] the requirement is now in danger of becoming empty" (PI, §107). J. L. Austin finds the model of analytic implication a shabby working model which "fails to fit the facts we really wish to talk about."[16] J. N. Findlay, paraphrased by William Lawhead, concurs: "The logic of strict entailment is a limited and impoverished paradigm of the ways in which thought typically functions."[17]

Wittgenstein appears to echo Mauthner's insights about contradiction when he states that "we shall see contradiction in a quite different light if we look at its occurrence and its consequences, as it were, anthropologically . . ." (RFM, p. 110). Mauthner's distinction between "talking-against" and "being-against" is mirrored in Wittgenstein's constant reminder that "the old logic contains more convention and physics than has been realized" (PG, p. 204). It is good that logicians recognize its conventional basis in language-games and forms of life, but bad that they continue to be subtlety influenced by physical models. " 'Anyone who understands negation knows that two negations yield an affirmation.' That sounds like 'Carbon and oxygen yield carbonic acid'. . . . Something here gives us the illusion of a fact of physics. As if we saw the result of a logical process" (PG, p. 52).

According to Wittgenstein, there is nothing iron-clad about this particular logical law that two negations yield an affirmation. To establish the law as a logical product of the concept of negation and the law of contradiction is simply to choose one way of organizing our thoughts and speech. "To forbid contradiction's occurrence is to adopt one system of expression, which may recommend itself highly. This does not mean that we cannot use a contradiction" (L 3, p. 71). This is what Wittgenstein means by the "civil status of a contradiction" (PI, §125). Just like any upstanding citizen in a community, a contradiction sometimes commands respect. The evangelical preacher who affirms that Jesus is fully man and fully God, and who in addition may admit that this directly contradicts the logic of "atheist philosophers," will surely gain the praise of millions of Americans. Or, the pervasive use of dou-

194 WITTGENSTEIN AND PHENOMENOLOGY

ble negation in the dialogue of many American TV series is an integral (="logical") part of the "in" speech. As Wittgenstein points out, the child who learns how to use negation correctly and then chooses to use double negation for an emphatic negation is surely not wrong (LFM, p. 194). In these 1939 lectures he even shows how one could actually remove the "contradiction" from double negation by simply replacing the conventional negation sign with another sign (LFM, p. 81).

Some of Wittgenstein's other examples on this point are equally illustrative. To tell a person "Leave the room and don't leave the room" might mean that I deliberately want to paralyze the person's action. Or, it might mean that the person is supposed to leave hesitantly in the same way that to say "the weather is fine and it is not fine" is to say that it is just "so-so" (LFM, p. 176). Another interesting example is based on the mathematical truth that any number times zero is zero, the proof of which involves the recognition of a contradiction. But, it is also perfect sense to say that if one sees three cows in a field and then multiplies these three cows by zero, one still has three cows (LFM, p. 135). Ultimately, one could also make ($\sim$ p. $\sim$ p) a true proposition and change one's imagery in such a way as to "make an absurd thing sound entirely natural (LFM, p. 187).

Wittgenstein wants to dispel the "infection" theory of the misuse of logic—i.e., if we allow one contradiction, then the entire structure of rational thought will come tumbling down. "Just as with tuberculosis: one suspects nothing and one day one is dead. So one also thinks: one day the hidden contradiction could perhaps appear and then the catastrophe is at hand" (WK, p. 120). "But it is vitally important to see that a contradiction is not a germ which shows a general illness" (LFM, p. 211). Indeed, a "healthy" person may be "filled with contradictions." Some contradictions are totally harmless and do not upset the cognitive homeostatis of our lives. We *normally* exclude contradiction and *normally* do not give it any meaning, because "recognizing the law of contradiction . . . [is] acting in a certain way we call 'rational' " (LFM, p. 201).

We must conclude that textual analysis does indeed support the thesis that Wittgenstein has joined the existential phenomenologists in Hegel's program of a "expanded reason," a dynamic rationality, which is subject to the conditions of history and society. Wittgenstein's concept of *Übersicht* takes on an even more Hegelian aura if R. J. Fogelin is correct in claiming that an *Übersicht* is a way of understanding identity-in-difference. E. T. Gendlin argues that Austin follows Wittgenstein and the phenomenologists in maintaining that the grounds for explication "are founded neither on formal logic nor on observed relationships.

They are based on an 'implicit' knowledge (if we call that 'knowledge'): on what is 'implicit' in experiencing, living, and acting in situation."[18] The foundations of logic are therefore pre-epistemological: they are found deep in our nature, in our needs, our purposes, and our forms of life. Mathematics, and therefore logic, is an "anthropological phenomenon," it is invention and not discovery (RFM, pp. 180, 47). The laws of logic are the expression of thinking habits (RFM, p. 41), and as long as we are in the habit of not thinking otherwise, then we will continue to infer as we do, and to hold some concepts as *a priori* and others as empirical (RFM, p. 45).

MERLEAU-PONTY AND "DYNAMIC" RATIONALITY

For students of philosophy (like myself) who have come to Husserl's phenomenology through the "back door," i.e., from Heidegger, Sartre, and Merleau-Ponty, many passages from the *Crisis* read like existential phenomenology. Husserl is fighting a battle on two fronts: one against psychologism, which wanted to explain logic in terms of empirical laws, and one against logicism, whose Platonism and formalism made it difficult for one to see how logic could be related to ordinary experience. Merleau-Ponty believes that Husserl's view of logic was similar to Hegel's in that it was a "logic of content": "Instead of a logical organization of the facts coming from a form that is superimposed upon them, the very content of these facts is supposed to order itself spontaneously in a way that is thinkable" (PrP, p. 52). But Hegel's attempt at a logic of content fails, primarily because he doesn't really allow the content to guide him. As Merleau-Ponty states: ". . . . it finally turns out be a logic which is ruling over the development of the phenomena" (like logicism) instead of logic itself becoming phenomenological, i.e. descriptive (PrP, p. 52). Both Husserl and Wittgenstein insist on a phenomenological method that allows the content and its structure *to show itself as it is* without metaphysical presuppositions. In the *Tractatus* logical form shows itself, while in the *Investigations* it is forms of life that reveal themselves.

In the *Crisis* Husserl holds to a strictly descriptive reason when he speaks of a logic which precedes science and whose structures conform "purely descriptively to the life-world" (K, p. 135). Husserl sounds surprisingly Hegelian when he speaks of reason as the organizing principle of history: "the movement of reason to actualize itself through stages of development," or "*ratio* in its incessant movement to clarify itself" (K, p. 273g). But Paul Ricoeur warns us not to interpret the Husserl of the *Crisis* as a philosopher who has given into historicism after a long career devoted to its defeat. History is necessary for the actualization of reason, but reason *does not evolve* by "deriving sense from senselessness." Rather, it is the temporal self-actualization of an eternal and infinite identity of sense."[19]

We have emphasized all along that the later Wittgenstein turns to a *Weltanschauungsphilosophie* through his concepts of language-games and forms of life. In Husserl's "Philosophy as a Rigorous Science" it is Dilthey's historicism that must be rejected, and his belief, as C. O. Schrag puts it, that "the comprehension which yields a sense of the historical is a process of grasping a life-form within the concrete context in which the individual himself stands."[20] The existential phenomenologists, also under the influence of Dilthey's life-philosophy, make a similar turn away from orthodox phenomenology by merging the life-world and rationality. Husserl always strove to protect the "eternal identity of sense" from the exigencies of history and society; Wittgenstein and the existential phenomenologists concluded that this was not possible, even though it seemed to destroy logic and therefore make philosophy, as traditionally understood, impossible.

According to Merleau-Ponty the life-world already contains a "pre-existent Logos" that is not the one of traditional logic. No sophisticated demonstration is needed to see this logic because "we witness every minute the miracle of related experiences," and our life-world is "this network of relationships" (PP, p. xx). This is the "broad" reason we have defined: reason is the capacity to "put together" a world that makes sense. The reason why traditional philosophy has found it difficult to relate the world and reason is that it has insisted upon the "crystalline purity" of strict reason, a reason untouched by history and society.

Therefore, any life-world is a rational world, just as Wittgenstein claims that "everything descriptive of a language-game is a part of logic" (OC, §56). Similarly, Merleau-Ponty contends that "rationality is precisely measured by the experiences in which it is disclosed. To say that there exists rationality is to say that perspectives blend, perceptions confirm each other, a meaning emerges" (PP, p. xix). If we keep in mind that the "conditions for consciousness" are found in forms or styles of life, then Merleau-Ponty agrees with Wittgenstein about the nature of contradiction: "I wish only to point out that the accusation of contradiction is not decisive, if the acknowledged contradiction appears as the very condition of consciousness" (PrP, p. 19). If indeed a life-world is built on contradictions, then we must accept them as the givens.

Merleau-Ponty believes that the demand of the absolute rationality of logicism is "only a wish, a personal preference which should not be confused with philosophy" (PrP, p. 24). This is parallel to Wittgenstein's observation that the crystalline purity of the old logic was not the result of investigation but a requirement, something imposed from the outside on experience. Experience itself shows a dynamic rationality that conforms to new ways of viewing the world and knowing it. As Merleau-Ponty maintains: "It would be a very romantic way of showing one's love for reason to base its reign on the disavowal of acquired knowledge" (PrP, p. 24). Logicism is safe in the same way as abstinence in sex: it is empty and useless if we are to know the true depth of life's experiences. The old logic is closed and hermetically sealed; but Merleau-Ponty's "rationality is neither a total nor an immediate guarantee. It is somehow open, which is to say that it is menaced" (PrP, p. 23). New knowledge is gained only at a risk.

As we shall see in our final chapter, Wittgenstein and the existential phenomenologists converge on the question of a linguistic phenomenology. Therefore, the meaning of *lego* as "I say or speak" becomes relevant at this point. Many classical Greeks thought that the only way to bring order to our thoughts (and thus reflect on the order of the world) was to speak, preferably in dialogue. (The Christian *logos*, the order of the world, is also spoken.) Therefore a more appropriate translation of the famous Greek definition of humankind, "*zōon logon echon*" (traditionally "the rational animal"), is "those living beings who *speak* reason" (cf. SZ, pp. 25, 165). This essential identification of language and reason was started by the Greeks, reaffirmed by Cicero in the merging of *ratio* and *oratio* in *De Officiis*, and reborn in Schopenhauer and Mauthner in the 19th Century. As Philip A. Hallie explains: "The Greek word *logos* and the logic that articulates its demands had to be translated by the Romans with the phrase *ratio et oratio*."[21] For Wittgenstein and the existential phenomenologists, philosophy's job is to investigate the ordinary "speaking-logic" of human beings in their own life-worlds. Heidegger declares that the "*saying* of Being, as of the destiny of truth, is the first law of thinking—not the rules of logic which can become rules only on the basis of the [spoken] law of Being" (BH, p. 241, my emphasis). Heidegger's cryptic "laws of Being" translates as the "existentials," the necessary conditions that make life in a *Dasein*-world possible.

Heidegger believes that Aristotle was on the track of a true phenomenological logic, but his theory of judgment ultimately ends up ignoring the true dialogical (=existential) basis of *logos* as a putting together and taking apart in speech itself (cf. SZ, p. 159). Aristotle's dialectic, just like the later Platonic dialectic, is not dialogue, but a pure *noesis* that works itself out independently of experience. When Aristotle does connect logic with the world it is through the subject-predicate paradigm, whose ontological correlates are substance and its necessary and accidental qualities. A metaphysics of substance and a subject-predicate logic dominated Western philosophy until the time of Kant and Hegel, whose rejection of the doctrine of substance provided the basis for the metaphysics of experience of life-philosophy and its 20th Century heir, existential phenomenology. This movement joins with Kant and Hegel in the freeing of metaphysics from substance, and the liberation of grammar from traditional logic (cf. SZ, p. 165).

THE LIBERATION OF GRAMMAR FROM LOGIC

We have already seen that Wittgenstein wanted to separate questions of meaning and sense (grammar) from questions of true and false judgments. In the *Philosophical Grammar* Wittgenstein argues that the subject-predicate paradigm does not generate one normative logical form, but "countless different logical forms" (PG, p. 205). The traditional subject-predicate model also leads us astray ontologically, because "the phrase 'bearer of a property' . . . conveys a completely wrong— an impossible—picture" (PG, p. 205). Wittgenstein's notion of language-games, which imagines a plurality of games generating just as many logical forms, "destroys grammatical prejudices and makes it possible for us to see the use of a word as it really is" (PG, p. 212). In other words, the analysis of language-games is Wittgenstein's tool for liberating grammar from traditional logic.

During the early modern period Aristotle's theory of judgment was merged with another methodological bias, *viz.*, the priority of epistemology. In order for humans to make sense and judge assertions to be true, they first have to know, clearly and distinctly, the concepts they are using and the rules of judgment. Wittgenstein's *On Certainty* is a radical critique of this philosophical method. Judging is not based on explicit knowledge, but on cultural conditioning and upbringing: "We do not learn the practice of making empirical judgment by learning rules: we are taught judgments and their connection with other judgments" (OC, §140). A person "must already judge in conformity with" other people, with those whom the person shares a *Weltbild* (OC, §§156, 162). If people are to use language to communicate, there must *already* be a pre-epistemological agreement in judgments (cf. PI, §242).

As we have seen the fundamental propositions of one's *Weltbild* (e.g., "The world exists and has had a long history") are not knowledge strictly speaking, but the *grounds* for one knowing anything at all (e.g., "Napoleon lost at Waterloo"). For Wittgenstein philosophy must return to pre-epistemological beginnings in the same way that Heidegger claims that the so-called epistemological problem "must be taken back ... into the existential analytic of *Dasein*" (SZ, p. 208). Henry LeRoy Finch's apt phrase has already been used: "making sense is not based upon knowing, but rather knowing itself must make sense."[22] In other words, knowledge and logic can never be separated from living in a "world" in a certain way, putting it together (*lego*) according to specific language-games and forms of life.

In 1943 Merleau-Ponty's critics accused him of "Protagoreanism," and favored a more traditional "intellectualism" to guard against the relativistic dangers of a phenomenology of perception. But Merleau-Ponty warns that pure reason will not necessarily clarify confused percepts. One would simply trade the ambiguities of a life-world for the antinomies of pure reason, and end up not doing justice to human experience at all (PrP, p. 18). As Merleau-Ponty states:

> The perceived world is the always presupposed foundation of all rationality, all value and all existence. This thesis does not destroy either rationality or the absolute. It only tries to bring them down to earth (PrP, p. 13).

Compare this with Wittgenstein:

> For the crystalline purity of logic [has got us] on to slippery ice where there is no friction and so in a certain sense the conditions are ideal, but also, just because of that, we are unable to walk. We want to walk; so we need *friction*. Back to the rough ground (PI, §107).

The existential phenomenologies of both Merleau-Ponty and Wittgenstein eschew clear and simple language-games which ignore friction and air resistance (PI, §130); their goals are to lead philosophy back to the rough ground of a life-world, a world conditioned by history and society. As the Norwegian Wittgensteinian Viggo Rossvaer states: "Wittgenstein's most important insight is that logic must accommodate itself with the world and not the world to logic."[23] Merleau-Ponty contends that "the phenomenon of truth . . . is known only through the praxis which *creates* it" and that "truth is another name for [cultural] sedimentation" (S, p. 96). Since Merleau-Ponty believes in a universal life-world whose common bond is perception, the *logos* of this world would be passive, while the cultural sediments would be active in their initiation but passive as tradition.

There is one important qualification to make about Wittgenstein's historicism which distinguishes him from more Hegelian life-philosophers and existential phenomenologists. For Wittgenstein reason and logic *do not evolve*; it is not even correct to say that they change. As Mauthner observed, each culture recognizes only one, unalterable logic. Therefore one life-world does not evolve into another as in the Hegelian progressive view of the history of Spirit; rather, one world-picture is replaced by another. (If this is true, then Wittgenstein's river metaphor is very misleading in its strong implication that one world-picture flows into another.) For example, if G. E. Moore is confronted with a tribe whose king claims that the world began with his coronation, Moore must persuade the king to take on Moore's world-picture (cf. OC, §262). There is no middle way between competing world-views; there is no historical progression from a more primitive one to a "modern" one. One is "converted" (or born into) a world-view, and it then becomes the "background against which I distinguish between true and false" (OC, §94).

Therefore, we must contrast those like Hegel who would synthesize all world-views in a universal *logos* with those like Wittgenstein and Spengler who wish to simply reveal the plurality of cultural *logoi*. For Spengler other cultures speak a "different language [-game], for other men there are different truths" (DW I, p. 25), but those within their own "*Weltbild* recognize only one logic, one world, and one truth (DW I, p. 99). Spengler distinguishes between an "organic" logic, which is instinctive, temporal, and true to life, and an "inorganic" logic, which is cognitive, atemporal, and based on the concept of lifeless extension (DW I, p. 117). Georg Simmel concurs in this life-philosophical view of logic by insisting that truth is not independent from life and by offering the following test: "If it is true it will preserve and support our life; if it is an error, it will lead us into ruin."[24] Heidegger claims to have used this test with regard to modern technology and discovered that technology has failed miserably.

This study so far has been almost exclusively exposition and has yet to take any critical distance from what are obviously some controversial views. One can see that phenomenology's insistence on a strictly descriptive methodology has led to the broad, dynamic rationality of Wittgenstein and the existential phenomenologists. But one crucial question remains: If philosophy is restricted to description and is barred from explanation or metaphysical speculation, does not description itself have to follow prescribed rules? If the existential phenomenologist is describing the form and structure of a life-world, is she not obligated to at least follow the law of non-contradiction? Is it possible, for example, to describe an orthodox Christian life-world as believing that Jesus is both a man-God and not a man-God? Are not self-contradictory descriptions illegitimate, and are not Wittgenstein and existential phenomenology forced back into some form of traditional logic? If we are to communicate at all, it appears that there must be non-dynamic rules for description that are not subject to society and history. Commentators have not been uncognizant of this problem in Wittgenstein. Specifically, Hilary Putnam maintains that a "form of life can never make a set of inconsistent axioms true,"[25] and that mathematical consistency always remains an objective fact. More generally I. M. Bochenski recognizes that "there are systems in which the principle of contradiction does not hold, but these systems must themselves be constructed without contradictions. . . ."[26]

In his book on the philosophy of history Patrick Gardiner rejects Dilthey's philosophy because he thinks that Dilthey is a very poor logician. But the life-philosopher can always rejoin by saying that life itself is a poor logician. Wittgenstein and the existential phenomenologists agree with all the life-philosophers on this basic point. These philosophers (plus some pragmatists) offer a radical alternative to traditional, as well as contemporary philosophical methods, which all at least agree in a self-justifying reason and a prescriptive logic. These methodologies believe in philosophical progress towards a common truth, and more or less continue the Cartesian search for clear and distinct ideas. Wittgenstein and the existential phenomenologists find no such clarity and precision in life and agree with Simmel that "life is the antithesis of form, and since only that which is somehow formed can be conceptually described, the concept of life cannot be freed from logical imprecision."[27] This means that philosophical methods based on Descartes and contemporary analysis cannot do justice to life itself. If philosophy cannot do that, then philosophy has surely betrayed itself.

10. Language and Hermeneutic

Only as a speaking being is a human human.

—*Heidegger (US, p. 11)*

[Outside of language] I cannot recognize the human in the human.

—*Wittgenstein (VB, p. 11)*

Man only becomes wholly man when he has acquired language.

—*Spengler (DW I, p. 80)*

Where word breaks off no thing may be.

—*Stefan George,* Das Wort

The limits of language...*mean the limits of* my *world.*

—*Wittgenstein (T, 5.62)*

Only where there is language is there world.

—*Heidegger (HD, p. 276)*

If we surrender the reins to language and not to life, *then the problems of philosophy arise.*

—*Wittgenstein (213, p. 521)*

[Hermeneutical Circle]: I cannot use language to get outside of language.
—*Wittgenstein (PR, p. 54)*

Rational thought is interpretation *in accordance with a scheme that we cannot throw off.*

—*Nietzsche*[1]

SEMANTIC HOLISM

Critics might complain that I have overlooked Gottlob Frege in my probing of Wittgenstein's intellectual background. Christopher Coope, *et al.*, believe that "the most important single·influence on Wittgenstein was Frege, and that this is true of the late as well as of the early work. . . ."[2] In his book *Wittgensteins Philosophische Grammatik*, Martin Lang agrees with me that Wittgenstein must be interpreted in terms of his continental background—that, for example, Wittgenstein is close to the "new" hermeneutic with his organic conception of language—but Lang also believes that Frege is the key to understanding Wittgenstein.[3] It is true that Wittgenstein did read most of Frege and recognized him as a "great thinker" (LFM, p. 144). His students remember that of the few books he kept in his quarters, a book of Frege and a dialogue of Plato were frequently those present. Like Husserl, Wittgenstein probably learned his anti-psychologism from Frege.

If we, however, begin to make an inventory of Fregean references, the points at which Wittgenstein disagrees with Frege overwhelm us. He was initially attracted to Frege's logic and realism in the *Tractatus*, but rejected them in the later works. Sometime between 1914 and 1918 Wittgenstein began to use something akin to Husserl's definition of *Sinn* and *Bedeutung* and not, significantly enough, Frege's. In the *Philosophical Grammar* Wittgenstein charges that Frege never was able to get beyond a subject-predicate logic (PG, p. 205; cf. 208, p. 17). In his 1939 lectures on mathematics he is ambivalent about Frege. At one point he says that "Frege made an enormous amount clear" (LFM, p. 168), but in an adjacent passage he says that what Russell and Frege did is "terrible muddle" and a "mass of confusions," partially because of Russell's symbolism (LFM, p. 167).

As we have seen, Wittgenstein cannot tolerate Frege's attempt at making logic into some form of "intellectual physics"; rather, he proposes a plurality of logics and accepts our "broad" reason, which is the "new kind of madness" of which Frege warned. Furthermore, he rejects the Fregean idea that logic can become the basis for a philosophy of mathematics. Indeed, Wittgenstein generally preferred Brouwer on the philosophy of mathematics. He liked Brouwer's attack on logic, found Brouwer's voluntarism compatible with his own, and agreed with him about the synthetic nature of arithmetic propositions. (Frege and Husserl thought they were analytic.) In addition, Frege chose the apriority of space while Wittgenstein and Brouwer chose the apriority of time. But the very thesis which Wittgenstein rejects in Brouwer is one which he enthusiastically endorses in Frege: holism, particularly in the form of "semantic" holism.

Frege's holistic dictum that "a word has a meaning only in the context of a sentence" is affirmed explicitly in both the *Tractatus* and the *Investigations* (T, 3.3; PI, §49). As Hacker has shown in his brilliant article "Semantic Holism: Frege and Wittgenstein," Frege propounded the holistic dictum as a way to preclude the psychologism of semantic atomism. Sense and meaning, unlike the subjective representations of psychologism, are "public, communicable, and fixed."[4] This attack on psychologism and the affirmation of the community of meaning are positions compatible with both Wittgenstein and the phenomenologists, although both ultimately reject that sense is eternally "fixed." But it takes some time for Wittgenstein to realize the full implications of a public *Sinn*, and only after he had critically assessed his own earlier Fregean tendencies, could he expand the holistic dictum far beyond what Frege himself intended. Only in the later period does Wittgenstein turn away, as Hacker explains, from "Fregean foundations in the calculus model, the truth-conditional principle, and mathematical analogy, to the more fundamental grounds of understanding, speech, and communication."[5]

To be sure, the basic Fregean insight remains: i.e., understanding always assumes an entire sentence. A sentence is like a move in chess: there is no such thing as a "half-sentence" in the same way that a knight cannot take a "half-move" (cf. 213, p. 1). Furthermore, the move (=sentence) has sense only within the context of the game. The holistic dictum is considerably expanded: not only is a sentence necessary for a word to have meaning, an entire language-world is necessary for a sentence to have sense. "To understand a sentence means to understand a language" (PI, §199; cf. BB, p. 5). The broader holistic dictum was already formulated and linked to the idea of meaning as use in the early 1930s. In a 1930 lecture he said: "A word only has meaning in a grammatical system, and what characterizes it is the way in which it is used (L 1, p. 36). A comment in a 1931 lecture gives us a clue to the enigmatic "meaning is a physiognomy" (PI, §568): "The word carries its meaning with it; it has a grammatical body behind it, so to speak" (L 1, p. 59). These insights allow Wittgenstein to merge his *Sprachphilosophie* with his *Lebensphilosophie*, for "only in the stream of thought and life do words have meaning" (Z, §173).

More important than Wittgenstein's expansion of Frege's holistic dictum, which Hacker claims is already implicit in Frege, are more fundamental differences. First, Wittgenstein gives up the determinacy of meaning, which is, in both Frege and the *Tractatus,* founded upon an ontology of metaphysical simples. Second, Wittgenstein's doctrine of intentionality, already discussed in Chapter Seven, clashes with Frege's claim that there is an external relation between an assertation and what might fulfill it. For Frege, as for Russell and Richards, there is a third "thing" that gets added in the process, e.g., the sensation that what we expected has indeed occurred. For Wittgenstein, however, there is an internal relation between, as Hacker phrases it, "the sense of a sentence and its assertability, or more generally, between its meaning and its use."[6]

THE FUSION OF *SPRACHPHILOSOPHIE* AND *LEBENSPHILOSOPHIE*

We have already mentioned the fact that when G. E. Moore sat in on Wittgenstein's lectures in the early thirties, he was quite critical of what was said, especially Wittgenstein's peculiar use of the word "grammar." Moore was so concerned about Wittgenstein's misuse of the term that he actually wrote up a small paper which articulated his criticisms. Sometime during 1931–32 Moore read the paper to Wittgenstein's class. In it was a comparison between two sentences: "Three men was [*sic*] working" and "Different colors can be in the same place in a visual field at the same time." Moore claims that the first obviously involves a violation of grammatical rules, but the second, even if sense-less, does not. Therefore, it makes no sense to say that the second sentence has anything to do with grammar (L 1, p. 97). Moore implies that the term "grammar" ought to be restricted to the rules of syntactical connection.

In his reply Wittgenstein admits that to call what he is doing "grammar" is to "express it badly," but he nonetheless goes on to defend his uncommon usage. He says that he is not worried about the agreement of verbs with their subjects because such mistakes are harmless. When he speaks of "grammar" it means that we are asking "Does it make any sense to say?" and if it doesn't make any sense, then it is a "vicious" violation of the rules of grammar. The violation is serious in the case of the color statement because it leads us to believe that two colors cannot be in the same place in the same way that two people cannot occupy the same chair (L 1, p. 98). This involves a fundamental confusion of physical and visual space, whose descriptions will obviously involve different grammars (cf. L 1, p. 69). The confusion between the physical and the phenomenal is one that phenomenologists have attempted to eradicate for a long time.

We have already made a case for the possibility that Wittgenstein's concept of grammar came from Husserl or early phenomenology in general. There is also always the possibility of Fritz Mauthner, who states that "I (like Luther) turned the whole of philosophy into grammar."[7] We have already excluded Richards and Ogden's *The Meaning of Meaning*, because Wittgenstein's use of the term is broader and antedates the appearance of this book by at least twelve years. With such an uncommon usage, a dictionary source seems highly unlikely, but among the definitions of "grammar" in the *Oxford English Dictionary* there is this one: "the fundamental principles or rules of an art or science." Under this definition we find such uses as "a small geographical grammar," "the grammar of entomology," and the "grammar of painting." The idea of grammar being a set of rules or a description of a thing's formal structure is very close to what Wittgenstein seems to have in mind.

The later works abound with the thesis that "meaning is use" and that the grammar of a word is the way in which it is used. "Grammar describes the use of words in the language" (PG, p. 60); or, "when you say 'suppose I believe . . .' you are presupposing the whole grammar of the words 'to believe,' the ordinary use, of which you are master" (PI, p. 192). But Wittgenstein's grammar goes beyond words, phrases, and sentences. When he talks about "the temporal character of facts" manifesting themselves grammatically (PG, p. 215), "the grammar of mental states" (PG, p. 82), or the grammar of color, sound, and number (PR, p. 53), then it seems that we have gone beyond linguistic analysis *per se* to a general description of the formal structures of phenomena and life itself. In 1932 he told his students that to multiply or to fix the length of the meter is to follow a rule of grammar (L 1, p. 92), which is generalized as the "rules of grammar by which we act and operate" (PG, p. 110). Therefore, one could confidently infer that *any* rule is a rule of "grammar."

Although many have been confused or at least uneasy about Wittgenstein's "grammar," some commentators have finally seen the broad sense in which it is used. Although Hacker believes that Wittgenstein is just "lax" when he uses "grammar" extralinguistically, he nonetheless admits that grammar involves investigating *all Darstellungsformen*.[8] Max Black recognizes that Wittgenstein's grammar is "vastly more liberal" than mere syntactical rules, but doubts whether this "capacious view" will be very illuminating.[9] Finch also realizes that Wittgenstein's grammar, which essentially includes all the forms of our *Weltbild*, "has a vastly extended meaning for [Wittgenstein], a meaning far wider than the ordinary one. Grammar (and this point has to be emphasized) is what replaces metaphysics and epistemology as the core of philosophy."[10] Since Wittgenstein equates grammar with phenomenology, and since the phenomenologists replace metaphysics and epistemology with their discipline, we may conclude that Wittgenstein's philosophical grammar is a general phenomenology of the basic structures of experience. Here are Wittgenstein's own words: "Thus, phenomenology would be the grammar of the description of those facts on which physics [or any other science] builds its theories" (PR, p. 51).

There are a number of commentators, especially Finch, who, have written to me about previous drafts of this work, who believe that we must be very careful to distinguish a phenomenology of experience from Wittgenstein's linguistic phenomenology. Finch is especially concerned about implying in any way that Wittgenstein believes, as Husserl does, that one can have a direct experience of essences apart from language. Finch's reservations are well founded, but my fear is that we will then set up a false dichotomy between language and experience, which does not exist either in Wittgenstein or existential phenomenology. When Don Ihde argues that "Husserl reduced things to transcendental experience; [but] Wittgenstein reduces things to linguistic usages,"[11] he is missing a major factor in Wittgenstein's concept of language-games: *viz.*, that they are founded on forms of life. As we have argued, forms of life are cultural, institutional, the crystallization of human actions, and serve as the equivalent of Husserl's "transcendental experience."

This fundamental ambiguity between "how we do it" and "how we say it" is a troublesome equivocation only if we insist that there is only an either/or choice between them, and that a linguistic phenomenology excludes a phenomenology of experience and vice versa. There is no question that Wittgenstein continued to believe that the "limits of *language* ... mean the limits of *my* world" (T, 5.62), and that he always believed that there is no direct extra-linguistic access to reality. In addition, he believed in the confines of the "hermeneutical circle"—that "I cannot use language to get outside of language" (PR, p. 54). But we must also keep in mind that Wittgenstein has a very broad definition of language. Some of his language-games are mostly action and few words; indeed, some of the examples of language-games such as "constructing an object from a description" and "solving a problem in practical arithmetic" (PI, §23), do not have to involve words at all. Wittgenstein's semantic holism must inevitably lead us to the co-extension of language and experience, for remember that he calls the "whole, consisting of language and the actions into which it is woven, the 'language-game' " (PI, §7).

This idea that "we are still using language (even if not *words*)" (L 1, p. 39) has a parallel in Merleau-Ponty and Heidegger. Heidegger believes that all art is essentially poetry (UK, p. 184), and this is simply the result of the merging of experience and language in his philosophy. For Merleau-Ponty all perception, and all action connected with it, including all uses of the human body, is a form of "primordial expression" (S, p. 67). For example, when a child learns a language, she primarily learns a "structure of conduct" (PrP, p. 99). William Lawhead, therefore, proposes a common definition of language for Wittgenstein and Merleau-Ponty: " 'Language' refers to all the various expressions and form-making activities through which persons project themselves toward the world in order to appropriate it, orient themselves toward it, and interact with the human community in ways that are personally and intersubjectively meaningful."[12] One might object that this identification of language and experience has the result of dissolving linguistic analysis into a philosophy of experience. But at least it has the advantage of preventing linguistic analysis from ignoring the life-world behind the mere words (cf. PE, p. 296). As Spiegelberg states: "Everywhere Wittgenstein tries to explore what goes on in our experience (*Erlebnis*), not merely to study the grammatical structure of the expressions we use in talking about it."[13] Therefore, when we said earlier that for Wittgenstein *Lebensphilosophie* takes precedence over *Sprachphilosophie*, the latter was being referred to in this narrow sense.

THE CRITIQUE OF ORDINARY LANGUAGE

Before turning to the linguistic philosophy of the existential phenomenologists, we must clarify the tension between an ideal language and ordinary language that we find in Wittgenstein's middle period. Right at the beginning of the *Philosophical Remarks* he states that his goal is no longer a "phenomenological language," or a "primary" language as he once called it. He now wants to concentrate on *our* language, and to separate the essential from the nonessential (PR, p. 51). This seems to indicate a turn away from the ideal language of the *Tractatus* to the ordinary language of the later period. At the same time, however, he is not just leaving language as he finds it, but is using a phenomenological reduction to separate the essential from the nonessential. On the very same page, where he began by rejecting phenomenological language, he proceeds to resurrect it. In order to separate out the essences, and to recognize "which parts of our language are wheels turning idly," we must *construct* a phenomenological language. In other words, in order to critique *our* language—i.e., ordinary language—we must devise a new language, the language of the phenomenological reductions.

This troublesome equivocation is found in conversations with Waismann that took place simultaneously with the writing of the *Remarks*. Here he states that he had earlier believed that in addition to ordinary language (*Umgangssprache*), there was a "primary" language that expressed "what we really know, *viz. Phänomene*" (WK, p. 45). But he makes it clear here at least that this view is mistaken and introduces a phrase which is the watchword for *The Blue Book* and the *Investigations*: ordinary language is in perfect order and we do not need any other language to free ourselves from philosophical difficulties. In Chapter V of the *Remarks* he repeats his disavowal of any distinction between ordinary and primary language. But he still compromises his position considerably by contending that since ordinary language is not always impartial, i.e., it sometimes expresses "a certain emotional overtone which doesn't belong to the essence of the phenomena," that an absolutely impartial phenomenological language would be necessary to critique ordinary language (PR, p. 84).

In other discussions he strongly implies that since ordinary language presupposes an uncritical physicalism, it is not adequate for revealing the phenomena themselves (PR, p. 98). Wittgenstein proposes that "we need a way of speaking with which we can represent the phenomena of visual space, isolated as such" (PR, p. 98). This project is integral to his general phenomenological program in the middle period, in which separate grammars of space, time, color, sound, etc. would be investigated in terms of their own *a priori* structures. It is therefore a "phenomenological language [that] isolates visual space and what goes on in it from everything else" (PR, p. 103). In contemporaneous manuscript material which I have not been able to verify, Spiegelberg has found a five-page discussion of "phenomenological language," which repeats for the most part the material of the *Remarks* except for the claim that "ordinary language is to some extent phenomenological though it does not allow for a separation of sense fields as does the phenomenological language."[14]

The critique of ordinary language continues in his discussion of Mach in Chapter XX of the *Remarks*. Here he chides Mach for following the impulses of ordinary language, which lead us to think that we can make a picture of our visual field. For Wittgenstein this shows a confusion between "physical and phenomenological language" (PR, p. 267). As other phenomenologists have shown, there is a distinct difference between how our visual field really does appear to us and how we have come to think that it does. The critical distance of the phenomenological reduction shows us "what we really know" and what we are really able to do. In the Big Typescript Wittgenstein describes a phenomenological language as one which gives a direct description of immediate experience without any hypothetical additions. As Husserl discovered, and as Wittgenstein continually implies in the middle period, ordinary language is burdened by one pervasive hypothetical addition: the naive physicalism of the "natural standpoint."

Wittgenstein finished the Big Typescript in 1933—the same year that he began dictating *The Blue Book* to his students. The mystery of the equivocation of ordinary and phenomenological language is not so much solved as it is deepened by the fact that *The Blue Book* contains some of the most enthusiastic defenses of ordinary language, a position that will remain for the rest of his life. For some reason the ambitious phenomenological program of 1930–33 is literally given up overnight. Although we continue to hear about grammar, it is the grammar of ordinary language, not primary language. And although we have argued that the grammar of the late period is still a phenomenology—a full life-world phenomenology—the attempt at isolating various grammars is precipitiously dropped. Furthermore, some commentators claim that the critique of the implicit naturalism of ordinary language is also abandoned; and if this is so, then one of the essential ingredients of any genuine phenomenology of language is missing.

In his article, "Husserl and Wittgenstein on Language," Paul Ricoeur contends that while the Tractarian view of language was too pure and alienated from life, the account of language in the later works is too close to life. The phenomenological reduction, which is so important in establishing an impartial idiom for phenomenological "seeing," is not present and therefore Wittgenstein's later philosophy does not qualify as phenomenology in any genuine sense. In a response to Ricoeur, Robert Arrington has shown that Ricoeur has overlooked some very important methodological assumptions of the *Investigations*. Ricoeur contrasts a view of language rooted in the "natural attitude" with Husserl's view of language "as a system of meanings intended and constituted by a consciousness free from the natural, causal influences of the world of fact."[15] Arrington answers Ricoeur with some of the same points that we have already established in our study: that Wittgenstein does have a theory of constitution and intentionality, that language-games are indeed "systems of meanings," that language is founded on forms of life which are transcendental conditions for experience, and that Wittgenstein has definitely left the natural standpoint in his pervasive acausalism and transcendentalism. As we have emphasized before, one does not necessarily give up the transcendental attitude by locating the transcendental conditions squarely in the life-world itself.

This also means that Wittgenstein, contrary to common conception, has not given up completely the critique of ordinary language that he proposed in his middle period. Wittgenstein is no doubt correct that the concept of time becomes a problem only when philosophers and physicists tear it out of the context of our ordinary ways of using "time" words. Nevertheless, a critical distance must still be established between ourselves and ordinary speech if such speech perpetuates and reinforces the common myths of language as the clothing of internal thought, of minds as separate from bodies, of private languages as intelligible, etc. With his idea of "depth" grammar Wittgenstein is admitting that the surface syntax of common parlance sometimes misleads us about true semantic meaning. Wittgenstein admits that ordinary language can "cramp" our mind, because it "holds [it] rigidly in one position," and that unconventional notation may help to alleviate such cramps (BB, p. 59). In his work John Austin has developed the implications of this Wittgensteinian thesis, and has declared that ordinary language has the first word to be sure, but not the last word. James Marsh sums up our argument beautifully:

> In this use of grammar, therefore, Wittgenstein achieves a critical transcendence of ordinary language which he himself often does not acknowledge. Wittgenstein's ordinary language is not the ordinary language of the man in the street. Such transcendence is necessary because our ordinary, actual usage covers up those aspects of things that remain most hidden because of their familiarity. Such grammar, both in its distance from the givens of the actual usage and its universality, seems to approximate the phenomenological notion of essence. Because Wittgenstein is inconsistent on this issue, phenomenology has the edge in the argument here.[17]

So, despite Wittgenstein's dictum "look and see" (PI, §66), we must also say "look, see, and think." Otherwise it would be true, as people like Brand Blanshard charge, that Wittgenstein has entirely destroyed philosophy.

In his article, "Heidegger and Wittgenstein on the Question of Ordinary Language," Thomas A. Fay reminds us that Heidegger is not even willing to let ordinary language have the first word. Fay is certainly correct in pointing out that Heidegger makes a firm distinction between genuine discourse, *Rede*, and *Gerede*, the ordinary talk ("chatter") of inauthentic humans. But we have argued that Wittgenstein's idea of depth grammar is a way of criticizing misleading "chatter," and one might propose a parallel between this depth grammar and Heidegger's *Rede*. After all, language as depth grammar is a transcendental form of life, just as *Rede* is an existential, which we have argued is equivalent to a Wittgensteinian *Lebensform*. The temptation to draw a comparison between Heidegger's "idle chatter" and Wittgenstein's "idling" of language is thwarted by a good observation by Karsten Harries: "When Wittgenstein likens language to an engine idling (PI, §132), he thinks of language which no longer functions as part of a language-game. . . . When Heidegger speaks of 'idle talk,' he thinks of language which does function as part of such a language-game which . . . is taken for granted."[18]

As we saw above, Wittgenstein proposes that when our mind is cramped by the rigidity of ordinary language, it may be relieved by the use of a new "notation," or a new language-game. Harries' strongest comparative point between Heidegger and Wittgenstein is the analogy between "inventing" a language-game (PI, §492) and Heidegger's idea of *Dichtung*. New language-games are certainly possible (PI, §23), they are "spontaneous, specific" (PI, p. 224), and they "provide a new way of looking at things" (PI, §§400–1). The poem then is a language-game which the poet plays with his readers: it has its own structure and its own "logic." The readers have to follow its "rules" if the aesthetic experience is to be consummated. As Harries declares: "This suggests that the establishment of a language-game is, as Heidegger calls poetry, a 'free act' establishing a new way of being in the world."[19]

This common ground between Wittgenstein and Heidegger also contains a significant difference. Wittgenstein would agree with Heidegger that philosophical "language strikes the everyday understanding as strange if not insane" (IM, p. 9; cf. OC, §467), but Wittgenstein believes that this is generally a bad sign for philosophy. By contrast, Heidegger contends that philosophy must criticize everyday (=inauthentic) understanding at every turn: "It is the very nature of philosophy never to make things easier but only more difficult. . . . It is the authentic function of philosophy to challenge historical *Dasein* . . . (EM, p. 9). Although Wittgenstein believes that new language-games, even poetic ones, can come into existence, he does not believe (except for hints at PI, §531) that philosophy can act in the same way as poetry in creating a "philosophical" language-game. He does allow us to correct some of the common errors of *Gerede*, but he would never declare a complete linguistic disaster; or as Arrington puts it: "There can be no suspicion of a [general] linguistic predicament."[20] But this is precisely what Heidegger believes, and Fay is correct in contrasting Heidegger and Wittgenstein on this crucial point. Therefore, one might say that not only is Wittgenstein's phenomenological program not very ambitious, it is morally and politically irresponsible as well.

Taking Heidegger as his lead, Fay is concerned that if we more or less exempt language-games and forms of life from thorough-going criticism, this could inevitably lead to reactionary political views of the most destructive sort. If a Wittgensteinian racist were to support his bigotry by saying "This is simply what I and my friends do," then the liberal Wittgensteinian has absolutely no recourse. (Note how impotent our "broad" descriptive reason is when it comes to trying to enforce an "ought.") The Wittgensteinian philosopher, whose job is simply to "note" language-games, is also in no position to morally judge. Fay is not the first commentator to see the reactionary implications of Wittgenstein's philosophy,[21] and signs of it are evident in his own life. Although he was known as a "left-winger" by the people of Southern Austria where he taught primary school, this was only because of his association with the school reform movement of the Austrian Social Democrats. His desire to visit Russia was probably more out of his love for Tolstoy than it was for the Russian Revolution. Support for Fay's thesis is found in Wittgenstein's completely uncritical support of Britain's war effort and his absolute disdain for his English colleagues, who, although they believed in the evil of Nazi Germany, still took a certain critical distance from the whole affair.

Even though I believe that Fay's thesis is tenable, there are some considerations which would qualify it in important respects. Even though it is clear that Heidegger was a "passive" Nazi in his 18-month tenure as the president of the University of Freiburg, he nonetheless signed all of the official memos "Heil Hitler" and fulfilled his duties without protest. So at least for a period, Heidegger did conform loyally to the current language-games and forms of life. One might then ask: What is the ultimate difference between "serving Being" and "serving" one's given forms of life? Fay criticizes Wittgenstein's view of language as being too "instrumental," but this is really not correct. We do not use language because it is useful, but simply because it is used. Therefore, it is our duty to "serve" language and the life-world it expresses. The famous *"Die Sprache spricht"* of Heidegger's *On the Way to Language* is indeed quite compatible with Wittgenstein's views. Language "speaks" and that is that. We should not try to dominate it; we should not try to improve it; we simply follow it. Therefore, one can also draw reactionary implications from Heidegger's philosophy of language. Fulfilling one's duties as a Nazi university president is not what one would characterize as "challenging historical *Dasein*."

"MOST DANGEROUS OF POSSESSIONS"

In his book on Wittgenstein and Heidegger, George F. Sefler summarizes Heidegger's linguistic phenomenology most succinctly: "Man's access to Being is linguistic. When Heidegger speaks of man's pre-predicative encounter with Being, this encounter is *not* pre-linguistic."[22] Early in his career Heidegger was dealing with philosophical grammar. His *"Habilitationsschrift"* of 1916, entitled *Die Kategorien- und Bedeutungslehre des Duns Scotus,* is a study of the medieval *"grammatica speculativa"* from the standpoint of Husserl's *Logical Investigations.* Although Scotus remains squarely within the tradition of a substance metaphysics, Heidegger shows that he nevertheless anticipates the doctrine of intentionality and the distinction between questions of sense and truth-falsity. In his detailed article on Heidegger's second book, John D. Caputo states that there are *"a priori* rules inherent in the modes of signification (*Bedeutung*) which dictate the order expressions are to follow if they are to make sense. These laws do not have a 'truth-value' but merely a 'syntactical value.' "[23]

In his interpretation of Scotus, Heidegger is definitely following Husserl, who in turn, as we have conjectured, might have influenced Wittgenstein's philosophical grammar. A transcendental grammar continues to be a principal concern of *Being and Time*: "We must inquire into the basic forms in which it is possible to articulate anything understandable" (SZ, p. 166). Like Wittgenstein, Heidegger believes that a genuine *Bedeutungslehre* will not come out of comparative linguistics or any other empirical science. He is not interested in the truth or falsity of empirical propositions, but only in the conditions that make language and a world possible (SZ, p. 162).

In the *Dasein*-analysis Heidegger discusses three basic existentials: state-of-mind, understanding, and discourse. The central importance of discourse can be seen in that "state-of-mind and understanding are characterized equiprimordially by discourse" (SZ, p. 133). Discourse is the formal framework for the way in which language is actually used and spoken; it is the "articulation of intelligibility" (SZ, p. 161). Heidegger observes that the Greeks had no word for language as such: they used instead the word "*logos*," which, as we have seen, comes from the verb "*lego*" meaning "to say." Heidegger therefore retranslates the famous Greek definition of humankind, "*zōon logon echon*" (traditionally "the rational animal") as "that living thing whose Being is essentially determined by the potentiality for discourse (*Redenkönnen*)" (SZ, p. 25).

Wittgenstein also believes that the unique characteristic of human beings is that they are the only animals that talk. "It is sometimes said that animals do not talk because they lack the mental capacity. And this means: 'they do not think, and that is why they do not talk.' But—they simply do not talk" (PI, §25). He hints that animals may have primitive forms of language, but like Heidegger, he believes that humans are unique in being able to articulate meanings and to be aware that they have done so. Both thinkers believe that special forms of existence accrue to beings that speak: forms of life or existentials. Because they can talk human beings can *then* be sincere, pretend, grieve, and be joyous.

Like Wittgenstein, Heidegger believes that the origin of meaning is not words or sentences, but a *Lebenswelt*. He does not follow Wittgenstein's strict distinction between the meaning *(Bedeutung)* of words and the sense *(Sinn)* of sentences, but he too would agree that neither *Bedeutung* nor *Sinn* are possible outside of an *Umgebung*. We have already used Wittgenstein's example of the meaning of the word "hope"—there will be as many meanings as there are situations. Both agree that "word-things do not get supplied with meanings" through ostensive definition (SZ, p. 161). Therefore, philosophy is wrong if it follows scientific linguistics in dividing up language into single words and phonemes. These are pure abstractions which do not lead us to the essence of language and the "life" that it embodies. The philosophies of language of both Wittgenstein and Heidegger are *existential* investigations as well as linguistic ones. Wittgenstein would certainly agree with Heidegger that an analysis of language cannot be abstract or piecemeal, but must be done in the context of life-in-the-world so that the "ontological-existential whole of the structure of *Rede*" can be grasped (SZ, p. 163).

Both Wittgenstein and Heidegger believe that the primary locus of intentionality is language itself. There is never an external relation between meaning-giving acts and meaningless matter; rather there is an internal relation, and intentionality itself constitutes this relation (see Chapter Seven). Heidegger scholar Jan Aler elaborates: "When listening attentively, one does not concentrate on the acoustic phenomenon but on what the other intends to say; one is not 'with' the linguistic phenomenon but 'with' the thing [intended]."[24] In addition, this means that language is not a system of word-things "present-to-hand" (*Vorhandenes*); rather, it is a relational system of internally related meanings "ready-at-hand" (*Zuhandenes*) (SZ, pp. 88, 161).

We must return to the question of ordinary language in order to qualify further the differences we proposed earlier between Heidegger and Wittgenstein. When Wittgenstein tells us that language may bewitch us (PI, §109), and warns us that giving into language may alienate us from life (213, p. 521), he is just as suspicious of ordinary language as Heidegger is. He would certainly agree with Heidegger's use of Hölderlin's claim that language is the "most dangerous of possessions" (HD, p. 270). Heidegger believes that we can forestall much of the misuse of language by examining the original meanings of words. We can thereby reach a more primordial means of expression of which every *Dasein* is capable.

Heidegger's emphasis on archaisms and etymologies is a means of stressing the fact that words have "lives," and that language can live again only if we are aware of the history of words. For example, research shows that the original word for "to say" in German (*sagan*) means "to show." So, original saying is always showing—an insight compatible with Wittgenstein's own views. Wittgenstein would also find confirmation of his semantic holism in a Heideggerian's observation that in some primitive language the basic linguistic unit is the sentence-word.[25] In the end, I do not see how Wittgenstein could have disagreed with the following statement from *Being and Time*:

> The ultimate business of philosophy is to preserve the *force of the most elemental words* in which *Dasein* expresses itself, and to keep the common unintelligibility which functions in turn as a source of pseudo-problems (SZ, p. 220).

Let us repeat a parallel statement from Wittgenstein: "If we surrender the reins to language and not to *life*, then the problems of philosophy arise" (213, p. 521). Although Wittgenstein himself does not engage in etymologies or a phenomenology of meaning-genesis, this Heideggerian assumption that the misuse of language causes the pseudo-problems of philosophy is right at the core of Wittgenstein's philosophy. Both Heidegger and Wittgenstein are acutely aware of the limits of language —"*Wo das Wort gebricht*"—(recall Wittgenstein's reference to Heidegger on this very point [WK, p. 68]), and both are very hesitant to say what is essentially unsayable. Wittgenstein simply prefers silence or showing, while Heidegger often offers poetry as our way to the unsayable.

MERLEAU-PONTY AND CREATIVE LANGUAGE

Merleau-Ponty continues Heidegger's search for a creative, philosophical speech that will be a critique of ordinary language, but will at the same time do justice to the fullness of lived experience. All three of our interlocutors agree that language can become ossified and stifle the movement of life itself. Cliches and other fixed meanings can obscure meaning and truth. Merleau-Ponty makes an important distinction between "verbalized" perception and "lived" perception— between what we think we see and what we really see if we look closely enough. In the following passage Merleau-Ponty reminds us of Heidegger: "Our view of man will remain superficial so long as we fail to go back to that origin, so long as we fail to find, beneath the chatter of words, the primordial silence . . ." (PP, p. 184).

Before we discuss the differences between Merleau-Ponty and Wittgenstein with regard to language, let us first lay out the common ground. Predictably enough, Merleau-Ponty rejects the concept of an ideal language and agrees with Wittgenstein that meaning is use: "I begin to understand the meaning of words through their place in a context of action, and by taking part in a communal life . . ." (PP, p. 179). Both thinkers also claim that the meaning of language is not exhausted in terms of its linguistic "atoms," and that language is not the "mere clothing of a thought which otherwise possesses itself in full clarity" (PrP, p. 8). In a significant sense language and thought are co-extensive, because, as Wittgenstein told his students in 1930, there is "no more direct way of reading thought than through language. Thought is not something hidden; it lies open to us" (L 1, p. 26).

Both Merleau-Ponty and Wittgenstein hold the revolutionary thesis that language dissolves the egocentric predicament; indeed, language is living proof of intersubjectivity. As Merleau-Ponty states: "Language leads us to a thought which is no longer ours alone, to a thought which is presumptively universal, though this is never the universality of a pure concept which would be identical for every mind" (PrP, p. 8). This means that there is no such thing as a private language, for "even solitary thought does not cease using the [intersubjective] language which supports it ... " (PrP, p. 8). As we saw in Chapter Seven, a "social" behaviorist holds that self-knowledge is parasitic on knowledge of others. In linguistic terms this means that we use language not only to express ourselves to others but to discover what our own intentions are (cf. S, p. 90).

In so far as both Merleau-Ponty and Heidegger stress the individual

originality of creative thinkers, this solid basis of intersubjectivity is
somewhat compromised. This is especially true of Heidegger, who describes the poet as one who is "apolis, without city and place, lonely,
strange, and alien . . . without statute and limit, without structure and
order, because they themselves as creators must first create all this"
(EM, p. 128). Heidegger's passion for the poet appears to undermine
his more sober ideas of the equiprimordiality of *Dasein* and world and
the apriority of *Mitsein*. As Harries phrases it: "Emphasizing poetry as
he does, Heidegger makes it impossible to do justice to a genuine
'we.' "[26]

Both Wittgenstein and Merleau-Ponty reject the notion that language
is an instrument contingent upon human achievement in the world.
For example, some might think that language would no longer be
needed if we could all read each other's minds. But Wittgenstein
strenuously objects: "Language is not an indirect method of communication, to be contrasted with 'direct' thought-reading. Thought-reading
could only take place through the interpretation of symbols and so
would be on the same level as language" (L 1, p. 25). This means that
language as a general symbolic system is a *necessary* component of
human life, i.e., it is a form of life which is neither merely instrumental
nor contingent on human evolution.

In his excellent dissertation William Lawhead offers a critique of
Wittgenstein's general linguistic conservatism from the standpoint of
Merleau-Ponty. Lawhead shows persuasively that the language-game
model is insufficient to eliminate the possibility of genuine philosophical speech. Wittgenstein sometimes gives the impression that
language-games are discrete and autonomous—that one does not overlap the other and that one could not be used to criticize the other. But
Wittgenstein himself admits that the boundaries are not clear (PI,
§§68–71), and that words "are used in a thousand different ways which
gradually merge into one another. No wonder that we can't tabulate
strict rules for their use" (BB, p. 28). As we have already seen, ordinary
language is not philosophically neutral: "it contains," as Lawhead explains, "fragments of many conflicting philosophical positions. Attempts to arrive at a consistent position without modifying ordinary
language will, no doubt, arbitrarily give favor to one part of the language while dismissing others as metaphorical or insignificant."[27]
Therefore, it is not possible to leave language as it is, and philosophical
speech then comes as naturally as poetic speech, both being just as authentic as any other linguistic mode. Furthermore, Lawhead supports
our thesis that Wittgenstein does indeed have a linguistic reduction:

"Hence, Wittgenstein has to 'bracket' ordinary language and thematize it to make its ordinariness stand forth *as* ordinary."[28]

Merleau-Ponty's linguistic reduction is more severe, primarily because he is convinced that an authentic philosophical speech is possible. Just as Heidegger, despite his poetic raptures, ultimately remains within *Dasein's* average everydayness (SZ, p. 16) (even the most creative of us do), Merleau-Ponty believes that the creative thinker should not confront the "given language" as "an enemy"; but "he destroys ordinary language . . . by realizing it. . . . It is entirely *ready* to convert everything new he stands for as a writer into an acquisition (S, p. 79). As T. S. Eliot expresses it: "And the end of all our exploring/ Will be to arrive where we started/ And know the place for the first time" ("Little Gidding" V). The linguistic reduction is like the poet Malraux's "coherent deformation," which throws the given language off center but only to recenter it (cf. S, p. 91); or "language [is] suddenly . . . thrown out of focus towards its meaning" (S, p. 44).

Merleau-Ponty admits that reading philosophy, like reading a poem, will be difficult in the beginning. We must begin with common meanings for the words the philosopher uses, but with patience we begin to learn his idiom, and ultimately, instead of alienating us from life, the good philosopher, with his non-ordinary language, is able to open up new vistas for us. The philosopher, like the poet, will "make [words] say something they have never said" (S, p. 91) and will thereby allow us to view the world anew. This is no different from a novice tracker gradually learning all the nuances of scent, animal prints, and landscape. Philosophical speech is not necessarily idling: in good philosophy it is simply engaging itself in new and illuminating ways. In the same way that an expert tracker "reads" things from a trail that the uninitiated has never seen, the philosopher reads between and behind accepted conventions. Merleau-Ponty phrases the point beautifully: "Just as the perceived world endures only through the reflections, shadows, levels, and horizons between things . . . so the works and thought of a philosopher are also made of certain articulations between things said" (S, p. 160). This reminds us somewhat of Wittgenstein's idea of philosophy's task as "finding and inventing *intermediate cases*" as an aid to gaining an *Übersicht* (PI, §122).

We must avoid the extremes to which both Wittgenstein and Heidegger tend in their least cautious moments: the former's reactionary "leaving everything as it is" and the latter's isolated poet attempting to create the world entirely anew. There is always a dialectic between the given expressions and the new ones, otherwise history would not have the continuity that it does and "true" discovery would not be possible. Revolutions in all disciplines would have no meaning without the historical background of the past. For Merleau-Ponty language and experience are co-extensive but not fused. Lawhead correctly observes that the dialectic of the lived and the said is what keeps us going—it makes history and a life-world possible. It is because we can make a distinction between experience and language that we are able to take the critical stance of philosophy itself. In contrast to the artist, the creative philosophical thinker has the task of bridging the gap, as Lawhead puts it, "between his existence as it is tacitly lived and understood and as it is explicitly articulated in speech."[29]

If language is the principal form of life, this means that it expresses a particular life-world; for language, as Harmon Chapman says, "is the life-world rendered articulate."[30] This explains then these cryptic pronouncements from Wittgenstein and Heidegger: "the limits of *language* . . . means the limits of *my* world" (T, 5.62), and "only where there is language is there world" (HD, p. 276). For Heidegger language discloses a world and expresses its *logos*, for the structure of language corresponds to the formal aspects of the world. This is so not because a differentiated world was there first, which we named through ostensive definition; rather, language articulates the world as differentiated. This talk of language as disclosing a life-world is the idiom of the "new" hermeneutic.

LANGUAGE AS HERMENEUTIC

The "new" hermeneutic, based on Heidegger and Gadamer, and carried out most vigorously by some German theologians, is distinguished from the "old" hermeneutic principally in the emphasis placed on language as the interpretative disclosure of a life-world. Traditional hermeneutic certainly recognized the problem of language, but this was mainly with regard to the mechanics of translation. If a text was adequately translated, then the role of language receded into the general hermeneutical background. For the old hermeneutic language was externally related to meaning, which was, as James M. Robinson phrases it, a "speechless profoundity." By contrast, Robinson describes the new hermeneutic as recognizing the "positive and indispensable role of language," the "unbroken linguisticality of understanding," and regarding the "language of the text . . . as an interpretative proclamation of . . . meaning and hence as our indispensable access to it."[31]

In the same way that our "broad" reason draws on forgotten meanings of the verb *legein*, the new hermeneutic appropriates the original meanings of the verb *hermēneuein*. For Heidegger modern logic is barren and inadequate because it does not know the significance of the "gathering" of *logos*. Similarly, traditional hermeneutic lost touch with the linguistic Greek meanings of *hermēneuein* and became mere mechanical exegesis. The etymology of *hermēneuein* is uncertain, but much evidence points to the meanings of "to say" and "to speak." There is no firm connection at all to the god Hermes, but still it is significant that he is credited with the discovery of language and writing, the media of all interpretation. The "saying" of ancient *hermēneia* is usually a proclamation or pronouncement which is simply accepted on its authority. (There is then a connection between our "passive" *logos* and this accepted "interpretation" of the nature of things.) The priest at the Delphic Oracle was called "*hermeois*," and Homer was considered the authoritative hermeneutical link between the gods and humankind. As Robinson states: "Here language is itself interpretation, not just the object of interpretation."[32]

Plato made a distinction between "the hermeneutical art" ([*hē*] *hermēneutikē* [*technē*]), which consisted of commands and pronouncements of the seer or herald, and the critical arts, where each individual is required to judge between the true and the false.[33] In hermeneutic people "only know what is said, but have not learned whether it is true" (*Statesman* 260 D). As we have already seen, Wittgenstein's emphasis on a passive reason, simply accepting how others have put the world together, is compatible with his general linguistic-hermeneutic conservatism about leaving language-games as they are. The new hermeneutic is principally passive; for example, it is primarily interested in permitting the life-world of the New Testament to show itself rather than in changing it in terms of our modern understanding. Therefore, the phenomenological hermeneutics of both Wittgenstein and Heidegger maintains the fundamental distinction between a strict description of sense and the determination of truth.

Heidegger's only reference to Wittgenstein is explicitly in the context of the concept of the "hermeneutical circle" (H, p. 31), the central axiom of the new hermeneutic. This concept is essentially identical with the thesis of semantic holism: in order to understand a word, one must understand the sentence, and in turn the language-games and forms of life in which it is found. In order to do justice to a text, one must stay within its circle of understanding. One applies an alien perspective to a text at the risk of completely destroying its meaning. In the *Philosophical Remarks* Wittgenstein expresses a related aspect of the hermeneutical circle: "I cannot use language in order to get outside of language" (PR,

p. 54). Meaning is not some eternal "speechless profoundity" that can be captured in strict objectivity by the techniques of traditional hermeneutic. Too often exegetes attempt to take the divine perspective on a text; they believe that it can be taken out of its milieu, its *Sitz-im-Leben*. They also believe that it is possible to strip ourselves of our own prejudices in interpreting the text. For Wittgenstein all seeing, thinking, and saying is interpretation (this is especially clear in the duck-rabbit discussion PI, pp. 194f, esp. p. 212), and there can never be any noninterpretative, purely noetic, understanding. Heidegger concurs: "Any mere pre-predicative seeing of the ready-at-hand is, in itself, something which already understands and interprets" (SZ, p. 149). As seeing and thinking are intelligible only within the "life" of words and language, Wittgenstein believes, like Heidegger, that language is hermeneutic.

The first exposition of Wittgenstein's link to hermeneutic phenomenology was a disguised one. Not too many commentators realized that Peter Winch's philosophical sociology, based primarily on Wittgenstein's concept of *Lebensformen*, restates in a general way the hermeneutic philosophy of Wilhelm Dilthey. In his use of the distinction between the *Geisteswissenschaften* and the *Naturwissenschaften* (manifested mainly in terms of the distinction between reasons and causes), the discussion of *Verstehen* and the doctrine of internal relations, and the return to the life-world by means of forms of life, Winch draws out the principal themes of a Wittgensteinian hermeneutic that is very close to the continental variety. We must, however, reiterate the fact that Wittgenstein, at least from his grammatico-phenomenological standpoint, does not make any ultimate distinction between a science of reasons and a science of causes. Furthermore, Wittgenstein would reject the hermeneutic theory of Dilthey and Schleiermacher, who, in their psychologistic leanings, wished to induce a *"Nacherleben"* of the composition of the text. As far as Karl-Otto Apel is concerned, Wittgenstein fulfills Dilthey's hermeneutical program much more successfully with his "objective description of the language-game, in whose context the meaning that is to be grasped, the intention, 'shows itself.' "[34]

For Dilthey the essential distinction between the natural sciences and the human sciences is the concept of *Verstehen*. The natural sciences are the "explaining" sciences while the human sciences are the "understanding" sciences. Heidegger continues the distinction between the two sciences, but de-psychologizes Dilthey's *Verstehen*. The latter thought it was a mental act, but the former makes it into a transcendental condition for the intelligibility of the world. Gadamer, as

Richard Palmer explains, follows Heidegger: "Understanding is conceived not in the traditional way as an act of human subjectivity but as the basic way of *Dasein's* being in the world."[35]

As we have seen, understanding, state-of-mind, and discourse are the most fundamental *a priori* structures of human Being. Understanding is not a mental process, but a formal framework that is the basis for the possibility of any understanding whatever. Heidegger goes beyond Kant's concept of *Verstand* in that *Verstehen* applies to all activities, noncognitive as well as cognitive. As Heidegger states: "Understanding always pertains to the whole basic states of Being-in-the-world" (SZ, p. 144). For Heidegger all "seeing" (*Sicht*) is grounded in understanding, and the basic *Sicht* of *Dasein* is, of course, the pre-predicative *Umsicht*. All forms of intuition, perception, and thinking are based on *Dasein's Umsicht* (SZ, p. 147).

In the preface to the *Investigations* Wittgenstein states that two of the main themes of the book are "meaning and understanding." Wittgenstein also has a basic "trinity" of understanding, discourse, and state-of-mind. Every understanding involves not only language, but is intimately connected with "how we find ourselves" (*wie man sich befindet*; hence Heidegger's *Befindlichkeit*). For both Heidegger and Wittgenstein we discover and understand the world via moods, for recall that humor and sadness are *Weltanschauungen,* ways of viewing the world. Like Heidegger, Wittgenstein de-psychologizes *Verstehen* and makes it a transcendental form of life. Combining Wittgenstein and Merleau-Ponty, Lawhead augments our point: "Rather than understanding being an interior process, it is the acquiring of a certain style of mobilization which enables one to participate in everyday discourse and commonly understood contexts."[36]

Wittgenstein does not always use the verb *"verstehen"* and the noun *"Verstehen"* in a technical, *a priori* way. For example, the meaning of the verb *"verstehen"* will simply depend upon its various uses (PI, §§531–32). But even here he implies that there is a basic concept that is essential for all uses of the word, a concept which he says elsewhere goes beyond the criterion of use: "But we *understand* the meaning of a word when we hear or say it; we grasp it in a flash, and what we grasp in this way is surely something different from the 'use' which is extended in time" (PI, §138; RFM, p. 40).

In the *Grammar* Wittgenstein offers the example of two people watching a chess game, one a non-player and the other a player. One would be tempted to claim that the difference between their respective "understandings" is an empirical difference, *viz.,* one knows the rules of the game and the other does not. "We can also say . . . that it is the knowledge of the rules which makes the first spectator have the particular experience he has. But this experience is not the knowledge of the rules. Yet we are inclined to call them both 'understanding' " (PG, pp. 49–50). He then gives a definition of understanding, which although not very clear, still appears very close to Heidegger's concept: "The understanding of language, as of a game, seems like a background against which a particular sentence acquires meaning" (PG, p. 50, cf. p. 88).

In *Being and Time* understanding is also the background for all interpretation and judgment: "The intelligibility of something has always been articulated, even before there is any appropriative interpretation of it" (SZ, p. 161). Any interpretation is already based in a "fore-having" and a "fore-sight," otherwise it would be without sense. In the *Grammar* Wittgenstein states that "the interpretation of written and spoken signs by ostensive definitions is not an application of language, but a part of the grammar" (PG, p. 88). Wittgenstein's own concept of "fore-having" can be clearly seen in the examples he uses: "If I say 'the color of this object is called violet,' I must already have denoted the color, already presented it for christening, with the words 'the color of that object' if the naming is to be able to take place" (PG, p. 88; cf. PI, §§138–9, 437). And Wittgenstein emphasizes in obvious Heideggerian fashion: "The interpretation remains at the level of generality preparatory to any application" (PG, p. 88).

Understanding always takes place in the framework of a system that is already laid out. Wittgenstein's semantic holism, an integral part of his hermeneutic phenomenology, is revealed when he contends that we will not find understanding as a mental process accompanying the act itself, but in the "*particular circumstances* which justify me in saying I can go on" (PI, §154). In a 1931 lecture we find this hermeneutic holism again: "If he understands path AC he must also understand path BC . . . he must understand in a system" (L 1, p. 54). Such a system then has a fore-structure of understanding, or as Wittgenstein says, "a paradigm that I could at any time compare the color with" (PR, p. 57). (Otherwise, how could I claim beforehand that I could recognize a color if it were presented to me?) Understanding then is always embedded in the world, which is a relational whole (Heidegger's *Bewandtnisganzheit*), and therefore F. Kerr is correct in maintaining that understanding is always "*Weltverständnis.*" Kerr finds this *Weltverständnis* in the "consensus" that constitutes Wittgenstein's forms of life: "Could we not say that this consensus in forms of life is the *a priori* interpretation of the world, the disclosure of the world, which is perceived, embodied, communicated, and of course constantly reactualized and modified in . . . any particular historical community?"[37]

In the passage dealing with chess used above, Wittgenstein suggests that *Verstehen* is an ability (*Können*) which we master. In the *Investigations* he proposes that understanding must be a "capacity" (*Fähigkeit*) rather than a feeling (PI, p. 181). In lectures of 1932–35 Wittgenstein told his students that understanding, rather than being a process accompanying the hearing or uttering of a word, is "being able to use a word in a sentence" (L 3, p. 79). Drawing an illuminating parallel to Heidegger, Gerd Brand, implicitly reminding Kerr that *Weltverständnis* is also *Seinsverständnis*, proposes that Wittgenstein's understanding is a *Seinskönnen*, a "Being-able-to" which is always there prior to any particular understanding. This "power" of understanding is, as Brand phrases it, "not something lying present-to-hand but a possibility, not a logical possibility, but a concrete possibility. Being-able-to is embedded in a situation and in human customs and institutions" (EW, p. 56). "Because language is an institutionalized Being-able-to, [I] can express every meaning, say something novel in the pre-existing system" (EW, p. 57), as well as claim that I could recognize my mother if she walked into the room, or that I understand how to play chess without actually playing a game. Understanding as *Seinskönnen* is therefore intimately related to the concept of operative intentionality, one, as Merleau-Ponty phrases it so well, "found beneath intentionality related to acts . . . another kind which is the condition of the former's possibility: namely an operative intentionality already at work before any positing of any judgment . . ." (PP, p. 429).

The key concept in the theory of interpretation (hermeneutic) of Heidegger and Gadamer is the idea that there are no free-floating, "objective" interpretations of the world. "Assertion is not a free-floating kind of behavior which, in its own right, might be capable of disclosing entities in general in a primary way: on the contrary, it always maintains itself on the basis of Being-in-the-world" (SZ, p. 156). And since understanding is not possible without discourse, language *is* hermeneutic; i.e., it reveals a world which is already laid out (*ausgelegt—Auslegung* = interpretation) for us—a world which we already understand in a general way. As we have seen, Wittgenstein's *Lebensformen* are based on social rules—rules, as Apel states, "that are also the *a priori* forms for the interpretation of the world."[38]

Wittgenstein always emphasizes that the rules of language-games are never free-floating, they are always found already established in a

Praxis (OC, §140), a *Weltbild*, or a *Lebensform*. Wittgenstein and Heidegger both agree that discourse is much more than just having the capacity of making vocal utterances—animals can do this. It is not merely an empirical difference of brain size or sophistication of vocal mechanisms—it is a formal difference. The uniqueness of human beings is their capacity to *discover* a world for the first time and to participate in forms of life. When humans speak, a qualitatively different and unique "world" opens up to them, one which is for the most part already interpreted for them. Therefore this hermeneutic component must be an integral part of the life-world phenomenology of Wittgenstein and the later phenomenologists.

One of the central themes of Gadamer's hermeneutic phenomenology is the "fusion of horizons" (*Horizontsverschmelzung*). One of the problems with historicizing the understanding is that it might preclude our being able to claim that we can translate successfully among languages and that we can have a genuine understanding of other cultures. Gadamer argues, however, that there is enough common ground between us and past cultures that a fusion of the horizons of the past and our horizon is possible. Rather than the *Nacherleben* theories of 19th Century hermeneuts, in which an attempt was made to *reconstruct* the past, Gadamer believes that we *integrate* what we can of the past into our own self-understanding. While the old hermeneuts engaged in a monologue with historical texts, the new hermeneut must participate in a dialogue. Gadamer therefore believes that the task of the new hermeneutic is to bring the text "out of the alienation in which it finds itself and into the living presence of conversation, whose fundamental procedure is always question and answer."[39]

As we have already indicated in previous discussion, Wittgenstein, probably because of strong Spenglerian influences, cannot accept this notion of *Horizontsverschmelzung*. More than Heidegger, Gadamer is influenced by Hegel's dialectical understanding of history, in which past and present are taken up in a new synthesis of human understanding. Wittgenstein and Spengler reject this Hegelian synthesis and emphasize cultural isolation instead. Albert Levi paraphrases Spengler very well: "Cultures are self-determining and impenetrable. When one looks at another it is through its own eyes, and when it appropriates, it is through the 'art of deliberate misunderstanding.' "[40] Wittgenstein and Spengler are then the fulfillment of Schleiermacher's dictum that all understanding is misunderstanding (cf. VB, p. 162).[41]

The concept of *Horizontsverschmelzung* is possible only on the basis of Hegel's unity of Spirit or the phenomenologists' idea of a universal life-world. Such notions would give firm philosophical basis for a meaning of *hermēneia* which we have not yet mentioned: *viz.*, the ability to *translate* from one language-culture to another. But Wittgenstein's linguistic isolationism appears to exclude this crucial aspect of the new hermeneutic. Significantly, Wittgenstein parts company with Heidegger on this point, for Heidegger believes that every human being will at least share the existentials and a single *Horizont*. Merleau-Ponty also speaks of the "unity of human style" and culture with "a single cumulative history—a single art" (S, p. 69). But Wittgenstein implies, for example, that we have nothing in common with the Egyptian style of art (PI, p. 230). Merleau-Ponty's support for the "fusion of horizons," and therefore his widest divergence from Wittgenstein, is clearly seen in this passage: "We understand by world not only the sum of things . . . but also the locus of their compossibility, the invariable style they observe, which connects their perspectives, permits transition from one to the other . . ." (VI, p. 13).

CONCLUSION

We must conclude that Wittgenstein and the existential phenomenologists have returned to the proto-phenomena of lived experience. This is "rough ground" and it will not yield clear and distinct ideas or answers. But the *Weltbild* is constant and reliable enough so that we are at least able to describe some of the inveterate forms of experience. Philosophizing then would be an attempt to get an *Übersicht* of the most fundamental features of the world and ourselves, not by gathering new facts—that is the task of science—but by reinvestigating the formal patterns of the facts that we already know.

In addition to this common ground we have also noted important differences. We have just discussed a major one: Wittgenstein's rejection of any universal life-world, one which could be the basis for truly common beliefs and styles of life. There are definitely shared forms of life, especially those which are closely connected with our common biology. In fact, at times Wittgenstein seems to support the fusion of horizons on this very basis: "The common behavior of mankind is the system of reference by means of which we interpret an unknown language" (PI, §206). But elsewhere Wittgenstein argues that to interpret the behavior of strange tribesmen, even if we have mastered their language, does not mean that we *understand* them (PI, p. 223). Therefore, cultural and linguistic differences are so great that forms of life and language-games diversify rather than unify. The results for philosophy are then quite predictable. In contrast to most all other philosophy, there is no way for the Wittgensteinian philosopher to speak for all people and for all times. Wittgenstein's radical contextualism and pluralism make him virtually unique among major philosophical figures.

Both Husserl and Wittgenstein considered themselves perpetual beginners, but Husserl definitely would have thought philosophy could do better than the following: "The most general remarks yield at best what looks like the fragments of a system" (PI, p. 228). Wittgenstein's phenomenological program is therefore far less ambitious than the other phenomenologists, and this fact is perhaps the clue for understanding this puzzling statement: "There is no such thing as phenomenology, but there are indeed phenomenological problems" (OCo, p. 9). This is Wittgenstein's way of saying that he recognizes the validity of the phenomenological method, but he refuses to engage in the risky, and probably impossible, task of a general "logic of phenomena." R. S. Rajan cautions us that "Wittgenstein's intense phenomenological description does not allow this kind of generality,"[42] for, as Wittgenstein himself says: "We are under the illusion that what is sublime, what is essential, about our investigation consists in its grasping one comprehensive essence" (Z, §444).

Notes

INTRODUCTION

1. Alfred Schütz, "William James' Concept of the Stream of Thought Phenomenologically Interpreted," *Philosophy and Phenomenological Research* 1 (1941), p. 442.
2. Arthur Danto, *Jean-Paul Sartre* (New York: Viking, 1975), p. xiii.
3. Quoted in the famous *Spiegel* interview, reprinted in *Philosophy Today* 20 (1976), p. 279.
4. Hubert Schwyzer, "Thought and Reality: the Metaphysics of Kant and Wittgenstein," *Philosophical Quarterly* 23 (1973), p. 205fn.
5. Karl Britton, "Portrait of a Philosopher" in *Ludwig Wittgenstein: The Man and His Philosophy*, ed. K. T. Fann (New York: Dell, 1967), p. 61.
6. M. O'C. Drury, *ibid.*, p. 68.
7. *The Philosophy of Rudolf Carnap*, ed. Paul A. Schlipp (LaSalle, Ill.: Open Court, 1963), p. 27.
8. Danto, *op. cit.*, p. xiii.
9. Gershon Weiler, *Mauthner's Critique of Language* (London: Cambridge University Press, 1970). Weiler speculates that Wittgenstein might have derived three concepts from the first thirty pages of Mauthner's *Beiträge einer Kritik der Sprache* (2 volumes, 1893–1902): the latter image found in the *Tractatus*, the idea of the growth of a language as analogous to the growth of a city (PI, §18), and basic idea behind the builder's language-game (pp. 298–306).
10. Michael Murray, "A Note on Wittgenstein and Heidegger," *Philosophical Review* 83 (1974), pp. 501–03.
11. Herbert Spiegelberg, "The Puzzle of L. Wittgenstein's *Phänomenologie* (1929–?)," *American Philosophical Quarterly* 5 (1968), pp. 244–56.
12. I thought that I got this quotation from G. J. Warnock's *English Philosophy Since 1900*, but I simply cannot find the reference.
13. F. Kerr, "Language as Hermeneutic in the Later Wittgenstein," *Tijdschrift voor Filosofie* 27 (1965), p. 517.
14. *The Philosophy of Rudolf Carnap*, p. 25.
15. Norman Malcolm, *Wittgenstein: A Memoir* (London: Oxford University Press, 1958), p. 2.

231

16. G. H. von Wright, "Wittgenstein's Views on Probability," *Revue Internationale de philosophie* 23 (1969), p. 260. Von Wright repeats this view in his review of the *Nachlass*. See his "The Wittgenstein Papers," *Philosophical Review* 78 (1969), p. 488.
17. Anthony Kenny, "From the Big Typescript to the *Philosophical Grammar*," *Acta Philosophica Fennica* 28 (1976), p. 46.
18. Malcolm, *op. cit.*, p. 2.
19. See *The Philosophy of Rudolph Carnap*, pp. 25–7.
20. Michael Dummett, "Wittgenstein's Philosophy of Mathematics," *Philosophical Review* 68 (1959), reprinted in Pitcher, p. 425.
21. J. L. Austin, *Philosophical Papers* (New York: Oxford University Press, 1961), p. 92.
22. Derek L. Phillips, *Wittgenstein and Scientific Knowledge: A Sociological Perspective* (London: Routledge & Kegan Paul, 1974), p. 98. See also Barry Stroud, "Wittgenstein and Logical Necessity," *Philosophical Review* 74 (1965), reprinted in Pitcher, pp. 489, 495; Henry LeRoy Finch, *Wittgenstein–The Later Philosophy* (Atlantic Heights, N.J.: Humanities Press, 1977) p. 156; and Rudolph Bensch, *L. Wittgenstein: Die apriorischen und mathematischen Sätzen in seinem Spätwerk* (Bonn: Bouvier Verlag, 1973). Bensch is convinced that Wittgenstein's "conventions" are not "free-floating" but are related to the world (pp. 51–2).
23. A. B. Levison, "Wittgenstein and Logical Necessity," *Inquiry* 7 (1964), p. 367.

CHAPTER ONE

1. Norman Malcolm, *Knowledge and Certainty: Essays and Lectures* (Englewood Cliffs, N.J.: Prentice-Hall, 1963). Excerpted in George Pitcher, ed. *Wittgenstein: The "Philosophical Investigations"* (New York: Doubleday Anchor, 1966), p. 91.
2. Stanley Cavell, "The Availability of Wittgenstein's Later Philosophy," *Philosophical Review* 71 (1962), reprinted in Pitcher, p. 161.
3. H. R. Smart, "Language-Games," *Philosophical Quarterly* 7 (1957), p. 232.
4. R. S. Rajan, "Cassirer and Wittgenstein," *International Philosophical Quarterly* 7 (1967), p. 592.
5. Robert L. Arrington, "Wittgenstein and Phenomenology," *Philosophy Today* 22 (1978), p. 295.
6. Peter Winch, *The Idea of a Social Science* (London: Routledge & Kegan Paul, 1958), p. 40. Derek L. Phillips also sees the central role that *Lebensformen* play, but he is not very clear about what they actually are. He is definitely wrong in thinking that differences in life forms are due to differences in biological and mental facts. See his *Wittgenstein and Scientific Knowledge*, p. 80.

   Peter McHugh, *et al.* have used Wittgenstein's *Lebensformen* as a basis for their *On the Beginning of Social Inquiry* (London: Routledge & Kegan Paul, 1974), pp. 49, 68, 76, 92, 171–76. In addition to seeing *Lebensformen* as cultural-historical, they correctly see that *Lebensformen* perform a transcendental function, i.e., they are the grounds of phenomena, much like Kant's *Bedingungen der Möglichkeit der Erfahrung*.

   A. A. Derksen in an article on philosophical sociology uses the term "form of life" and defines it as a community with its own criteria, rules, and concepts which are socially established. It can also be used more specifically as "characteristic features of a community such as magic, science, religion, etc." (*Philosophy of the Social Sciences* 8 [1978], p. 210).

7. In philosophy of religion the following authors deal with forms of life: Alan Keightley, *Wittgenstein, Grammar, and God* (London: Epworth Press, 1976); Kai Nielsen, "God and Forms of Life," *Indian Journal of Philosophy* 1 (1972), pp. 45–66, and "Religion and the Appeal to Forms of Life," *Agora* 3 (1976), pp. 67–71; Patrick Sherry, *Religion, Truth, and Language-Games* (New York: Macmillan, 1977); Dallas M. High, *Language, Persons, and Beliefs* (New York: Oxford, 1967); Jens Glebe-Møller, *Wittgenstein og Religionen* (Copenhagen: Gads Forlag, 1969); D. Z. Phillips, *Death and Immortality* (London: St. Martins, 1970) and *The Concept of Prayer* (London: Routledge & Kegan Paul, 1965); W. D. Hudson, *Ludwig Wittgenstein: The Bearing of his Philosophy upon Religious Beliefs* (Richmond: John Knox Press, 1968). Phillips and Hudson have several more books and articles in this area. For a detailed bibliography of articles on forms of life see the Bibliography under "Wittgenstein and Forms of Life."

8. Hanna Pitkin, *Wittgenstein and Justice* (Berkeley: University of California Press, 1972), p. 132.

9. John Hunter, "Forms of Life in Wittgenstein's *Philosophical Investigations*," *American Philosophical Quarterly* 5 (1968), pp. 233–43. Reprinted in E. D. Klemke, ed. *Essays on Wittgenstein* (Urbana: University of Illinois Press, 1971), pp. 276, 277, 278.

10. Malcolm, *Knowledge and Certainty*, p. 93.

11. Hunter, *op. cit.*, p. 282.

12. James Shekelton, "Rules and *Lebensformen*," *Midwest Studies in Philosophy* 1 (1976), p. 131.

13. One might argue that Wittgenstein has been proved wrong by the recent success in training apes to use sign language, which they in turn have taught to their companions and offspring. Researchers working with these apes would certainly claim that these animals are participating in human life forms such as hoping, pretending, etc. But critics such as Herbert Terrace of Columbia argue that these apes are still unable to master the grammar of language and are therefore only imitating human language and life forms. See Terrace's *Nim: A Chimpanzee Who Learned Sign Language* (New York: Knopf, 1979).

14. Timothy Binkley, *Wittgenstein's Language* (The Hague: Nijhoff, 1973), p. 213. C. A. van Peursen concurs: "The forms of life are rather the manner of action shared by people of a particular time and culture (*Ludwig Wittgenstein: An Introduction to His Philosophy*, trans. Rex Ambler [London: Faber and Faber, 1969], p. 108).

15. Majorie Grene, *Philosophy In and Out of Europe* (Berkeley: University of California Press, 1976), p. 151.

16. Anthony Kenny, *Wittgenstein* (London: The Penquin Press, 1973), p. 224.

17. P. M. S. Hacker, *Insight and Illusion: Wittgenstein on Philosophy and the Metaphysics of Experience* (London: Oxford University Press, 1972), p. 241.

18. See Peter French, "Wittgenstein's Limits of the World," *Midwest Studies in Philosophy* 1 (1976), p. 115. I am also indebted to Henry LeRoy Finch's chapter on forms of life in which he shows how Wittgenstein is different from sociological theorists. Finch argues that even the descriptive methodology of Levi Strauss' neo-structuralism is not what Wittgenstein had in mind. In contrast K. W. Rankin believes that the "descriptive analysis" of the Evans-Pritchard and Levi-Strauss schools is compatible with Wittgensteinian methodology. See Rankin's "Wittgenstein on Meaning, Understanding, and Intending," *American Philosophical Quarterly* 3 (1966), p. 2.

19. See McHugh, *et al., op. cit.*; see also Stephen A. Erickson, *Language and Being: An Analytic Phenomenology* (New Haven: Yale, 1970), p. 111; and Igance Verhack, "Wittgen-

stein's Deictic Metaphysics: An Uncommon Reading of the *Tractatus*," *International Philosophical Quarterly* 18 (1978), p. 437.

CHAPTER TWO

1. D. S. Shwayder, "Wittgenstein on Mathematics" in Peter Winch, ed. *Studies in the Philosophy of Wittgenstein* (London: Routledge & Kegan Paul, 1969), p. 66. For an extensive bibliography on this topic, see the entry "Kant and Wittgenstein" in the Bibliography.
2. Eva Schaper, "Kant's Schematism Reconsidered," *Review of Metaphysics* 18 (1964), p. 292.
3. Henry LeRoy Finch, *Wittgenstein–The Early Philosophy* (Atlantic Heights, N.J.: Humanities Press, 1971), p. 267.
4. Hacker, *Insight and Illusion*, p. 139. Of the five philosophers who Hacker believes exerted the most influence on Wittgenstein—Frege, Russell, Schopenhauer, Hertz, and Brouwer—the last three are Kantian thinkers.
5. French, "Wittgenstein's Limits of the World," p. 114.
6. Bruce Wilshire observes that Husserl's transcendental method is based on Kant's philosophy (*William James and Phenomenology* [Bloomington: Indiana University Press, 1968], pp. 4–5). We document Heidegger's Kantianism in Section IV. Merleau-Ponty sees himself as fulfilling the true goals of the critical philosophy by completing the "critique of dogmatism" (PrP, p. 19). For more on this see Thomas Langan's *Merleau-Ponty's Critique of Reason* (New Haven: Yale University Press, 1966). The most complete discussion of Kant and Husserl is found in Iso Kern's book *Husserl und Kant* (The Hague: Nijhoff, 1964).
7. S. K. Wertz writes the most extensive remarks against the Kantian interpretation of Wittgenstein, although his case is weakened by ignoring Wittgenstein's explicit transcendentalism, and by not mentioning his explicit resurrection of Kant's synthetic *a priori* ("On Placing Wittgenstein in History," *Southern Journal of Philosophy* 11 [1973], pp. 337–50). W. W. Bartley believes that the *Tractatus* is "not only *non*-Kantian but *pre*-Kantian in spirit." (Bartley is definitely correct in terms of the *Tractatus*' explicit ontology.) Bartley concludes that Wittgenstein moved "from a pre-critical, pre-Kantian position to a post-Kantian, Hegelian-style position *without the benefit of Kant*," (*Wittgenstein* [London: Quartet Books, 1977], pp. 46–7, 116). Although he believes Wittgenstein is a transcendental philosopher, the Norwegian Audun Øfsti argues that Wittgenstein's idea that the constitution of objects is culturally based is more Hegelian than Kantian (*Språk og Fornuft* [Oslo: Universitetsforlaget, 1975], p. 107). This only means that life-philosophy as a "sociological" neo-Kantianism was additionally influenced by Hegelianism.
8. Ross Mandel, "Heidegger and Wittgenstein: A Second Kantian Revolution" in Michael Murry, ed. *Heidegger and Modern Philosophy* (New Haven: Yale University Press, 1978).
9. David Pears, *Wittgenstein* (London: Collins, 1971), p. 28.
10. Alexander Maslow, *A Study of Wittgenstein's "Tractatus"* (Berkeley: University of California Press, 1961), p. xiv.
11. Erik Stenius, *Wittgenstein's "Tractatus": A Critical Exposition of its Main Lines of Thought* (Oxford: Blackwell, 1960), p. 218.
12. Quoted in Garth Hallett, *A Companion to Wittgenstein's "Philosophical Investigations"* (Ithaca: Cornell University Press, 1977), p. 768.

13. S. M. Engel, "Wittgenstein and Kant," *Philosophy and Phenomenological Research* 30 (1970).

14. James Griffin, *Wittgenstein's Logical Atomism* (London: Oxford University Press, 1964). Allan Janik and Stephen Toulmin also discuss Hertz's influence in the *Wittgenstein's Vienna* (New York: Simon & Schuster, 1973), pp. 139, 179–85, 188–91. Also see Hacker for more on Hertz's influence (*op. cit.*, pp. 2–4).
    G. C. Lichtenberg and Otto Weininger were other strong Kantians who had profound influence on Wittgenstein. In an article on Weininger and Wittgenstein, Janik states that Weininger "came to regard the neo-Kantian theory of knowledge of Dilthey and the ethics of the *Critique of Practical Reason* as the essential basis for any scientific study of character" ("Wittgenstein and Weininger" in *Wittgenstein and His Impact on Contemporary Thought* [Proceedings of the Second Annual Wittgenstein Symposium, 1977] [Vienna: Hölder-Pichler-Tempsky, 1978] p. 27).

15. B. F. McGuiness, "Philosophy of Science in the *Tractatus*," *Revue internationale de philosophie* 23 (1969), p. 155.

16. T. H. Morawetz, "Wittgenstein and Synthetic *A Priori* Judgments," *Philosophy* 49 (1974), pp. 433–4.

17. Cavell, "The Availability . . . ," p. 175.

18. Quoted in S. M. Engel, *op. cit.*, p. 494.

19. Jonathan Bennett, *Rationality* (London: Routledge & Kegan Paul, 1964), p. 2.

20. Janik and Toulmin, *Wittgenstein's Vienna*, p. 121.

21. Engel, *op. cit.*, p. 508. Hubert Schwyzer also notes that Kant "derives the categories from the forms of judgment (forms of sentences, *the ways in which we speak*)" ("Thought and Reality," p. 202fn).

22. Wilshire, *op. cit.*, p. 191. A reader whose comments came to me late reminds me that Kant mentions "phenomenology" as a "doctrine of appearances" in Chapter Four of *The Metaphysical Foundations of Natural Science*, trans. James Ellington (Indianapolis: Bobbs-Merrill, 1970).

23. Paul Ricoeur, *Husserl: An Analysis of his Phenomenology*, trans. E. G. Ballard and L. E. Embree (Evanston: Northwestern, 1967), p. 180. James Ellington disagrees with the conclusion of this paragraph. He believes that Kant's commitment to Euclidean geometry and Newtonian physics is incidental to the genuine phenomenological investigation that takes place in the first Critique. See his introduction to *The Metaphysical Foundations of Natural Science*, p. xxx.

24. Ricoeur, *Husserl*, p. 184. A nice formulation of intentionality is also found at KRV, p. 323.

25. Allan Janik, "Schopenhauer and the Early Wittgenstein," *Philosophical Studies* (Irish) 15 (1966), p. 81.

26. Ricoeur, *op. cit.*, p. 192.

27. Schwyzer, *op. cit.*, p. 201fn.

28. Viggo Rossvaer, *Kant og Wittgenstein* (Oslo: Universtitetsforlag, 1971), p. 401.

29. Karsten Harries, "Two Conflicting Interpretations of Language in Wittgenstein's *Investigations*," *Kant-Studien* 56 (1968), p. 402. P. F. Strawson also agrees that transcendental conditions need not be located in the mind (*The Bounds of Sense* [London: Methuen, 1966], p. 15). Hacker is therefore wrong to claim that after 1929, Wittgenstein "cut out the transcendental twaddle" (*Insight and Illusion*, p. 81).

30. Wilshire, *James and Phenomenology*, p. 203.

31. Mandel, "Heidegger and Wittgenstein," p. 266.

32. M. C. Dillon, "Gestalt Theory and Merleau-Ponty's Concept of Intentionality," *Man and World* 4 (1971), p. 453.

33. Hans-Georg Gadamer, *Truth and Method* (New York: Seabury Press, 1975), p. 214. In a footnote to this claim, Gadamer tells of a conversation in 1923 in which Heidegger told him how much Simmel's philosophy meant to him (p. 521). Otto Pöggeler also stresses the strong influence of Dilthey during Heidegger's *Sein und Zeit* period. *Der Denkweg Martin Heideggers* (Tübingen: Neske, 1963), pp. 35–6, 105.
34. Stenius, *op. cit.*, p. 219.
35. Stephen Erickson, "Meaning and Language," *Man and World* 1 (1968), p. 585fn.
36. Rossvaer, *op. cit.*, p. 401.
37. See Hacker, *op. cit.*, Schwyzer, *op. cit.*, and Wilshire, *Metaphysics* (New York: Western Publishing Co., 1969), who connects Wittgenstein with the "task of first-philosophy or metaphysics [which] reminds us of what lies in the background of any special study or activity, and to recall us from our absorption in the speciality to a comprehensive grasp of its presuppositions and consequences" (p. 32).
38. Mandel, *op. cit.*, p. 265.
39. Quoted in E. B. Greenwood, "Tolstoy, Wittgenstein, and Schopenhauer," *Encounter* (London) 36 (1973), p. 72.
40. Hacker, *op. cit.*, p. 146.

CHAPTER THREE

1. Georg Simmel, quoted in M. F. Sciacca, *Philosophical Trends in the Contemporary World*, trans. A. T. Salerno (Notre Dame, Ind.: University of Notre Dame Press, 1964), p. 28.
2. Wilhelm Dilthey, *Gesammelte Schriften* (Stuttgart: Teubner, 1958), Vol. 5, p. cxii.
3. *Ibid.*, Vol. 1, p. xii.
4. Majorie Grene, *Philosophy in and out of Europe* (Berkeley: University of California Press, 1976), p. 151.
5. Patrick Sherry, "Is Religion a Form of Life?" *American Philosophical Quarterly* 9 (1972), p. 161.
6. K. E. Trandøy, "Recollections of Wittgenstein," *Acta Philosophica Fennica* 28 (1976), p. 19.
7. Josef Simon, "*Leben*" in *Handbuch philosophischer Grundbegriffe* (Munich: Kösel Verlag, 1973), Vol. 3, p. 857.
8. Bernard Kaplan, "Some Considerations of Influences on Wittgenstein," *Idealistic Studies* 1 (1971), p. 80.
9. Herman Feigl, quoted in George Pitcher, *The Philosophy of Wittgenstein* (Englewood Cliffs, N.J.: Prentice-Hall, 1964), p. 8fn.
10. I. M. Bochenski, *Contemporary European Philosophy*, trans. D. Nicholl and K. Aschenbrenner (Berkeley: University of California Press, 1956), p. 101.
11. "A Biographical Sketch" in Norman Malcolm, *Wittgenstein: A Memoir*, p. 5.
12. Hacker, *Insight and Illusion*, p. 73.
13. A. P. Griffiths, "Wittgenstein, Schopenhauer, and Ethics" in *Understanding Wittgenstein*, p. 98, cf. p. 109.
14. Hacker, *op. cit.*, p. 64. Patrick Gardiner, *Schopenhauer* (Middlesex: Penquin Books, 1967), p. 226fn. Gershon Weiler proposes that Wittgenstein got the ladder image from Fritz Mauthner (*Mauthner's Critique of Language*, p. 296).
15. Engel, *Wittgenstein's Doctrine of the Tyranny of Language* (The Hague: Nijhoff, 1975), Chapter Four. S. K. Wertz probably has a better argument that William James is the

source of the phrase "craving for generality" ("On Wittgenstein and James," *New Scholasticism* 46 [1972]).
16. Gardiner, *op. cit.*, p. 119.
17. Hacker, *op. cit.*, p. 70.
18. Janik, "Schopenhauer and the Early Wittgenstein," p. 81. See also Gardiner, p. 169.
19. Hacker, *op. cit.*, p. 76.
20. Kaplan, *op. cit.*, p. 80.
21. Calvin O. Schrag, "The Life-World and Its Historical Horizon" in *Patterns of the Life-World*, eds. James M. Edie, *et al.* (Evanston: Northwestern University Press, 1970), p. 111.
22. Karl-Otto Apel, *Analytic Philosophy of Language and the "Geisteswissenschaften"* (Dortrecht: Reidel, 1967), p. 41.
23. Kaplan, *op. cit.*, p. 82.
24. Janik and Toulmin, *Wittgenstein's Vienna*, p. 230. Toulmin gives credit for this point to Robert Fogelin of Yale in a foreward to S. M. Engel's *Wittgenstein's Doctrine of the Tyranny of Language*, p. xi.
25. Eduard Spranger, *Types of Men*, trans. P. J. W. Pigers (Tübingen: Niemeyer, 1928), p. 13.
26. *Ibid.*, p. viii.
27. *Ibid.*, p. 30, 35.
28. *Ibid.*, p. 29.
29. In *The Conflict in Modern Culture and Other Essays*, ed. K. P. Etzkorn (New York: Teacher's College Press, 1968), p. 20.
30. *Ibid.*, p. 21.
31. *Ibid.*, p. 26.
32. Oakes, "Introduction" to Simmel's *The Problem of the Philosophy of History* (New York: Free Press, 1977), p. 33.
33. R. H. Weingartner, *Experience and Culture: The Philosophy of Georg Simmel* (Middletown, Conn.: Wesleyan University Press, 1960), p. 37.
34. Simmel, *The Problem of the Philosophy of History*, p. 159. See also Simmel's "How is Society Possible?" in M. Natanson, ed. *The Philosophy of the Social Sciences* (New York: Random House, 1963), p. 84.
35. Quoted in R. H. Weingartner, "Form and Content" in *Essays on Sociology, Philosophy & Aesthetics*, ed. Kurt H. Wolff (New York: Harper & Row, 1959), p. 51.
36. Quoted in Weingartner, *Experience and Culture*, p. 55.
37. Weingartner, "Form and Content," p. 49.
38. "The Conflict in Modern Culture," p. 20. L. E. J. Brouwer appears to agree with Simmel on this point when he contends that exactness in mathematics is not based on a "practical certainty that . . . will never lead to a misunderstanding in human relations" (CW I, p. 86).
39. Quoted in Weingartner, *Experience and Culture*, p. 62.
40. *Ibid.*, pp. 63–4.
41. As Weingartner states: "Broadly speaking, Simmel arrives at his theory of world-forms by way of a generalized Kantianism" ("Form and Content," p. 60). See Simmel's "How is Society Possible?" *passim*, and "The Conflict of Modern Culture," p. 42.
42. Weiler, *Mauthner's Critique of Language*, p. 55.
43. Von Wright quoted in Hallett, *A Companion*, p. 774. Von Wright also states that "many readers will no doubt be struck by the strongly Spenglerian nature of Wittgenstein's attitude to his times. . . . The fact is that Wittgenstein *was* influenced

by Spengler" ("Wittgenstein in Relation to His Times" in *Wittgenstein and His Impact*, p. 76).

44. W. H. Dray, "Oswald Spengler" article in *The Encyclopedia of Philosophy*, ed. Paul Edwards (New York: Macmillan, 1967), Vol. 7, p. 528.

45. Hallett, *op. cit.*, p. 774 and von Wright, "Wittgenstein in Relation to His Times," p. 77. Engel argues that it was Schopenhauer, not Spengler, from whom he derived the term (*Wittgenstein's Doctrine of the Tyranny of Language*, p. 76fn).

46. See DW I, pp. 113, 121. Spengler uses the word "*Urphänomen*" in Goethe's sense to describe cultural styles on pp. 105, 205.

47. *Wittgenstein–The Later Philosophy*, pp. 68, 270. Wittgenstein refers to Goethe often (see Hallett, *op. cit.*, pp. 765–66) and Goethe's *Farbenlehre* is the basis for *On Color*.

48. *Ibid.*, p. 55. I have offered my own translation due to the garbled rendering by Atkinson. Like Simmel, Spengler also uses the term "*Weltform*" as synonymous with *Weltbild* and *Weltanschauung* (DW I, p. 98).

49. Hallett, *op. cit.*, p. 747.

50. Hacker, *Insight and Illusion*, p. 100. "To someone like Wittgenstein who found in Schopenhauer both inspiration and insight, there is a *prima facie* likelihood that Brouwer's emphasis on the primacy of the will would have an intrinsic appeal. The fundamental idea that neither language, nor mathematics, nor logic are anything but free creations of the human will imposing an order on reality may well have appeared a deeply liberating conception" (p. 102). See also Charles Parson's article on Brouwer in the *Encyclopedia of Philosophy*, Volume One, p. 400. Brouwer's heavy use of eastern philosophy might also be due to Schopenhauer, who inspired a whole generation of continental thinkers in this area.

51. Bertrand Russell, *The Autobiography of Bertrand Russell 1914–44* (Boston: Little, Brown & Co., 1968), p. 297.

52. Michael Dummett, *Elements of Intuitionism* (Oxford: Oxford University Press, 1977), p. 2.

53. V. H. Klenk, *Wittgenstein's Philosophy of Mathematics* (The Hague: Nijhoff, 1976), p. 19.

54. Dummett, *op. cit.*, pp. 3–4, cf. p. 366.

55. Smart, "Language-Games," p. 232.

CHAPTER FOUR

1. J. T. Price, *Language and Being in Wittgenstein's "Philosophical Investigations"* (The Hague: Mouton, 1973), pp. 83, 108, 82.

2. David Pole, *The Later Philosophy of Wittgenstein* (London: The Athalone Press, 1958), p. 1.

3. Cavell, "The Availability . . . , p. 184.

4. In a letter to Moore (May 5, 1930) Russell admits that Wittgenstein's "theories are certainly important and certainly very original. Whether they are true, I do not know; I devoutly hope they are not, as they make mathematics and logic almost incredibly difficult." Later in a formal report to the Trinity Council on Wittgenstein's philosophical progress, based on reading about a third of TS 209 (a version of our current *Philosophical Remarks*), Russell's declares that "as a logician who likes simplicity," he hopes that Wittgenstein's views are not valid (*The Autobiography of Bertrand Russell*, Vol. 2, pp. 297, 301).

5. Karl Britton, "Portrait of a Philosopher" in K. T. Fann, ed. *Ludwig Wittgenstein: The Man and His Philosophy*, p. 56.

6. J. N. Findlay, "My Encounters with Wittgenstein," *Philosophical Forum* 4 (1973), p. 167.
7. Hilary Putnam, *Language, Belief, and Metaphysics*, ed. Kiefer and Munitz (Albany: SUNY Press, 1970), p. 60.
8. Paul Bernays, "Comments on L. Wittgenstein's *Remarks on the Foundation of Mathematics*" *Ratio* 2 (1959), p. 6. As early as 1939 Wittgenstein was sensitive to the criticism he had received because of his views on mathematics. He reports that his critics believe that he is "undermining mathematics, introducing Bolshevism" into it (LFM, p. 67). But all that he wants to do is to draw an important distinction between discovering something and inventing something.
9. Dummett, "Wittgenstein's Philosophy of Mathematics," reprinted in Pitcher, pp. 427, 430.
10. Matthew Fairbanks, "James and Wittgenstein," *The New Scholasticism* 40 (1966), p. 331.
11. James E. Marsh, "The Triumph of Ambiguity," *Philosophy Today* 19 (1975), p. 243.
12. Samuel B. Mallin, *Merleau-Ponty's Philosophy* (New Haven: Yale University Press, 1979), p. 204.
13. Robert J. Fogelin, *Wittgenstein* (London: Routledge & Kegan Paul, 1976), pp. 196, 197.
14. P. F. Strawson, Review of the *Philosophical Investigations, Mind* 63 (1954), reprinted in Pitcher's anthology, p. 62.
15. In addition to direct references to the Gestalt psychologists, Wittgenstein was closely associated with the Austrian Gestaltist Karl Bühler, who was the intellectual leader of the Austrian school reform movement, of which Wittgenstein was an enthusiastic participant. For more on the Bühler connection see Bernard Kaplan, "Some Considerations of Influences on Wittgenstein," p. 82; and W. W. Bartley, "Theory of Language and Philosophy of Science as Instruments of Education Reform: Wittgenstein and Popper as Austrian Schoolteachers," *Boston Studies in the Philosophy of Science* 14 (1974), pp. 307–337.
16. Gerd Brand, "The Material *A priori* and the Foundation for its Analysis in Husserl," *The Later Husserl and the Idea of Phenomenology*, ed. A. Tymieniecka *Analecta Husserliana*, Volume II (Dortrecht: Riedel, 1972), p. 128.
17. Hacker, *Insight and Illusion*, p. 136.
18. *Ibid*.
19. Ricoeur, "Husserl and Wittgenstein on Language" in E. N. Lee and M. Mandelbaum, ed. *Phenomenology and Existentialism* (Baltimore: The Johns Hopkins Press, 1967), p. 211.
20. Janik and Toulmin, *Wittgenstein's Vienna*, p. 184.
21. Rossvaer, *Kant og Wittgenstein*, p. 453fn.
22. Janik and Toulmin, *op. cit.*, p. 183. Bolzano called ideal logical constructions *Vorstellungen an sich* and von Wright finds Wittgenstein and Bolzano in such close agreement on the concept of probability that he states that "it seems appropriate to talk of one definition of probability here and call it the Bolzano-Wittgenstein definition" "Wittgenstein's Views on Probability," *Revue internationale de philosophie* 23 [1969], p. 264). Although von Wright doubts that Wittgenstein ever read any Bolzano, this is still more evidence of Wittgenstein's strong continental roots.
23. Brand Blanshard, *et al.*, Symposium on Internal Relations, *Review of Metaphysics* 21 (1967), p. 272.
24. H. Malmgren, "Internal Relations in the Analysis of Consciousness," *Theoria* 41 (1975), p. 67.

25. Karsten J. Struhl, "Language-Games and Forms of Life," *Journal of Critical Analysis* 11 (1970), p. 25.
26. Malcolm, "Wittgenstein on the Nature of Mind" in Nicholas Rescher, ed. *Studies in the Theory of Knowledge* (Oxford: Blackwell, 1970), p. 22. Referring to Peter Winch's work, Blanche L. Premo states that "social relations are internal relations and therefore belong to the same logical type as those between ideas or between propositions" ("The Early Wittgenstein and Hermeneutics," *Philosophy Today* 16 [1972], p. 63, fn. 59).
27. Bruce Aune, Symposium on Internal Relations, p. 237.
28. Blanshard, *Reason and Belief* (New Haven: Yale University Press, 1975), pp. 499–500.

CHAPTER FIVE

1. See Spiegelberg's supplement to "The Puzzle . . ." which will be reprinted in *The Context of the Phenomenological Movement,* forthcoming from Nijhoff.
2. Quoted in *ibid.,* item #3 of the supplement.
3. Spiegelberg, "The Puzzle . . . ," p. 252.
4. See Spiegelberg, *The Phenomenological Movement* (The Hague: Nijhoff, 2nd ed., 1969), p. 9. Colin McGinn cites these important differences between Mach and Husserl: (1) there is no doctrine of essences in Mach; (2) Husserl definitely rejects, like Wittgenstein, Mach's idea of simplification through "thought economy"; (3) for Husserl and Wittgenstein meaning is immanent in experience, but Mach believes that meaning is conferred in conventionalist fashion; and (4) Mach has a "phenomenalist reduction" to sense data, while Wittgenstein and Husserl have a "phenomenological reduction" to the *modes* in which experience is given. See McGinn's "Mach and Husserl," *Journal of the British Society for Phenomenology* 3 (1972), p. 154f. I have interpolated my own observations about Wittgenstein.
5. Janik and Toulmin, *Wittgenstein's Vienna,* p. 182.
6. Quoted in McGinn, *op. cit.,* p. 146.
7. Finch, *The Later Philosophy,* p. 175.
8. See Arnulf Zweig's "Goethe" article in the *Encyclopedia of Philosophy,* Vol. 3, p. 363.
9. Anthony Kenny, *Wittgenstein* (Cambridge: Harvard University Press, 1973), p. 225.
10. Spiegelberg, "The Puzzle . . . ," p. 247fn.
11. Max Black, *A Companion to Wittgenstein's "Tractatus"* (Ithaca: Cornell University Press, 1964), pp. 136–7. C. A. van Peursen also sees parallels between the two thinkers on the themes of grammar and *Sachverhalte* ("Husserl and Wittgenstein," *Philosophy and Phenomenological Research* 20 [1959], pp. 182–4).
12. Barry Smith, "Wittgenstein and the Background of Austrian Philosophy" in *Wittgenstein and His Impact,* p. 33.
13. Marsh, "The Triumph of Ambiguity," p. 251.
14. Quoted in Malcolm, *A Memoir,* p. 69fn.
15. "A name means an object. The object is its meaning" (T, 3.203). As Hallett remarks: "In one all-important respect, though, the *Tractatus* terminology does resemble Frege's. In both the *Bedeutung* is a referent, an object of some sort" (*Wittgenstein's Definition of Meaning as Use* [The Bronx: Fordham University Press, 1967], p. 25).
16. Smith, "Wittgenstein and the Background . . . ," p. 33. Smith also observes in an unpublished piece, "Palaeontological Reflections on the *Tractatus*" (some of which has found its way into his "Law and Eschatology in Wittgenstein's Early Thought," *In-*

quiry 21 [1978], pp. 425–41), that since Wittgenstein was very interested in the psychology of music, at least in his early Cambridge days, that he could not have avoided reading or reading about Carl Stumpf's two volume work *Tonpsychologie* (1883/90).

17. John Hems, "Husserl and/or Wittgenstein," *International Philosophical Quarterly* 8 (1968), pp. 547–578. Reprinted in Harold A. Durfee, *Analytic Philosophy and Phenomenology* (The Hague: Nijhoff, 1976), p. 82.

18. Ricoeur, *Husserl . . .* , p. 176.

19. Brand, "The Material *A priori . . .* ," p. 128.

20. Hems, *op. cit.*, p. 80.

21. Ricoeur, *Husserl . . . .* , p. 176.

22. Richard Schmitt, "Phenomenology and Analysis," *Philosophy and Phenomenological Research* 23 (1963), p. 107.

23. Hallett, *A Companion . . .* , p. 762.

24. Quoted in Gary Gutting, "Husserl and Logical Empiricism," *Metaphilosophy* 2 (1971), p. 206.

25. Don Ihde, "Wittgenstein's Phenomenological Reduction" in *Phenomenological Perspectives*, ed. P. Bossert (The Hague: Nijhoff, 1975), p. 48.

26. Aron Gurwitsch, *Studies in Phenomenology and Psychology* (Evanston: Northwestern University Press, 1966), p. 426.

CHAPTER SIX

1. Raymond Herbenick, "Merleau-Ponty and the Primacy of Reflection" in *The Horizons of the Flesh*, ed. Garth Gillan (Carbondale, Ill.: Southern Illinois University Press, 1973), pp. 93–94.

2. Hems, "Husserl and/or Wittgenstein," p. 66.

3. Philip J. Bossert, "The Explication of 'The World' in Constructionalism and Phenomenology," *Man and World* 6 (1973), p. 231.

4. Gurwitsch, "Problems of the Life-World" in *Phenomenology and Social Reality*, ed. M. Natanson (The Hague: Nijhoff, 1970), p. 46. As David Carr states: "There is no denying the Heideggerian flavor of these later considerations of Husserl, and the question of influence is properly raised" ("Husserl's Problematic Concept of the Life-World" in *Husserl: Exposition and Appraisal*, ed. and trans. F. A. Elliston and P. McCormick [Notre Dame: Notre Dame University Press, 1977], p. 211).

5. Hans-Georg Gadamer, *Truth and Method*, p. 217.

6. Gadamer, "The Science of the Life-World" in *The Later Husserl and the Idea of Phenomenology*, p. 180.

7. Robert Ehman, "The Phenomenon of World" in *Patterns of the Life-World*, ed. J. Edie, *et al.* (Evanston: Northwestern University Press, 1970), p. 85.

8. Helmut Wagner, "The Bergsonian Period of Alfred Schütz," *Philosophy and Phenomenological Research* 38 (1978), p. 189.

9. A. K. Saran, "A Wittgensteinian Sociology?" *Ethics* 75 (1965), p. 195.

10. See Bibliography entry "Wittgenstein and Polanyi" for more on this important connection.

11. Gurwitsch, "Problems of the Life-World," p. 49.

12. George F. Sefler, *Language and World* (Atlantic Heights, N.J.: Humanities Press, 1974), pp. 94–5.

13. *Ibid.*, p. 96.

14. Hacker, *Insight and Illusion*, p. 213.

15. Jens Glebe-Møller, *Wittgenstein og Religionen* (Copenhagen: Gads forlag, 1969), pp. 244–5.

16. Karl-Otto Apel, "Wittgenstein und Heidegger," *Philosophisches Jahrbuch* 75 (1967), p. 384.

17. Although at one time I thought that the comparison between forms of life and existentials was original with me, I discovered that Dagfinn Føllesdal at least had an inkling of this idea in his article "Husserl and Heidegger on the Role of Actions in the Constitution of the World" in *Essays in Honor of Jaakko Hintakka*, eds. E. Saariene, *et al.* (Dortrecht: Reidel, 1979), p. 371.

18. Ingvar Horgby, "The Double Awareness in Heidegger and Wittgenstein," *Inquiry* 2 (1959), p. 246.

19. From a discussion at a conference on Heidegger and Language held at The Pennsylvania State University, September, 1969, cited in a footnote in *On Heidegger and Language*, ed. Joseph J. Kockelmans (Evanston: Northwestern University Press, 1972), p. 110.

20. This is the opinion of Apel, "Heidegger und Wittgenstein," p. 389 and *Analytic Philosophy of Language and the "Geisteswissenschaften"* (Dortrecht: Reidel, 1967), p. 49. See also D. I. Couprie, "Wittgenstein I: Transcendentalfilosof, Ja or Neen?" *Tijdschrift voor Filosofi* 32 (1970), fn. 6.

CHAPTER SEVEN

1. John W. Cook, "Human Beings" in Peter Winch, ed. *Studies in the Philosophy of Wittgenstein* (London: Routledge & Kegan Paul, 1969), p. 117.

2. Hems, "Husserl and/or Wittgenstein," p. 68.

3. Hallett, *A Companion* . . . , p. 625.

4. C. W. K. Mundell, " 'Private Language' and Wittgenstein's Kind of Behaviorism," *Philosophical Quarterly* 16 (1966), p. 35.

5. C. S. Chihara and J. A. Fodor, "Operationalism and Ordinary Language: A Critique of Wittgenstein," *American Philosophical Quarterly* 2 (1965), p. 282fn.

6. See Day's "On Certain Similarities between the *Philosophical Investigations* of Ludwig Wittgenstein and the Operationism of B. F. Skinner," *Journal of the Experimental Analysis of Behavior* 12 (1969), pp. 489–506. See Waller's "Chomsky, Wittgenstein, and the Behaviorist Perspective," *Behaviorism* 5 (1977), p. 49fn. He is definitely wrong when he implies that Wittgenstein is a materialist (p. 45).

7. Hems, *op. cit.,* pp. 77–8.

8. See C. A. van Peursen, *Ludwig Wittgenstein,* p. 92; Henry LeRoy Finch, *The Later Philosophy,* pp. 65–67; J. T. Price, *Language and Being* . . . , pp. 62–63; Timothy Binkley, *Wittgenstein's Language,* p. 81; R. W. Miller, "Wittgenstein in Transition" (A Review of the *Philosphical Grammar*), *Philosophical Review* 86 (1977), pp. 525–6.

9. Cook, *op. cit.,* pp. 130–1.

10. Dennis O'Brien, "The Unity of Wittgenstein's Thought" in *Philosophy Today No. 1* (New York: Macmillan, 1968), p. 60.

11. Day, *op. cit.,* pp. 492, 499, 502, and *passim.*

12. Begelman, "Wittgenstein," *Behaviorism* 4 (1976), p. 203.

13. Skinner's uncritical effusion about the achievements of Darwin is embarrassing for philosophers familiar with the serious theoretical problems of Darwinism in all of its forms. Skinner claims that the key word in Darwin's great work is "origin" (AB, p.

Notes 243

224), and yet Darwin himself admitted that the origin of flowering plants was a great mystery to him. In the contemporary debate it is still questionable whether or not natural selection itself is able to explain the development of new species. Even with the genetic reforms of neo-Darwinism, which place great emphasis on mutations, there are serious problems with the so-called "hopeful monster" thesis.

14. J. B. Watson, *Behaviorism* (New York: Norton, 1930), p. 7.
15. Quoted in Day, p. 497.
16. "The Causation of Behavior," *Acta Philosophica Fennica* 28 (1976), p. 290.
17. Hems, *op. cit.*, p. 81.
18. Ihde, "Wittgenstein's Phenomenological Reduction," p. 55.
19. Hems, *op. cit.*, p. 68.
20. Pitkin, *Wittgenstein and Justice*, p. 324.

CHAPTER EIGHT

1. Garth Hallett, *Wittgenstein's Definition of Meaning as Use* (The Bronx: Fordham University Press, 1967), p. 6. "It is the essence of philosophy not to depend on experience, and this is what is meant by saying that philosophy is *a priori*" (L 3, p. 97).
2. Arthur Pap, *The "A Priori" in Physical Theory* (New York: King's Crown Press, 1946), p. viii.
3. Quine's essay first appeared in the *Philosophical Review* 60 (1951) and appears as Chapter Two in his *From the Logical Point of View* (Cambridge: Harvard University Press, 1961). This particular reference is found in Section 4.
4. Saul Kripke, "Naming and Necessity" in *Semantics of Natural Language*, ed. D. Davidson and G. Harman (Dordrecht: Reidel, 1972), pp. 263, 274–5, 314, 326.
5. Mikel Dufrenne, *Jalons* (The Hague: Nijhoff, 1966), pp. 188–207.
6. Peter Zinkernagel, *Conditions for Description* (London: Routledge & Kegan Paul, 1962), pp. 39–47.
7. "Is There a Factual *A priori*?" trans. W. Sellars in Feigl and Sellars, eds., *Readings in Philosophical Analysis* (New York: Appelton Century Crofts, 1949).
8. Cf. Iso Kern, *Kant und Husserl* (The Hague: Nijhoff, 1964), p. 61.
9. Brand, "The Material *A priori* . . . ," p. 130.
10. George J. Seidel, "Constitution in Mikel Dufrenne," *The Modern Schoolman* 47 (1970), p. 171.
11. Brand, "The Material *A priori*," p. 130.
12. Hallett, *Meaning as Use*, p. 193.
13. Brand, "The Material *A priori*," pp. 130, 142.
14. Robert Sokolowski, *The Formation of Husserl's Concept of Constitution* (The Hague: Nijhoff, 1964), p. 212.
15. See Hems, "Wittgenstein and/or Husserl," p. 62 and Black, *A Companion* . . . , p. 95.
16. Kern, *op. cit.*, p. 59.
17. Thomas Lagan, *Merleau-Ponty's Critique of Reason* (New Haven: Yale University Press, 1966), p. 8.
18. As Dufrenne states: "The material *a priori* on the other hand is the meaning spontaneously expressed by the appearance of a horse and not the empirical meaning derived from observations of its physiology" (NA, p. 83). Incidentally, there are many analytic subtleties (e.g., his claim that not all essences are *a priori*) in Dufrenne's book which we have not had time to point out or discuss.

19. Michael Sukale, *Comparative Studies in Phenomenology* (The Hague: Nijhoff, 1977), p. 119.
20. See Gary Gutting, "Husserl and Logical Empiricism," p. 203.
21. Finch, "Wittgenstein's Last Word," p. 392.
22. Harrison Hall, "The *A priori* and the Empirical in Merleau-Ponty's *Phenomenology of Perception*," *Philosophy Today* 23 (1979), p. 304.
23. *Ibid.*, p. 305.
24. William Lawhead, "Wittgenstein and Merleau-Ponty on Language and Critical Reflection" (doctoral dissertation, University of Texas, 1977), p. 173. Again it is instructive to note that Pap also describes his approach to the *a priori* as "dynamic" or "developmental" (*op. cit.*, p. 4). Lothar Eley argues that the exact, objective *a priori* of *mathesis* is always constituted within the "life-world" *a priori*. See his *Die Krise des A Priori* (The Hague: Nijhoff, 1966), p. 116.
25. E. K. Specht, *The Foundations of Wittgenstein's Late Philosophy*, trans. D. E. Walford (Manchester: Manchester University Press, 1969), p. 169. Some African languages have only three color words, so language does not only limit what we can say, but it also appears to limit what we can *see*. See D. L. Phillips, *Wittgenstein and Scientific Knowledge*, p. 42.
26. This is the term used by Pap to describe the same phenomenon (*op. cit.*, p. 4). Wittgenstein criticizes the theory of analyticity in another way: "The tendency to generalize the case seems to have a strict justification in logic . . . [but] we are under the illusion that what is essential about our investigation consists in its grasping *one* comprehensive essence" (Z, §444). I am indebted to Rudolf Bensch for his discussion of "bachelors are unmarried males" (*L. Wittgenstein: Die apriorischen und mathematischen Sätzen in seinem Spätwerk* [Bonn: Bouvier Verlag, 1973], pp. 50–52). At times Wittgenstein implies that meaning is not always use. If this is so, then this total ban on analyticity may be mitigated somewhat.
27. Wittgenstein annoys us with his inconsistencies: in 1923–3 lectures he conjures up a fictitious natural history in which it would make sense to remember the future (L 3, p. 15).
28. Finch, "Wittgenstein's Last Word," p. 384.
29. Weingartner, "Form and Content," p. 54.
30. Hall, *op. cit.*, p. 309.

CHAPTER NINE

1. John Passmore, *A Hundred Years of Philosophy* (Harmondsworth: Penguin Books, 1968), p. 106.
2. Robert C. Solomon, ed., *Nietzsche: A Collection of Critical Essays* (New York: Doubleday Anchor, 1973), p. 3.
3. Lothar Ely, "Life-World Constitution of Propositional Logic and Elementary Predicate Logic," *Philosophy and Phenomenological Research* 32 (1972), p. 322.
4. Smart, "Language-Games," p. 228.
5. French, "Wittgenstein's Limits of the World," p. 117.
6. Thomas Fay, *Heidegger: The Critique of Logic* (The Hague: Nijhoff, 1977), p. 85.
7. See Louis Couturat's article in *Leibniz*, ed. Harry G. Frankfurt (Doubleday Anchor, 1972), p. 30.
8. Quoted in *ibid.*

9. Rajan, "Cassirer and Wittgenstein," pp. 607, 608.

10. Winch, *The Idea of a Social Science*, p. 100.

11. *Ibid.*, p. 57.

12. Levison, "Wittgenstein and Logical Necessity," p. 369.

13. Weiler, *Mauthner's Critique of Language*, p. 221.

14. *Ibid.*, p. 231.

15. *Ibid.*, p. 248.

16. J. L. Austin, *Philosophical Papers*, ed. Urmson and Warnock (New York: Oxford University Press, 1961), p. 30.

17. Lawhead, "Wittgenstein and Merleau-Ponty on Language," p. 243. From my last minute reading of *Wittgenstein's Lectures, Cambridge 1932–35*, I found these appropriate passages: "I once said that logic describes the use of language in a vacuum"; and "Now who uses the calculus of T and F? I would say that it has no use. Taken as a calculus it is dull and useless, and so is Russell's calculus" (L 3, pp. 99, 139).

18. E. T. Gendlin, "What are the Grounds of Explication? A Basic Problem in Linguistic Analysis and in Phenomenology," *The Monist* 49 (1965), cited in Durfee, *Analytic Philosophy and Phenomenology*, p. 243.

19. Ricoeur, Husserl . . . , p. 158.

20. C. O. Schrag, "The Life-World and its Historical Horizon" in *Patterns of the Life-World*, p. 111.

21. Philip A. Hallie, "Stoicism" in the *Encyclopedia of Philosophy*, Vol. 8, p. 20.

22. Finch, "Wittgenstein's Last Word," p. 392.

23. Rossvaer, *Kant og Wittgenstein*, p. 401.

24. Simmel, "The Conflict in Modern Culture," p. 19.

25. Putnam, "Analyticity and Apriority," *Midwest Studies in Philosophy* 4 (1979), p. 425.

26. Bochenski, *The Methods of Contemporary Thought* (Dortrecht: Reidel, 1965), p. 79.

27. Simmel, "The Conflict of Modern Culture," p. 26.

CHAPTER TEN

1. Friedrich Nietzsche, *The Will to Power*, ed. Walter Kaufmann (New York: Vintage, 1968), p. 286 (my emphasis).

2. Coope, *et al.*, *A Wittgenstein Workbook* (Berkeley: University of California Press, 1970), pp. 5–6.

3. Martin Lang, *Wittgensteins Philosophische Grammatik* (The Hague: Nijhoff, 1971), pp. 7, 10.

4. Hacker, "Semantic Holism: Frege and Wittgenstein" in *Wittgenstein: Sources and Perspectives*, ed. C. G. Luckhardt (Ithaca: Cornell University Press, 1979), p. 226.

5. *Ibid.*, p. 233.

6. *Ibid.*, p. 237.

7. Quoted in Weiler, "On Fritz Mauthner's Critique of Language," *Mind* 67 (1958), p. 85. Wittgenstein acknowledges that "Luther said that theology is the grammar of the word of 'God' " (L 3, p. 32), and perhaps this is a clue to his cryptic phrase "theology as grammar" (PI, §373).

8. Hacker, *Insight and Illusion*, p. 151.

9. Black, "*Lebensform* and *Sprachspiel* in Wittgenstein's Later Work" in *Wittgenstein and His Impact*, p. 329.

10. Finch, *The Later Philosophy*, p. 149.

11. Ihde, "Wittgenstein's Phenomenological Reduction," p. 54.
12. Lawhead, "Wittgenstein and Merleau-Ponty on Language," pp. 88–9.
13. Spiegelberg, *The Phenomenological Movement*, Vol. 2, p. 670.
14. Spiegelberg, Supplement to "The Puzzle . . . ," item #2.
15. Paraphrased by Robert L. Arrington, "Wittgenstein and Phenomenology," *Philosophy Today* 22 (1978), p. 288.
16. John L. Austin, "A Plea for Excuses" in *Philosophical Papers*, p. 133.
17. Marsch, "The Triumph of Ambiguity," pp. 251–2. There is also appropriate material from Wittgenstein's lectures of 1932–35: "We are pulling ordinary grammar to bits"; "the common-sense answer is itself no solution"; and a discussion in which he claims that the grammar of ethical and theological terms will be different from ordinary grammar (L 3, pp. 31, 109, 32).
18. Harries, "Wittgenstein and Heidegger: The Relationship of the Philosopher to Language," *The Journal of Value Inquiry* 2 (1968), p. 288.
19. *Ibid.*, p. 289.
20. Arrington, *op. cit.*, p. 298.
21. See J. C. Nyiri, "Wittgenstein's New Traditionalism" *Acta Philosophica Fennica* 28 (1976), pp. 503–509. Nyiri reminds us of Wittgenstein's comments to his friend Paul Engelmann in which Wittgenstein considered all revolutionary convictions as immoral (p. 504). Nyiri also mentions Spengler as probably the most profound influence with regard to Wittgenstein's conservatism. His desire to go to Russia was not only because of his admiration for Tolstoy and Dostoevsky, but also because Spengler had predicated that Russian culture would be the "spring" of the dying "winter" of "Faustian" culture (p. 505).
22. Sefler, *Language and the World*, p. 190.
23. John D. Caputo, "Phenomenology, Mysticism, and the *'Grammatica Speculativa':* A Study of Heidegger's *'Habilitationsschrift,'* " *The Journal of the British Society for Phenomenology* 5 (1974), p. 107.
24. Jan Aler, "Heidegger's Conception of Language in *Being and Time*" in *On Heidegger and Language*, p. 53.
25. The Heideggerian theologian is Heinrich Ott, "Hermeneutic and Personal Structure of Language," in *On Heidegger and Language*, p. 178.
26. Harries, "Wittgenstein and Heidegger," p. 290.
27. Lawhead, "Wittgenstein and Merleau-Ponty," p. 116.
28. *Ibid.*, p. 136.
29. *Ibid.*, p. 199.
30. Quoted in *ibid.*, p. 62.
31. James M. Robinson, "Hermeneutic Since Barth" in *The New Hermeneutic*, eds. Robinson and John B. Cobb, Jr. (New York: Harper & Row, 1964), pp. 6–7.
32. *Ibid.*, p. 2.
33. See *ibid.*, p. 9.
34. Apel, "Wittgenstein and the Problem of Hermeneutical Understanding" in *Towards a Transformation of Philosophy*, trans. G. Adey and D. Frisby (London: Routledge & Kegan Paul, 1980), p. 207. See also his *Analytic Philosophy of Language . . .*, p. 43.

    Robert Innis, in his introduction to Brand's *The Essential Wittgenstein*, points out that in *Truth and Method* Gadamer spends much time developing the hermeneutical aspects of the concept of game. As Innis states: "The analogy is striking between the interpretative moves of philosophical hermeneutics which studies the interpretative moves of other hermeneutical projects and Wittgenstein's study of the various 'moves' constituting the grammars of multifarious and heterogeneous language-games" (EW, p. xiii). He sums up his comparison: "One will see . . . the shared concern with the unavoidably interpretative and finite character of our behavior in the world, the linguistically constituted relativity of our standpoints, and perhaps most importantly, the dissolution of the pretense of an objective metaphysics functioning as a super-science" (*ibid.*).

35. Richard E. Palmer, *Hermeneutics* (Evanston: Northwestern University Press, 1969), p. 215.
36. Lawhead, "Wittgenstein and Merleau-Ponty," p. 35.
37. F. Kerr, "Language as Hermeneutic in the Later Wittgenstein," *Tijdschrift voor Filosofie* 27 (1965), p. 518. Kerr offers other insightful statements: "Wittgenstein is simply a phenomenologist of language as disclosure of the consensus embodied in the human community"; and "Is language . . . the hermeneutic of the consensus which is the *a priori* of the human form of life?" (pp. 507, 506).
38. Apel, *Analytic Philosophy of Language* . . . , p. 50.
39. Gadamer, *Truth and Method*, p. 331.
40. Albert Levi, *Philosophy and the Modern World* (Bloomington, Ind.: Indiana University Press, 1959), p. 120.
41. Quoted in Apel, "Wittgenstein and the Problem . . . ," p. 2.
42. Rajan, p. 609.

Bibliography

WITTGENSTEIN AND FORMS OF LIFE

Arnhart, Larry, "Language and Nature in Wittgenstein's *Philosophical Investigations*," *Journal of Thought* 10 (1975), pp. 194–199.

Binkley, Timothy, "Natural History" in *Wittgenstein's Language*. The Hague: Nijhoff, 1973, pp. 94–111.

Black, Max, "*Lebensform* and *Sprachspiel* in Wittgenstein's Later Work" in *Wittgenstein and His Impact on Contemporary Thought*. Proceedings of the Second International Wittgenstein Symposium, 1977. Vienna: Hölder-Pichler-Tempsky, 1978, pp. 325–31.

Farhang, Zabeeh, "On Language-Games and Forms of Life" in E. D. Klemke, ed., *Essays on Wittgenstein*. Urbana: University of Illinois, 1971, pp. 432–349.

Finch, Henry LeRoy, "Forms of Life" in his *Wittgenstein–The Later Philosophy*. Atlantic Heights, N.J.: Humanities Press, 1977, pp. 89–102.

French, Peter, "Wittgenstein's Limits of the World," *Midwest Studies in Philosophy* 1 (1976) pp. 114–125.

Gier, Nicholas F., "Wittgenstein and Forms of Life," *Philosophy of the Social Sciences* 10 (1980), pp. 241–258.

Glebe-Møller, Jens. *Wittgenstein og Religionen*. Copenhagen: Gads Forlag, 1969.

High, Dallas M., "Form of Life" in *Language, Persons, and Beliefs*. New York: Oxford, 1967, pp. 99–130.

Hunter, J. F. M., "Forms of Life in Wittgenstein's *Philosophical Investigations*," *American Philosophical Quarterly* 5 (1968), pp. 233–243, reprinted in Klemke, *op. cit.*, pp. 273–297. Cited from Klemke.

Nielsen, Kai, "God and Forms of Life," *Indian Journal of Philosophy* 1 (1972), pp. 45–66.

————, "Religion and the Appeal to Forms of Life," *Agora* 3 (1976), pp. 67–71.

Petrie, Hugh, "Science and Metaphysics" in Klemke, pp. 138–169.

Shekelton, James "Rules and *Lebensformen*," *Midwest Studies in Philosophy* 1 (1976), pp. 125–132.

Sherry, Patrick, "Is Religion a Form of Life?" *American Philosophical Quarterly* 9 (1972), pp. 159–167.

Struhl, Karsten J., "Language-games and Forms of Life," *Journal of Critical Analysis* 11 (1970), pp. 25–31.

Sutherland, Stuart R., "On the Idea of a Form of Life," *Religious Studies* 11 (1975), pp. 293–306.

van Peursen, C. A., "Forms of Life" in *Ludwig Wittgenstein: An Introduction to His Philosophy*, trans. R. Ambler. London: Faber & Faber, 1969, pp. 95–113.

KANT AND WITTGENSTEIN

Bernays, Paul, Review of *Remarks on the Foundation of Mathematics, Ratio* 2 (1959), pp. 1–22.

Cavell, Stanley, "The Availability of Wittgenstein's Later Philosophy," *Philosophical Review* 71 (1962), pp. 67–93. Reprinted in G. Pitcher, ed., *Wittgenstein: The "Philosophical Investigations."* New York: Macmillan, 1966, pp. 151–185. Also reprinted in Cavell's *Must We Mean What We Say?* New York: Scribner's, 1969, pp. 44–72.

Couprie, D. L., "Wittgenstein I: Transcendentalfilosof, Ja of Neen?" *Tijdschrift voor Filosofi* 32 (1970), pp. 197–213.

Engel, S. Morris, "Wittgenstein and Kant," *The Monist* 53 (1969), pp. 656–669.

———, "Kant and Wittgenstein," *Philosophy and Phenomenological Research* 30 (1970), pp. 483–513.

Fang, J., "Wittgenstein vs. Kant in a Philosophy of Mathematics" in *Akten des XIV. Internationalen Kongresses für Philosophie*. Vienna: Herder, 1968, pp. 233–36.

Finch, Henry LeRoy, "Wittgenstein and Kant on Objects" in his *Wittgenstein: The Early Philosophy*. Atlantic Heights, N.J.,: Humanities Press, 1971, pp. 264–67.

Gill, J. H., "On Reaching Bedrock," *Metaphilosophy* 5 (1974), pp. 277–90.

Harries, Karsten, "Two Conflicting Interpretations of Language in Wittgenstein's *Investigations*," *Kant-Studien* 59 (1968), pp. 397–409.

Hartnack, Justus, "Kant and Wittgenstein," *Kant-Studien* 60 (1969), pp. 131–34.

Mandel, Ross, "Heidegger and Wittgenstein: A Second Kantian Revolution" in Michael Murray, ed., *Heidegger and Modern Philosophy*. New Haven: Yale University Press, 1978, pp. 259–70.

Maslow, Alexander. *A Study of Wittgenstein's "Tractatus."* Berkeley: University of California Press, 1961.

Morawetz, Thomas, "Wittgenstein and Synthetic *A Priori* Judgments," *Philosophy* 49 (1974), pp. 433–4.

Pears, David. *Wittgenstein*. London: Collins, 1971, pp. 25–41.

Rossvaer, Viggo. *Kant og Wittgenstein*. Oslo: Universitetsforlaget, 1971.

Schaper, Eva, "Kant's Schematism Reconsidered," *Review of Metaphysics* 18 (1964), pp. 291–2.

Schwyzer, Hubert, "Thought and Reality: the Metaphysics of Kant and Wittgenstein," *Philosophical Quarterly* 23 (1973), pp. 193–206.

Schwayder, D. S., "Wittgenstein on Mathematics" in Peter Winch, ed., *Studies in the Philosophy of Wittgenstein*. London: Routledge and Kegan Paul, 1969, pp. 66–116.

Specht, E. K. *The Foundations of Wittgenstein's Late Philosophy*, trans. D. E. Walford. Manchester: Manchester University Press, 1969, pp. 176–9.

Stegmüller, W., "Ludwig Wittgenstein als Ontologe, Isomorphietheoretiker, Transzendentalphilosoph und Konstruktivist," *Philosophische Rundschau* 13 (1965), pp. 116–52.

Stenius, Erik, "Wittgenstein as a Kantian Philosopher" in his *Wittgenstein's Tractatus*. London: Oxford, 1960, pp. 214–226.

Wertz, Spenzer K., "On Placing Wittgenstein in History," *Southern Journal of Philosophy* 11 (1973), pp. 337–350.

SCHOPENHAUER AND WITTGENSTEIN

Engel, S. Morris, "Schopenhauer's Impact on Wittgenstein," *Journal of the History of Philosophy* 7 (1969), pp. 285–302.

Gardiner, Patrick, "Schopenhauer and Wittgenstein," a chapter in his *Schopenhauer*. Harmondsworth: Penguin, 1963, pp. 275–82.

Greenwood, E. B., "Tolstoy, Wittgenstein, and Schopenhauer," *Encounter* (London) 36 (1973), pp. 60–72.

Griffiths, A. Phillips, "Wittgenstein, Schopenhauer, and Ethics" in *Understanding Wittgenstein*, ed. G. Vesey. Ithaca: Cornell University Press, 1974, pp. 96–116.

Janik, Allan, "Schopenhauer and the Early Wittgenstein," *Philosophical Studies* (Irish) 15 (1966), pp. 76–95.

WITTGENSTEIN'S GENERAL HISTORICAL BACKGROUND

Bartley, W. W. *Wittgenstein*. New York: J. B. Lippincott, 1973.

Drury, M. O'C., "Some Notes on Conversations with Wittgenstein," *Acta Philosophica Fennica* 28 (1976), pp. 22–39.

Findlay, J. N., "My Encounters with Wittgenstein," *Philosophical Forum* 4 (1973), pp. 167–185.

Hacker, P. M. S. *Insight and Illusion: Wittgenstein on Philosophy and the Metaphysics of Experience*. London: Oxford University Press, 1972. Good for Kant, Schopenhauer, and Brouwer.

Haller, Rudolf, "Ludwig Wittgenstein und die Österreichische Philosophie," *Wissenschaft und Weltbild* 21 (1968), pp. 77–87.

Hallett, Garth. *A Companion to Wittgenstein's "Philosophical Investigations,"* Ithaca: Cornell University Press, 1977, pp. 759–775.

Janik, Allan, and Toulmin, Stephen. *Wittgenstein's Vienna*. New York: Simon and Schuster, 1973.

Janik, Allan, "Wittgenstein and Weininger" in *Wittgenstein and His Impact*, pp. 25–29.

Kaplan, Bernard, "Some Considerations of Influences on Wittgenstein," *Idealistic Studies* 1 (1971), pp. 73–88.

Nyiri, J. C., "Wittgenstein's New Traditionalism," *Acta Philosophica Fennica* 28 (1976), pp. 583–9.

Smith, Barry, "Law and Eschatology in Wittgenstein's Early Thought," *Inquiry* 21 (1978), pp. 425–41.

——— , "Wittgenstein and the Background of Austrian Philosophy" in *Wittgenstein and His Impact*, pp. 31–35.

Toulmin, Stephen, "Ludwig Wittgenstein," *Encounter* (London) 32 (1969), pp. 58–71.

Tranøy, K., "Recollections of Wittgenstein," *Acta Philosophica Fennica* 28 (1976), pp. 11–21.

von Wright, G. H., "Wittgenstein in Relation to His Times" in *Wittgenstein and His Impact*, pp. 73–78.

Wallace, Kyle, "Nietzsche's and Wittgenstein's Perspectivism," *Southwest Journal of Philosophy* 4 (1973), pp. 101–107.

Weiler, Gershon, "On Fritz Mauthner's Critique of Language," *Mind* 67 (1958), pp. 80–87.

———. *Mauthner's Critique of Language.* London: Cambridge University Press, 1970.

WITTGENSTEIN AND EXISTENTIALISM

Cavell, Stanley, "Existentialism and Analytic Philosophy," *Daedalus* 93 (1964), pp. 946–974. A Comparison of Wittgenstein and Kierkegaard.

Gallagher, Michael P., "Wittgenstein's Admiration for Kierkegaard," *The Month* 39 (1968), pp. 43–49.

Leiber, Justin, "Linguistic Analysis and Existentialism," *Philosophy and Phenomenological Research* 32 (1971), pp. 47–56. Wittgenstein and Camus compared.

Lübbe, H., "Wittgenstein—ein Existentialist?" *Philosophisches Jahrbuch* 69 (1962).

Salamun, K., "Wittgenstein und die Existenzphilosophie" in *Wittgenstein and His Impact*, pp. 65–69.

WITTGENSTEIN, FREGE, AND HUSSERL

Smith, Barry, "Frege, Husserl, and the Ontology of Reference," *Journal of the British Society for Phenomenology* 9 (1978), pp. 111–125.

Solomon, Robert C., "Sense and Essence: Frege and Husserl," *International Philosophical Quarterly* 10 (1970), pp. 378–401. Reprinted in Durfee, pp. 31–54. Also reprinted in Solomon's *Phenomenology and Existentialism.* New York: Harper & Row, 1972, pp. 258–281.

WITTGENSTEIN, HUSSERL, AND PHENOMENOLOGY

Arrington, Robert L., "Wittgenstein and Phenomenology," *Philosophy Today* 22 (1978), pp. 287–300.

Brand, Gerd. *The Essential Wittgenstein*, trans. Robert E. Innis. New York: Basic Books, 1979.

Copelston, F. C., "Wittgenstein frente a Husserl," *Revista Portuguesa de Filosofia* (Braga) 21 (1965), pp. 134–49.

Dufrenne, Mikel. *Jalons.* The Hague: Nijhoff, 1966. A chapter on Husserl and Wittgenstein, pp. 188–207.

Findlay, J. N., "Phenomenology" in *Encyclopedia Britannica*, 1964 ed.

Hems, John, "Husserl and/or Wittgenstein," *International Philosophical Quarterly* 8 (1968), pp. 547–578. Reprinted in Durfee, pp. 55–86. Durfee pages cited.

Ihde, Don, "Wittgenstein's Phenomenological Reduction," *Phenomenological Perspectives*, ed. P. Bossert. The Hague: Nijhoff, 1975, pp. 47–60.

Mohanty, J. N. *Edmund Husserl's Theory of Meaning.* The Hague: Nijhoff, 1964.

Munson, Thomas N., "Wittgenstein's Phenomenology," *Philosophy and Phenomenological Research* 23 (1962), pp. 37–50.

Ricoeur, Paul, "Husserl and Wittgenstein on Language" in *Phenomenology and Existentialism*, ed. E. N. Lee and M. Mandelbaum. Baltimore: Johns Hopkins, 1967, pp. 207–217.

Rosenberg, Jay F., "Intentionality and Self in the *Tractatus*," *Nous* 2 (1968), pp. 341–358.

Seligman, David B., "Wittgenstein on Seeing Aspects and Experiencing Meaning," *Philosophy and Phenomenological Research* 37 (1976), pp. 205–217.

Spiegelberg, Herbert, "The Puzzle of Wittgenstein's *Phänomenologie* (1929–?)," *American Philosophical Quarterly* 5 (1968), pp. 244–256. This article will be reprinted with a supplement in *The Context of the Phenomenological Movement*, a collection of Spiegelberg's articles, forthcoming from Nijhoff.

Taylor, Earl, "*Lebenswelt* and *Lebensform*: Husserl and Wittgenstein on the Goal and Method of Philosophy," *Human Studies* 1 (1978), pp. 184–200.

TeHennepe, Eugene, "The Life-World and the World of Ordinary Language" in J. Edie, ed., *An Invitation to Phenomenology*. Chicago: Quadrangle, 1965, pp. 133–146.

van Peursen, C. A., "Husserl and Wittgenstein," *Philosophy and Phenomenological Research* 20 (1959), pp. 181–197.

WITTGENSTEIN AND HEIDEGGER

Apel, Karl-Otto, "Wittgenstein und Heidegger," *Philosophisches Jahrbuch* 75 (1967), pp. 358–396.

Behl, L., "Wittgenstein and Heidegger," *Duns Scotus Philosophical Association Convention Report* 27 (1963), pp. 70–115.

Cavell, Stanley, "Leopards in Connecticut," *The Georgia Review* 30 (1976), pp. 240–241.

Erickson, Stephen. *Language and Being: An Analytic Phenomenology*. New Haven: Yale University Press, 1970.

Fay, Thomas A., "Early Heidegger and Wittgenstein on World," *Philosophical Studies* (Irish) 21 (1973), pp. 161–171.

————— , "Heidegger and Wittgenstein on the Question of Ordinary Language," *Philosophy Today* 23 (1979), pp. 154–159.

Gier, Nicholas F., "Wittgenstein and Heidegger: A Phenomenology of Forms of Life," *Tijdschrift voor Filosofie* 43 (1981).

Goff, R. A., "Wittgenstein's Tools and Heidegger's Implements," *Man and World* 1 (1968), pp. 447–62.

Harries, Karsten, "Wittgenstein and Heidegger: The Relationship of the Philosopher to Language," *The Journal of Value Inquiry* 2 (1968), pp. 281–291.

Heaton, J. M., McCormick, Peter, Schaper, Eva, "Saying and Showing in Heidegger and Wittgenstein," *Journal of the British Society for Phenomenology* 3 (1972), pp. 27–45.

Horgby, Ingvar, "The Double Awareness in Heidegger and Wittgenstein," *Inquiry* 2 (1959), pp. 235–264.

Hottois, Gilbert, "Aspects du rapproachment par K.-O. Apel de la philosophie de M. Heidegger et de la philosophie de la Wittgenstein," *Revue internationale de philosophie* 30 (1976), pp. 450–485.

Mandel, Ross, "Heidegger and Wittgenstein" in *Heidegger and Modern Philosophy*, pp. 259–70.

Mood, John J., "Poetic Languaging and Primal Thinking: A Study of Barfield, Wittgenstein, and Heidegger," *Encounter* (Indianapolis) 26 (1965), pp. 417–433.

Morrison, James C., "Heidegger's Criticism of [early] Wittgenstein's Conception of Truth," *Man and World* 2 (1969), pp. 551–573.

Murray, Michael, "A Note on Wittgenstein and Heidegger," *Philosophical Review* 83 (1974), pp. 501–503.
Sefler, George F. *Language and the World: A Methodological Synthesis within the Writings of M. Heidegger and L. Wittgenstein.* Atlantic Heights: The Humanities Press, 1974.
Weil, G. M., "Esotericism and the Double Awareness," *Inquiry* 3 (1960), pp. 61–72.

WITTGENSTEIN AND BEHAVIORISM

Begelman, D. A., "Wittgenstein," *Behaviorism* 4 (1976), pp. 201–207.
Chihara, C. S. and Fodor, J. A., "Operationalism and Ordinary Language: A Critique of Wittgenstein," *American Philosophical Quarterly* 2 (1965), pp. 281–295.
Costall, Alan, "The Limits of Language: Wittgenstein's Later Philosophy and Skinner's Radical Behaviorism," *Behaviorism* 8 (1980), pp. 123–131.
Day, Willard F., "On Certain Similarities Between the *Philosophical Investigations* of Ludwig Wittgenstein and the Operationism of B. F. Skinner," *Journal of the Experimental Analysis of Behavior* 12 (1969), pp. 489–506.
Gier, Nicholas F., "Wittgenstein. Intentionality, and Behaviorism." *Metaphilosophy* 12 (1981).
Holborow, L. C., "Wittgenstein's Kind of Behaviorism?" *Philosophical Quarterly* 17 (1967), pp. 345–57.
Johnson, Charles W., "On Wittgenstein," *Behaviorism* 5 (1977), pp. 39–42.
Mundell, C. W. K., " 'Private Language' and Wittgenstein's Kind of Behaviorism," *Philosophical Quarterly* 16 (1966), pp. 35–46.
Waller, Bruce, "Chomsky, Wittgenstein and the Behaviorist Perspective," *Behaviorism* 5 (1977), pp. 43–59.

WITTGENSTEIN AND MERLEAU-PONTY

Epstein, Michele F., "The Common Ground of Merleau-Ponty and Wittgenstein's Philosophy of Man," *Journal of the History of Philosophy* 13 (1975), pp. 221–234.
Kemp, Peter, "Den faenomenologiske sprogfilosofi og Wittgenstein" in *Filosofiske Portraetter.* Copenhagen: Vinten forlag, 1973, pp. 107–115. First appeared in *Exil* (1969).
Kwant, R. G., "Merleau-Ponty en Wittgenstein," *Tijdschrift voor Filosofie* 32 (1970), pp. 3–29.
Lawhead, William F., "Wittgenstein and Merleau-Ponty on Language and Critical Reflection," doctoral dissertation, University of Texas, 1977.
Marsh, James L., "The Triumph of Ambiguity: Merleau-Ponty and Wittgenstein," *Philosophy Today* 19 (1975), pp. 243–255.
Munson, Thomas, "The Pre-Objective Reconsidered," *Review of Metaphysics* 12 (1958), pp. 624–632.
Spurling, Laurie. *Phenomenology and the Social World.* London: Routledge and Kegan Paul, 1977, pp. 62–72, 175–179.

WITTGENSTEIN AND HERMENEUTICS

Apel, Karl-Otto. *Analytic Philosophy of Language and the "Geisteswissenschaften."* Dortrecht: Reidel, 1967. Originally published in *Philosophisches Jahrbuch* 72 (1965), pp. 239–289.

———, "Wittgenstein und das Problem des hermeneutischen Verstehens," *Zeitschrift für Theologie und Kirche* 63 (1966), pp. 49–87. English translation in *Towards a Transformation of Philosophy*, trans. G. Adey and D. Frisby. London: Routledge & Kegan Paul, 1980, pp. 1–45.

Fahrenbach, Helmut, "Die Logische-Hermeneutische Problemstellung in Wittgensteins *Tractatus*," in R. Buhner, *et al.* eds. *Hermeneutik und Dialektik: Hans-Georg Gadamer zum 70. Geburtstag.* Tübingen: J. C. B. Mohr, 1970, pp. 26–54.

Gadamer, Hans-Georg, "Die Phänomenologische Bewegung," *Philosophische Rundschau* 11 (1963), pp. 42ff.

Kerr, F., "Language as Hermeneutic in the Later Wittgenstein," *Tijdschrift voor Filosofie* 27 (1965), pp. 489–520.

Premo, Blanche L., "The Early Wittgenstein and Hermeneutics," *Philosophy Today* 16 (1972), pp. 43–65.

JAMES, WITTGENSTEIN, AND PHENOMENOLOGY

Cerf, Walter H., "An Approach to Heidegger's Ontology," *Philosophy and Phenomenological Research* 1 (1940), pp. 177–190. Heidegger and James are compared.

Coope, Christopher, *et al* eds. *A Wittgenstein Workbook.* Berkeley: University of California Press, 1970. Appendix 2 on "Passages Parallel to Wittgenstein's *Philosophical Investigations* and *Zettel* in James' *The Principles of Psychology*.

Edie, James M., "John Wild's Interpretation of William James's Theory of the Free Act," *Man and World* 8 (1975), pp. 136–140.

———, "William James and Phenomenology," *Review of Metaphysics* 22 (1970), pp. 481–526.

Fairbanks, Matthew, "Wittgenstein and James," *The New Scholasticism* 40 (1966), pp. 331–340.

Gurwitsch, Aron, "William James' Theory of the 'Transitive Parts' of the Stream of Consciousness," *Philosophy and Phenomenological Research* 3 (1943), pp. 449–477.

Husserl, Edmund, "Persönliche Anzeichungen," *Philosophy and Phenomenological Research* 16 (1956), pp. 293–302.

Ross, Robert R. N., "William James—The Wider Consciousness," *Philosophy Today* 20 (1976), pp. 134–148.

Schütz, Alfred, "William James' Concept of the Stream of Thought Phenomenologically Interpreted," *Philosophy and Phenomenological Research* 1 (1941), pp. 442–452.

Wertz, S. K., "On Wittgenstein and James," *The New Scholasticism* 46 (1972), pp. 446–448.

Wilshire, Bruce. *William James and Phenomenology.* Bloomington, Ind.: Indiana University Press, 1968.

WITTGENSTEIN AND POLANYI

Daly, C. B., "Polanyi and Wittgenstein" in *Intellect and Hope*, ed. Thomas A. Langford. Durham, N.C.: Duke University Press, 1968, pp. 136–68.

Gill, Jerry H., "Saying and Showing: Radical Themes in Wittgenstein's *On Certainty*," *Religious Studies* 10 (1974), pp. 279–290.

Hall, Ronald L., "Wittgenstein and Polanyi: The Problem of Privileged Self-Knowledge," *Philosophy Today* 23 (1979), pp. 267–278.

GENERAL COMPARISONS OF LINGUISTIC
ANALYSIS AND PHENOMENOLOGY

Arrington, Robert L., "Can There Be a Linguistic Phenomenology?" *Philosophical Quarterly* 25 (1975), pp. 289–304.

Ayer, A. J., "Phenomenology and Linguistic Analysis II" in Dufree, pp. 232–242.

Bossert, Philip J., "The Explication of 'The World' in Constructionalism and Phenomenology," *Man and World* 6 (1973), pp. 231–251. Husserl and Goodman are compared.

Cayard, W. W., "Bertrand Russell and Existential Phenomenology," *Journal of the West Virginia Philosophical Society* (1976), pp. 17–22.

Danto, Arthur. *Sartre*. New York: Viking, 1975. Sartre's philosophy is translated into the terminology of analytic philosophy.

Durfee, H. A., ed. *Analytic Philosophy and Phenomenology*. The Hague: Nijhoff, 1976.

Føllesdal, Dagfinn, "Meaning and Experience" in *Mind and Language*, ed. Samuel Guttenplan. Oxford: Clarendon Press, 1975, pp. 25–44.

Gill, Jerry H., "Linguistic Phenomenology," *International Philosophical Quarterly* 13 (1973), pp. 535–50.

Gorner, Paul, "Husserl and Strawson," *Journal of the British Society of Phenomenology* 2 (1971), pp. 2–9.

Grene, Marjorie. *Philosophy In and Out of Europe*. Berkeley: University of California, 1976.

Gutting, Gary, "Husserl and Logical Empiricism," *Metaphilosophy* 2 (1971), pp. 197–226.

Ihde, Don, "Some Parallels between Analysis and Phenomenology" in Durfee, pp. 179–189. Quine and Ricoeur Compared.

Kung, Guido, "Language Analysis and Phenomenological Analysis," *Akten des XIV. Internationalen Kongresses für Philosophie*, pp. 247–53.

_____ , "The Role of Language in Phenomenological Analysis," *American Philosophical Quarterly* 6 (1968), pp. 330–334.

_____ , "Ingarden on Language and Ontology: A Comparison with some Trends in Analytic Philosophy," in *The Later Husserl and the Idea of Phenomenology, Analecta Husserliana*. Dortrecht: Reidel, 1972, Vol. 2, pp. 204–217.

"Linguistic Analysis and Phenomenology," topic of entire issue of *The Monist* 49 (1965).

Lübbe, Hermann, "Sprachspiele und Geschichte: Neopositivismus und Phänomenologie im Spätstadium," *Kant-Studien* 50 (1960), pp. 220–243.

Mays, W. and Brown, S., eds. *Linguistic Analysis and Phenomenology*. Lewisburg, Pa.: Bucknell University Press, 1972.

Murray, Michael, "Heidegger and Ryle: Two Versions of Phenomenology," *Review of Metaphysics* 27 (1973), pp. 88–111.

Pivcevic, Edo. *Phenomenology and Philosophical Understanding*. London: Cambridge University Press, 1975.

Roche, Maurice. *Phenomenology, Language, and the Social Sciences*. London: Routledge and Kegan Paul, 1973.

Rosen, Stanley. *Nihilism: A Philosophical Essay*. New Haven: Yale University Press, 1969.

Schmitt, Richard, "Phenomenology and Analysis," *Philosophy and Phenomenological Research* 23 (1963), pp. 101–110.

———, "Phenomenology and Metaphysics," *Journal of Philosophy* 59 (1962), pp. 421–428.

Solomon, Robert C., "Wittgenstein and Cartesian Privacy," *Philosophy Today* 16 (1972).

Taylor, Charles, "Phenomenology and Linguistic Analysis I" in Dufree, pp. 217–231.

Tibbetts, Paul, "The Levels of Experience Doctrine in Modern Philosophy of Mind," *Studi Internazionale di Filosofia* 3 (1971), pp. 15–32.

Tillman, Frank, "Transcendental Phenomenology and Analytic Philosophy," *International Philosophical Quarterly* 7 (1967), pp. 32–40.

———, "Phenomenology and Philosophical Analysis," *International Philosophical Quarterly* 6 (1976), pp. 465–480.

Tranǿy, K., "Contemporary Philosophy: Analytic and Continental," *Philosophy Today* 8 (1964), pp. 155–168.

Tugendhat, Ernst, "Phänomenologie und Sprachanalyse" in *Hermeneutik und Dialektik*, Vol. 2, pp. 3–23. English translation by P. McCormick and F. Elliston (also editors) in *Husserl: Exposition and Appraisals*. Notre Dame: Notre Dame University, 1977, pp. 325–337.

van Peursen, C. A. *Phenomenological and Analytical Philosophy*. Pittsburgh: Duquesne, 1972.

Weinzweig, Majorie, "Phenomenology and Ordinary Language Philosophy," *Metaphilosophy* 8 (1977), pp. 116–46.

MISCELLANEOUS WORKS ON WITTGENSTEIN

Bensch, Rudolph. *L. Wittgenstein: Die apriorischen und mathematischen Sätzen in seinem Spätwerk*. Bonn: Bouvier Verlag, 1973.

Black, Max. *A Companion to Wittgenstein's "Tractatus."* Ithaca, N.Y.: Cornell University Press, 1964.

Britton, Karl, "A Portrait of a Philosopher" in Fann's *Wittgenstein: The Man and His Philosophy*, pp. 56–63.

Cook, John W., "Human Beings" in *Studies in the Philosophy of Wittgenstein*, ed. P. Winch. London: Routledge & Kegan Paul, 1969.

Coope, Christopher, et al., eds. *A Wittgenstein Workbook*. Berkeley: University of California Press, 1970.

Dummett, Michael, "Wittgenstein's Philosophy of Mathematics," *Philosophical Review* 68 (1959), pp. 324–48, cited from Pitcher's anthology on the *Investigations*.

Engel, S. M. *Wittgenstein's Doctrine of the Tyranny of Language*. The Hague: Nijhoff, 1975.

Fann, K. T. *Wittgenstein's Conception of Philosophy*. Berkeley: University of California Press, 1971.

———, ed. *Wittgenstein: The Man and His Philosophy*. New York: Dell Publishing Co., 1967.

Finch, Henry LeRoy, "Wittgenstein's Last Word: Ordinary Certainty," *International Philosophical Quarterly* 15, (1978), pp. 383–395.

Findlay, J. N., "My Encounters with Wittgenstein," *Philosophical Forum* 4 (1973), pp. 167–85.

Fogelin, Robert J. *Wittgenstein*. London: Routledge & Kegan Paul, 1976.

Griffin, James. *Wittgenstein's Logical Atomism*. London: Oxford University Press, 1964.

Hacker, P. M. S., "Semantic Holism: Frege and Wittgenstein" in *Wittgenstein: Sources and Perspectives*, pp. 213–42.

Hallett, Garth. *Wittgenstein's Definition of Meaning as Use*. New York: Fordham University Press, 1967.

WITTGENSTEIN AND PHENOMENOLOGY

Hudson, W. D. *Ludwig Wittgenstein: The Bearing of his Philosophy upon Religious Beliefs.*
Richmond: John Knox Press, 1968.
Keightley, Alan. *Wittgenstein, Grammar, and God.* London: Epworth Press, 1976.
Kenny, Anthony. *Wittgenstein.* Cambridge: Harvard University Press, 1973.
———, "From the Big Typescript to the *Philosophical Gramar,*" *Acta Philosophica Fennica* 28
(1976), pp. 41–53.
Klenk, V. H. *Wittgenstein's Philosophy of Mathematics.* The Hague: Nijhoff, 1976.
Lang, Martin. *Wittgensteins Philosophische Grammatik.* The Hague: Nijhoff, 1971.
Levison, A. B., "Wittgenstein and Logical Necessity," *Inquiry* 7 (1964), pp. 367–73.
Luckhardt, C. G., ed. *Wittgenstein: Sources and Perspectives.* Ithaca: Cornell University
Press, 1979.
McGuiness, B. F. "Philosophy of Science in the *Tractatus,*" *Revue internationale de philosophie*
23 (1969), pp. 155–66.
Malcolm, Norman. *Wittgenstein: A Memoir.* London: Oxford University Press, 1958.
———. *Knowledge and Certainty: Essays and Lectures.* Englewood Cliffs, N.J.: Prentice-Hall,
1963. Excerpted and cited from Pitcher's anthology.
Miller, R. W., "Wittgenstein in Transition" (Review of the *Philosophical Grammar*),
Philosophical Review 86 (1977).
O'Brien, Dennis, "The Unity of Wittgenstein's Thought" in *Philosophy Today No. 1.* New
York: Macmillan, 1968.
Øfsti, Audun. *Språk og Fornuft.* Oslo: Universitetsforlaget, 1975.
Phillips, Derek L. *Wittgenstein and Scientific Knowledge: A Sociological Perspective.* London:
Routledge & Kegan Paul, 1974.
Phillips, D. Z. *Death and Immortality.* London: St. Martin's Press, 1970.
Pitcher, George. *The Philosophy of Wittgenstein.* Englewood Cliffs, N.J.: Prentice-Hall,
1964.
———. *Wittgenstein: The "Philosophical Investigations."* New York: Macmillan, 1966.
Pitkin, Hanna F. *Wittgenstein and Justice.* Berkeley: University of California Press, 1972.
Pole, David. *The Later Philosophy of Wittgenstein.* London: The Athalone Press, 1958.
Price, Jeffrey Thomas. *Language and Being in Wittgenstein "Philosophical Investigations."* The
Hague: Mouton, 1973.
Rajan, R. Sundara. "Cassirer and Wittgenstein," *International Philosophical Quarterly* 7
(1967), pp. 591–610.
Saran, A. K., "A Wittgensteinian Sociology?" *Ethics* 75 (1965), pp. 195–200.
Smart, H. R. "Language-Games," *Philosophical Quarterly* 7 (1957).
Stoutland, Frederick, "The Causation of Behavior," *Acta Philosophica Fennica* 28 (1976),
pp. 286f.
Strawson, P. F., Review of the *Philosophical Investigations, Mind* 63 (1954), pp. 70–99. Re-
printed and cited from Pitcher's anthology, pp. 22–64.
Stroud, Barry, "Wittgenstein and Logical Necessity," *Philosophical Review* 74 (1965), pp.
504–518. Reprinted and cited from Pitcher's anthology, pp. 477–96.
Verhack, Igance, "Wittgenstein's Deictic Metaphysics: An Uncommon Reading of the
Tractatus," *International Philosophical Quarterly* 18 (1978), pp. 433–44.
Winch, Peter. *The Idea of a Social Science.* London: Routledge & Kegan Paul, 1958.
von Wright, G. H., "The Wittgenstein Papers," *Philosophical Review* 78 (1969), pp.
483–503.
———, "Wittgenstein's Views on Probability," *Revue internationale de philosophie* 23 (1969),
pp. 259–83.
———, "Biographical Sketch" in Malcolm's *Memoir.*
———, "Wittgenstein in Relation to His Times" in *Wittgenstein and His Impact*, pp. 73–78.

OTHER WORKS CITED

Aler, Jan, "Heidegger's Conception of Language in *Being and Time*" in *On Heidegger and Language*, trans. and ed. Joseph J. Kockelmans. Evanston: Northwestern University Press, 1972, pp. 33–64.

Arrington, Robert L., "Can There Be A Linguistic Phenomenology?" *Philosophical Quarterly* 25 (1975), pp. 289–304.

Austin, John L. *Philosophical Papers*. New York: Oxford University Press, 1961.

Bennett, Jonathan. *Rationality: An Essay Toward an Analysis*. London: Routledge & Kegan Paul, 1964.

Blanshard, Brand. *Reason and Belief*. New Haven: Yale University Press, 1975.

———, *et al.*, A Symposium on Internal Relations, *Review of Metaphysics* 21 (1967).

Bochenski, I. M. *Contemporary European Philosophy*, trans. D. Nicholl and K. Aschenbrenner. Berkeley: University of California Press, 1965.

———, *The Methods of Contemporary Thought*. Dortrecht: Reidel, 1965.

Brand, Gerd, "The Material *A priori* and the Foundation for its Analysis in Husserl" in *The Later Husserl and the Idea of Phenomenology*, ed. A. Tymieniecka, *Analecta Husserliana*, Volume II, Dortrecht: Reidel, 1972, pp. 128–148.

Caputo, John D., "Phenomenology, Mysticism, and the 'Grammatica Speculativa': A Study of Heidegger's 'Habilitationsschrift,' " *Journal of the British Society for Phenomenology* 5 (1974), pp. 101–117.

Carr, David, "Husserl's Problematic Concept of the Life-World" in *Husserl: Exposition and Appraisal*, eds. and trans. F. A. Elliston and P. McCormick. Notre Dame: Notre Dame University Press, 1977.

Dillon, M. C., "Gestalt Theory and Merleau-Ponty's Concept of Intentionality," *Man and World* 4 (1971), pp. 436–459.

Dilthey, Wilhelm. *Gesammelte Schriften*, 12 volumes. Stuttgart: Teubner, 1958.

Dray, W. H., "Oswald Spengler" in *The Encyclopedia of Philosophy*, ed. Paul Edwards. New York: Macmillan, 1967, Vol. 7, pp. 527–530.

Dummett, Michael. *Elements of Intuitionism*. Oxford: Oxford University Press, 1977.

Edie, James M., *et al.*, eds. *Patterns of the Life-World: Essays in Honor of John Wild*. Evanston: Northwestern University Press, 1970.

Ely, Lothar, "Life-World Constitution of Propositional Logic and Elementary Predicate Logic," *Philosophy and Phenomenological Research* 32 (1972), pp. 322–40.

———. *Die Krise des Apriori*. The Hague: Nijhoff, 1966.

Erickson, Stephen A., "Meaning and Language," *Man and World* 1 (1968), pp. 563–586.

Fay, Thomas A. *Heidegger: The Critique of Logic*. The Hague: Nijhoff, 1977.

Findlay, J. N. *Meinong's Theory of Objects and Value*. Oxford: The Clarendon Press, 1963.

Føllesdal, Dagfinn, "Husserl and Heidegger on the Role of Actions in the Constitution of the World" in *Essays in Honor of Jaakko Hintikka*, eds. E. Saariene, *et al.* Dortrecht: Reidel, 1979.

Frankfurt, Harry G., ed. *Leibniz*. New York: Doubleday Anchor, 1972.

Gadamer, Hans-Georg. *Truth and Method*. New York: The Seabury Press, 1975.

———, "The Science of the Life-World" in *The Later Husserl and the Idea of Phenomenology*, pp. 173–85.

Gill, Jerry H., "Linguistic Phenomenology," *International Philosophical Quarterly* 13 (1973), pp. 535–550.

Gurwitsch, Aron. *Studies in Phenomenology and Psychology*. Evanston: Northwestern University Press, 1966.

———— , "Problems of the Life-World" in *Phenomenology and Social Reality*, ed. M. Natanson. The Hague: Nijhoff, 1970.

Hall, Harrison, "The *A priori* and the Empirical in Merleau-Ponty's *Phenomenology of Perception*," *Philosophy Today* 23 (1979), pp. 304–9.

Hallie, Phillip A., "Stoicism" in *The Encyclopedia of Philosophy*, Vol. 8, pp. 19–22.

Herbenick, Raymond, "Merleau-Ponty and the Primacy of Reflection" in *The Horizons of the Flesh*, ed. Garth Gillan. Carbondale, Ill.: Southern Illinois University Press, 1973, pp. 92–113.

Kern, Iso. *Husserl und Kant*. The Hague: Nijhoff, 1964.

Kockelmans, Joseph, ed. and trans. *On Heidegger and Language*. Evanston: Northwestern University Press, 1972.

Kripke, Saul, "Naming and Necessity" in *Semantics of Natural Language*, ed. D. Davidson & G. Harman. Dortrecht: Reidel, 1972.

Langan, Thomas. *Merleau-Ponty's Critique of Reason*. New Haven: Yale University Press, 1966.

McGinn, Colin, "Husserl and Mach," *Journal of the British Society for Phenomenology* 3 (1972), pp. 146–57.

McHugh, Peter, *et al. On the Beginning of Social Inquiry*. London: Routledge & Kegan Paul, 1974.

Mallin, Samuel B. *Merleau-Ponty's Philosophy*. New Haven: Yale University Press, 1979.

Malmgren, H., "Internal Relations in the Analysis of Consciousness," *Theoria* 41 (1975), pp. 61–83.

Natanson, Maurice, ed. *The Philosophy of the Social Sciences*. New York: Random House, 1963.

Nietzsche, Friedrich, *The Will to Power*, trans. W. Kaufmann and R. J. Hollingdale. New York: Vintage Books, 1967.

Ott, Heinrich, "Hermeneutic and Personal Structure of Language of *Being and Time*" in *On Heidegger and Language*, pp. 169–193.

Palmer, Richard E. *Hermeneutics: Interpretation Theory in Schleiermacher, Dilthey, Heidegger, and Gadamer*. Evanston: Northwestern University Press, 1969.

Pap, Arthur. *The "A priori" in Physical Theory*. New York: King's Crown Press, 1946.

Passmore, John. *A Hundred Years of Philosophy*. Harmondsworth: Penguin Books, 1968.

Pöggeler, Otto. *Der Denkweg Martin Heideggers*. Tübingen: Neske, 1963.

Putnam, Hilary, "Analyticity and Apriority," *Midwest Studies in Philosophy* 4 (1979).

Quine, W. V., "Two Dogmas of Empiricism," *Philosophical Review* 60 (1951). Reprinted as Chapter Two in *From the Logical Point of View*. Cambridge: Harvard University Press, 1961.

Ricoeur, Paul, *Husserl: An Analysis of His Phenomenology*, trans. E. G. Ballard and L. E. Embree. Evanston: Northwestern University Press, 1967.

Robinson, James M., "Hermeneutic Since Barth" in *The New .Hermeneutic*, ed. Robinson and John B. Cobb, Jr. New York: Harper and Row, 1964, pp. 1–77.

Russell, Bertrand. *The Autobiography of Bertrand Russell–1914–1944*. Boston: Little, Brown & Co., 1968.

Sallis, John. *The Gathering of Reason*. Athens: University of Ohio Press, 1980.

Schlipp, Paul A., ed. *The Philosophy of Rudolph Carnap*. LaSalle, Ill.: Open Court, 1963.

Schlick, Moritz, "Is There a Factual *A priori*?" in *Readings in Philosophical Analysis*, ed. Sellars and H. Feigl. New York: Appleton Century Crofts, 1949, pp. 277–285.

Schrag, Calvin O., "The Life-World and Its Historical Horizon" in *Patterns of the Life-World*, pp. 107–22.

Sciacca, M. F. *Philosophical Trends in the Contemporary World,* trans. A. T. Salerno. Notre Dame, Ind.: University of Notre Dame Press, 1964.

Seidel, George J., "Constitution in Mikel Dufrenne," *The Modern Schoolman* 47 (1970), pp. 169–175.

Simmel, Georg. *The Conflict in Modern Culture and Other Essays,* ed. K. P. Etzkorn. New York: Teacher's College Press, 1968.

———. *The Problem of the Philosophy of History,* trans. Guy Oakes. New York: Free Press, 1977.

Sokolowski, Robert. *The Formation of Husserl's Concept of Constitution.* The Hague: Nijhoff, 1966.

Solomon, Robert C., ed. *Nietzsche: A Collection of Critical Essays.* New York: Doubleday Anchor, 1973.

Spiegelberg, Herbert. *The Phenomenological Movement.* Two Volumes. The Hague: Nijhoff, 2nd edition, 1969.

Spranger, Eduard. *Types of Men,* trans. P. J. W. Pigers. Tübingen: Niemeyer, 1928.

Sukale, Michael. *Comparative Studies in Phenomenology.* The Hague: Nijhoff, 1977.

Terrace, Herbert. *Nim: A Chimpanzee Who Learned Sign Language.* New York: Knopf, 1979.

Watson, J. B. *Behaviorism.* New York: Norton, 1930.

Weingartner, R. H. *Experience and Culture: The Philosophy of Georg Simmel.* Middletown, Conn.: Wesleyan University Press, 1960.

Wilshire, Bruce. *Metaphysics: An Introduction to Philosophy.* New York: Western Publishing Company, 1969.

Wolff, Kurt H., ed. *Essays on Sociology, Philosophy & Aesthetics.* New York: Harper & Row, 1959.

Zinkernagel, Peter. *Conditions for Description.* London: Routledge and Kegan Paul, 1962.

Zweig, Arnulf, "Goethe" in *The Encyclopedia of Philosophy,* Vol. 3, pp. 362–4.

Index